Babel,

Multiculturalism, G

the New World Order
by
Kerry Bolton

Babel, Inc.

Multiculturalism, Globalisation, and the New World Order

by

Kerry Bolton

Copyright © 2013 Black House Publishing Ltd

ISBN-13: 978-0-9927365-2-1

Black House Publishing Ltd

Kemp House

152 City Road

London

UNITED KINGDOM

EC1V 2NX

www.blackhousepublishing.co.uk

Email: info@blackhousepublishing.co.uk

Contents

Foreword

The New True Enemy

If a book is a tool that brings affective forces into the world, then one may measure a book by its strengthening or weakening affects; by whether or not it makes possible the will to attack one's enemies and to defend one's people; by how much purpose and resolve it provides those in the thick of a life and death struggle; and by how much "territory" it liberates from one's enemies. In light of these criteria, Dr. Kerry Bolton's *Babel, Inc. : Multiculturalism, Globalization, and the New World Order* has the potential to be truly explosive.

Babel, Inc. continues the critical analysis that Dr. Bolton began in *Revolution from Above* (2011).[1] But whereas that book on the close bonds between the power structure of global capitalism and supposedly oppositional Marxist ideologies and movements gave the reader a sense of distance – as if reading about the machinations and absurdities of an alien species – this book does not afford such a luxurious feeling in the reader. In fact, it affects a changing wind and a reappraisal of the forces aligned against the contemporary Right and the world's peoples and traditions that face certain extinction.

For while it has long been common to read Rightist ruminations on race, immigration, and even ethnological characteristics, only recently has the Right devoted much critical thought to capitalism and the liberal State. Bolton, in his characteristically energetic style, not only makes it possible to know how the United States and its neoliberal allies are combining multinational corporate Money Power with the contemporary moral and truth regime known as multiculturalism to create a new type of human creature, but he also succeeds in making

---

1   Kerry Bolton, Revolution from Above: Manufacturing 'Dissent' in the New World Order (London: Arktos Media, 2011).

this arrangement the primary target of Rightist agitation and revolt. For unlike the Left, which is utterly complicit in the very State-sponsored liberalism that it purports to oppose, the Right's anti-liberalism and transvaluational tendencies have allowed it to remain free of the sense-and-capital making apparatuses of the liberal State.

Despite this freedom, though, the Right has said very little about the State or capitalism. Perhaps this is because both are darlings of Marxist ideologues, or because the Right has always been fond of nationalism and Statism and weary of homo economicus. In any case, Bolton has ensured that the State and its capitalist "culture of death" will no longer be ignored.

The Creation of Homo Globicus

At the heart of *Babel, Inc.* is an exposé of multiculturalism as a "social control mechanism" that scorches the earth in preparation for the coming of the rationale of global capitalism: homo globicus. This global man will be at home anywhere in the world because the world will be homogeneously liberal. If that idea seems farfetched now, perhaps at the conclusion of *Babel, Inc.* it will seem less a possibility than a growing reality.

Homogeneity is the key that unlocks the ontological functions of multiculturalism. While globalists, corporate spokesmen, political leaders, and academics speak in glowing terms of a relativist multicultural humanism based on political and economic freedom, they are actively engaged in a two-pronged attack on human particularity and the defense thereof.

First, multiculturalism is a moral regime that links progressive liberal ideals of tolerance, ecumenicalism, and cosmopolitanism in order to aggressively condemn racism or pride in one's particularity. This moral and epistemological element links the liberal intelligentsia with Leftist ideologues and activists, not only against the world's various media-created racist and fascist villains, but also in the service of the liberal State and capitalism.

Second, the State, having finally shed the pretense of existing as the will of a people, uses this moral regime at the bidding of the capitalist oligarchs – that actually make the State possible – to spread a monolithic culture of liberal politics, feminism, anti-racism, and identity-based hyper-consumption. It calls for "one world, one race," – the flip side of multiculturalism – and actively undermines any attempts to preserve the standards, values, and traditions of local peoples, wherever they exist. Just as the State uses the World Trade Organization and World Monetary Fund to control the underdevelopment of the Third World, it uses global capitalism as a talisman to unlock any societies, peoples, States, or regions that remain overly local, xenophobic, or archaic, essentially capturing space for the purpose of its homogeneic valuation.

But when that talisman does not properly entice, war is an ever-present possibility. Indeed, Bolton provides an indispensible explanation of the wars in the name of homo globicus that have laid the foundation of the contemporary geopolitical reality. War and identity, then, are merely capitalism by other means. In this unipolar world, allies are merely markets, and people are merely consumers; most of who will gladly embrace the possibilities of unencumbered consumption, credit, and leisure promised by the global American man.

Join the Fight!

Others though will fight. They will fight homo globicus as homo insurrectus. They will fight to defend their particular values and traditions, their people, and, in a sense, their humanity. However, they will not fight to defend their State or nation, for, as Bolton demonstrates, these are the enemies of the people, being friends only of capitalist oligarchs and liberal humanist consumers. In place of Statist and nationalist solutions, Bolton posits new collective arrangements like the geopolitical vectors and blocs explained by Alexander Dugin and based in the ethnic and civilizational heritages being subsumed by liberalism, multiculturalism, and global capitalism.[2]

Ultimately, however, the will to fight must be stirred and nourished in each man, woman, and child that understands the price to be paid for homo globicus. For the Afrikaner, Serb, or Basque the war has long since begun, but for others it is long overdue. The only certainty is that this modern Babel is coming to each and all. States will not fight it because they are beholden to its rewards; nor will bourgeois men and women because it is their inheritance and, more importantly, their instinctual constitution. The smooth spaces – territorial, ontological, or epistemological – that either resist being captured or extricate themselves from the flood of homogenization find themselves at the frontlines of a war. It is a war of ideas and concepts; of territory and space; but also of men and women. The enemy is in each and every one of us, but it is also in very specific States, corporations, and governmental agencies.

The failure or success of *Babel, Inc.* will be measured neither in dollars nor readers; it will not be because of the efforts of Dr. Bolton, even though he has identified our potential enslavers. Instead, the energies brought into the world by *Babel, Inc.* place the onus of the book's ultimate value squarely on the reader, for it is his or her responsibility to do something – to act! – with those affective forces.

---

2   Alexander Dugin, The Fourth Political Theory. Mark Sleboda and Michael Millerman. trans. John Morgan ed. (London: Arktos Media, 2011).

Babel, Inc.

For all of the supposed "inevitability" of homo globicus, the United States, the global capitalist oligarchs, and the lackeys of both, are working extremely hard to ensure his victory: they know the power of ideas and the threat of even the smallest breach in the web that they weave. It is time that we follow suit and embrace the power of our ideas, to seek out and create breaches, and to become an enemy worthy of such a powerful threat.

Mark Dyal

September 2013

Mark W. Dyal is a cultural anthropologist specializing in Western European resistances to globalization and the homogenizing forces of liberal modernity. He has a PhD in Anthropology and a Masters in Black Studies. In his short time writing for New Right journals and websites, he has demonstrated a wide range of philosophical and historical interests, from contemporary artisan production to post-modern anti-philosophy, while remaining focused on the Nietzschean critique of modernity. His most recent series of essays sccks to move the New Right toward a more revolutionary stance against the liberal State.

His essays can be found online at Counter-Currents (www.counter-currents.com), Attack the System (www.attackthesystem.com), and his own site (www.markdyal.com). He publishes essays in academic presses as well, and has just signed with Arktos Media to publish his first book later this year. The book will be on Ultras (a very political Southern European version of soccer hooligans) and the fight against globalization, Americanization, and liberalization in Rome, Italy.

Introduction

If Hitlerism allegedly aimed at the creation of a 'master race,' the 'one world, one race' ideology is its mirror image: the elimination of all distinct peoples and their replacement with a homogeneous, dumbed-down global slave race, without attachments to any land, culture, lineage, or ethnicity. That this drive for global uniformity is being undertaken in the name of 'celebrating our differences' and 'respect for all cultures' (other than the European) is fooling the masses into thinking that the aim is quite opposite to what is really intended. It is what we can call *deconstruction* for the purpose of *reconstruction*: The deconstruction of a cohesive cultural or national entity in the name of multiculturalism, for the purpose of reconstructing a society that has no ethno-cultural foundation at all, but has been reduced to a produce-and-consume society, with the aim of a global factory and a global shopping mall.

Doublethink: Destroying Diversity by Proclaiming Diversity

Multiculturalism is a self-contradiction. Its propaganda slogans include oxymorons such as 'unity in diversity,' proclaim that we are 'all different and should celebrate those differences' while simultaneously proclaiming: 'one race, the human race.' The Left rants and protests against globalisation, while adopting the same aim as the globalists: 'open borders.' Every race has the right to 'self-determination' unless they are Europeans. On the other hand, when the Right raises the same banner it is decried with the challenge that 'there is no such thing as race.' Indigenous rights are promoted—but only for non-European indigenes. 'Minority rights' are promoted, but only when the minority is non-White; otherwise 'majority rights' are promoted, but only when the majority is non-

White. If one happens to be a Zionist, then the contention will be that 'multiculturalism is a moral duty in every land other than Israel, and among every people other than Jews.'

The arguments of the globalists and their Left-wing and liberal stalwarts are buttressed by a system of mental acrobatics that George Orwell described as 'doublethink': 'The power of holding two contradictory beliefs in one's mind simultaneously, and accepting both of them. . . .'[3] Hence the slogans of the regime in *Nineteen Eighty-Four*: 'War is peace. Freedom is slavery. Ignorance is strength.' The multicultural equivalent is 'unity in diversity,' 'diversity is strength,' and the like.

Orwell has his protagonists in *Nineteen Eighty-Four* describe 'doublethink': 'But if thought corrupts language, language can also corrupt thought.' 'It's a beautiful thing, the destruction of words.' 'Power is in tearing human minds to pieces and putting them together again in new shapes of your own choosing.'

'Doublethink' today is the language of 'political correctness.' The most draconian of laws are enacted in 'democratic societies' in the interests of 'human rights.' It is the same type of doublethink that enables the most tyrannical state to call itself a 'Democratic People's Republic.' The French Revolution undertook the 'Reign of Terror' in the name of 'Liberty, Equality, Fraternity.' The same outlook prevails today in terms of political doctrine. As will be seen, it has even been suggested in our liberal-democratic states that medication could be used on people deemed 'racist.'

---

3   George Orwell, *Nineteen Eighty-Four* (London: Martin Secker and Warburg, 1949), part 1, ch. 3, p. 32.

A Symptom of Decay

The multiculturalism and immigration that are being used in the process of globalisation are repeating aspects of a cycle of decline that has taken place in long-dead Civilisations. We in the Western Civilisation are not unique. We stand analogously where the Greeks, Romans, and others stood in the dying cycles of their Civilisations. When a culture comes to be based on the pursuit of wealth and neglects its moral, religious, social, and ethnic foundations, the measure of people becomes their ability to produce and consume in the economy of what has become an ossified Civilisation. Material well-being becomes the dominant aim; what today is called the 'American Dream' which is what the globalists want for the entire world. At this time of a culture's cycle, when economic considerations dominate, and hence when the ruling class is an oligarchy or an elite of money, rather than a trained and disciplined nobility, the measure of a potential citizen is based on how that person might contribute to the economy.

Immigration brings with it the alien customs of a multitude of cultures. The habits and thoughts of former colonial subjects and slaves have an increasingly important and eventually dominant role in a Civilisation. Over the course of centuries, the Civilisation is altered until little is left of its founding élan and ethos. Those few with foresight try to warn of an approaching collapse, and are vilified or laughed at as 'alarmists,' 'racists, 'extremists,' and 'xenophobes.' 'A prophet is not without honour, but in his own country, and among his own kin, and in his own house.'[4]

The English scholar Professor C. Northcote Parkinson, writing on the fall of Rome, commented that the Roman conquerors were subjected 'to cultural inundation and grassroots influence.' Because Rome extended throughout the world, the economic opportunities accorded by Rome

---

4   Mark 6:4.

3

drew in all the elements of the subject peoples, 'groups of mixed origin and alien ways of life.' 'Even more significant was what the Romans learnt while on duty overseas, for men so influenced were of the highest rank.' Parkinson quotes Edward Gibbon's *Decline and Fall of the Roman Empire*, referring to the Roman colony of Antioch:

> . . . Fashion was the only law, pleasure the only pursuit, and the splendour of dress and furniture was the only distinction of the citizens of Antioch. The arts of luxury were honoured, the serious and manly virtues were the subject of ridicule, and the contempt for female modesty and reverent age announced the universal corruption of the capitals of the East . . .[5]

The Roman traditional ethos of severity, austerity and disdain for softness that Emperor Julian attempted to reassert was greeted by 'fashionable society' with 'disgust.'[6] Parkinson remarks that 'there is just such a tendency in the London of today, as there was still earlier in Boston and New York.'[7] The Rome and Antioch that were being described existed in the analogous cultural epochs of the present Western Civilisation, and hence the attitudes of the Roman citizens in it's epoch of decay, as described by Parkinson and Gibbon, will sound familiar to the reader today.

With a change in the values of a culture, and the focus on material comfort, birth rates decline. It is a factor that was observed in ancient Civilisations, just as it is among the European populations today. Centuries ago this shortfall in population was made up by slaves, mercenaries, and immigrants. Today the same situation pertains to the policies

5   Edward Gibbon, *The History of the Decline & Fall of the Roman Empire* (London: Reprint Society, 1961), vol. II, ch. 24.
6   C. Northcote Parkinson, *East and West* (London: John Murray, 1963), 100–101.
    7 I bid., 100.

The Goths Sack Rome by German artist Ludwig Thiersch

of having an ageing population supported by immigrants from still prolific regions such as Asia, Africa, and Latin America. Hence the economic argument in favour of alien immigration into European nations is based on the need to supplement the declining European population. States are now nothing other than pieces of real estate for the purposes of economic function. According to the economic rationale for immigration, it does not matter where immigrants come from, as long as they provide labour or investments. At any rate, since Europeans, Asians, Africans, and Latinos all have the same desire to become cogs in the production process and 'make it' in terms of money, a global consumer culture will allow those of all races to integrate as units of the economic process. Differences in culture, race, ethos, élan, or religion no longer matter, because there is increasingly a common faith in what the Bible calls the 'love of *Mammon*.'[8] Behind this façade of the happy shopper of the global mall and the smiling idiot of the global village stands the raw power of the global oligarchy. To paraphrase Karl Marx, 'shopping is the opiate of the people.'

---

8   I Timothy 6–10.

Introduction

The process of depopulation and immigration was observed in ages past in other Civilisations that were at the same cycle in which we now exist. The philosopher-historian Oswald Spengler, in his morphology on the rise and fall of cultures, observed on the phenomenon of population decline that birth control was deplored by Polybius as the ruin of Greece. Women were no longer regarded as potential mothers, as the procreator of a family lineage, but only as companions. The 'emancipation of woman,' or 'feminism' as it is today called, applauded almost universally as 'progressive,' is simply another replay of what has taken place in Alexandria, Rome, or Athens thousands of years ago.[9] This 'feminism' has 'emancipated' women from the family and integrated them into the production process. It is why the globalists are so avid in funding and promoting feminism[10] as they are in regard to multiculturalism and immigration.

'The father of many children is for the great city a subject of caricature.'[11] This state of 'appalling depopulation' 'lasts for centuries,' until the Civilisation has collapsed and has become historically passé. Analogous epochs of depopulation in each of the Civilisations are traced by Spengler: the Egyptian New Empire from the XIX Dynasty onwards, the Mayan, the measures to encourage population increase in China in the 3rd century BC, and the emptiness of Samarra by the 10th century BC. Augustus Caesar attempted to reverse the decline of Rome with marriage-and-children laws. Soldiers recruited from the barbarian subject peoples were sought to fill the depopulated countryside.

Here again, we can see the analogy between these Civilisations

---

9   Oswald Spengler, *The Decline of the West* (London: Allen and Unwin, 1971), 2:105.

10 For the globalist sponsorship of feminism by the same interests that promote multiculturalism and 'open borders,' see K. R. Bolton, *Revolution from Above* (London: Arktos Media, 2011), 'New Left from Old' (Feminism), 160–200.

11 Spengler, *The Decline of the West*, 2:105–7.

and our own: while overpopulation effects the non-European states, the ageing populations of Western states (and other White states such as Russia in particular) are being replaced with Asian and Muslim immigrants, whose high birth rates account for their population increases. Spengler concludes from these analogous epochs, writing of the cosmopolitan Cities as symbolic of the Late or senile cycle:

> This, then is the conclusion of the city's history; growing from primitive barter-centre to Culture-city and at last to world-city, it sacrifices first the blood and soul of its creators to the needs of its majestic evolution, and then the last flower of that growth to the spirit of Civilisation— and so, doomed, moves on to final self-destruction.[12]

The Modern Babel

However one relates to the Bible, whether as literal or as allegorical, one of the great lessons relevant to the matter of multiculturalism and the push for 'one world, one race' by the lovers of Mammon and the worshippers of the Golden Calf, is the mythic Tower of Babel. It shows how the powerful have been full of *hubris* since ancient times. They tried to arrogate the powers of God and create, even then, what is today called by friend and foe alike, a 'new world order.' This account in Genesis is prescient of modern times:

> And they said, go to, let us build us a city and a tower, whose top may reach unto heaven; and let us make us a name, lest we be scattered abroad, upon the face of the whole earth. And the Lord came down to see the city and the tower, which the children of men builded. And the Lord said, behold, the people is one, and they have all one language, and this they begin to do: and now nothing will be restrained from them, which they

---

12   Ibid., 107.

have imagined to do. Go to, let us go down, and there confound their language, that they may not understand one another's speech. So the Lord scattered them abroad from thence upon the face of the earth and they left off to build the city. Therefore is the name of it called Babel . . .[13]

Such a work is alluded to in the fragments of Babylonian tablets, of a tower destroyed by the gods and the languages of humanity confounded.[14] Our modern Babel is called 'globalisation,' whereby a moneyed elite has arrogated to itself godlike powers to recreate humanity in an image of its choosing and for the sake of its own power. This global Babel requires the deconstruction of identities with the aim of reconstructing a single identity based on the ever-shifting requirements of mass production and consumption.

Perhaps several thousand years from now, a Chinese archaeologist will unearth the remains of a collapsed tower while excavating New Beijing, or what was in ancient times known as New York, and discover torn and scattered fragments of the 'United Nations Charter,' and conclude that here was another failed attempt by deluded man to play God and build for himself an edifice to his own glory, only to cause his whole civilisation to collapse as others have before it.

---

13   Genesis 11:4–9.

14   George Smith, *The Chaldean Account of Genesis* (Minneapolis: Wizard Bookshelf, 1977 [1876]), 8, 9, 13, 48, 158–61.

No Colour, No Country:
the Nature of Capitalism

Whoever criticizes capitalism, while approving immigration, whose working class is its first victim, had better shut up. Whoever criticizes immigration, while remaining silent about capitalism, should do the same.[15]

—Alain de Benoist, French philosopher, founder of the
Nouvelle Droite

The Old Left knew exactly what the nature of capitalism was and the use of multiculturalism and immigration to expand the labour market. The Old Left was therefore in the forefront of demanding immigration restrictions and ethnic policies that would preserve national identities.

Now, however, the rank-and-file of the Left, whether social democrats, communists, or anarchists, are clueless in regards to the nature of capitalism and multiculturalism, and their leaders exploit what is today called 'identity politics' to recruit disaffected minorities in the name of feminism, 'gay rights,' 'human rights,' 'children's rights,' 'minority rights,' 'majority rights,' *ad infinitum*. As IBM's Jacques Maisonrouge[16] commented several decades ago, 'Down with borders' is just as much a corporate slogan as it is a slogan of the New Left youth who were rioting in Paris at the time, and this remains true today.

Today the Left pontificates about the 'racist' nature of capitalism. According to Marxist theory, capitalism uses racism to divide the working class, which is supposed to be international and not loyal to country, class loyalty superseding any other loyalty or bond of kinship.

---

15 Alain de Benoist, 'Immigration: The Reserve Army of Capital,' p. 4, http://www. alaindebenoist.com/pdf/immigration_reserve_army_of_the_capital-anglais.pdf.

16 'Jacques G. Maisonrouge,' IBM, http://www-03.ibm.com/ibm/history/exhibits/ builders/builders_maisonrouge.html.

This is nonsense. Capitalism has long used immigration to move different ethnic groups throughout the world according to the needs of production, like pieces on a global chessboard, each with their own functions. Hence, Indians were sent to Fiji to cut sugar cane, and Chinese were sent to South Africa, Canada, the United States, New Zealand, and Australia to work on railways. Now capitalism also uses multiculturalism to create a nebulous class of willing wage slaves without identity other than as units of production and consumption. More recently Polynesians were encouraged to migrate to New Zealand when it was still a manufacturing country, and now the Asian middle and upper classes are encouraged to migrate to New Zealand for their money, since New Zealand is no longer a labour-intensive economy, and is being forced into an Asian economic bloc. While I am not generally given to citing Wikipedia as a reliable source on anything, its entry on 'Free Migration' succinctly states of these matters:

> Free migration or open immigration is the position that people should be able to migrate to whatever country they choose, free of monetary charge. Although the two are not the same issue, free migration is similar in spirit to the concept of free trade, and both are advocated by free market economists on the grounds that economics is not a zero-sum game and that free markets are, in their opinion, the best way to create a fairer and balanced economic system, thereby increasing the overall economic benefits to all concerned parties. Many libertarians, liberals, socialists, and anarchists advocate open immigration, notwithstanding other noteworthy differences among these political ideologies.[17]

Immigration undermines national identity and national boundaries that are hindrances to global marketing and production. In an analysis reminiscent of Old Labour before

---

17 'Free Migration,' Wikipedia, http://en.wikipedia.org/wiki/Free_migration.

it was taken over by Marxists and other internationalist elements, the celebrated American scholar Professor Noam Chomsky, heralded by the Left as a seminal influence, explained the character of capitalism relative to race that is particularly cogent in describing the crux of the issue:

> See, capitalism is not fundamentally racist—it can exploit racism for its purposes, but racism isn't built into it. Capitalism basically wants people to be interchangeable cogs, and differences among them, such as on the basis of race, usually are not functional. I mean, they may be functional for a period, like if you want a super exploited workforce or something, but those situations are kind of anomalous. Over the long term, you can expect capitalism to be anti-racist—just because it's anti-human. And race is in fact a human characteristic—there's no reason why it should be a negative characteristic, but it is a human characteristic. So therefore identifications based on race interfere with the basic ideal that people should be available just as consumers and producers, interchangeable cogs who will purchase all the junk that's produced—that's their ultimate function, and any other properties they might have are kind of irrelevant, and usually a nuisance.[18]

The Old Labour movements understood the nature of capitalism. Marx predicted in *The Communist Manifesto* that capitalism would become international, transcending imperial and national boundaries, and that in so doing the 'proletariat' would also become international and an international revolutionary working class would thereby be formed to overthrow world capitalism and establish world communism, stating:

> National differences and antagonisms between

---

18   Noam Chomsky, *Understanding Power: The Indispensable Chomsky* (New York: The New Press, 2002), 88–89.

peoples are daily more and more vanishing, owing to the development of the bourgeoisie, to freedom of commerce, to the world market, to uniformity in the modern of production and in the conditions of life corresponding thereto. The supremacy of the proletariat will cause them to vanish faster.[19]

Marx and Engels similarly wrote 'on the Free Trade question':

Generally speaking, the protectionist system today is conservative, whereas the Free Trade system has a destructive effect. It destroys the former nationalities, and renders the contrasts between workers and middle class more acute. In a word, the Free Trade system is precipitating the social revolution. And only in this revolutionary sense do I vote for Free Trade.[20]

Where Marxism differs from non-Marxist Old Labour is that Marx regarded the internationalisation of capitalism as a positive part of the dialectical process of history[21] that would break down national boundaries, enabling the working class to also become international. The Old Labour pioneers saw the internationalist character of capitalism as something to be fought. Marx was correct in predicting the globalisation of capital, however his dialectical outlook on history was wrong in seeing this as a step towards socialism. Rather, it is a step towards a world economy ruled by oligarchs, a class that does transcend race, culture, and nation. This has formed a global 'elite' or oligarchy that is promoting 'one world, one race' in tandem with the bogus Left.

---

19 Karl Marx, *The Communist Manifesto* (Moscow: Progress Publishers, 1975), 71.

20 Karl Marx and Friedrich Engels, 'Speech on the Question of Free Trade Delivered to the Democratic Association of Brussels at Its Public Meeting of January 9, 1848,' in *Collected Works*, vol. 6 (London: Lawrence & Wishart, 1976).

21 For an explanation of dialectics and how both Capitalism and Marxism use it, see K. R. Bolton, *Revolution from Above* (London: Arktos Media, 2011), 'Capitalist and Marxist Dialectics,' 9–14.

Babel, Inc.

The Fallacy of 'White Privilege'

The grassroots worker's movement opposed the internationalising tendencies of capitalism, and their demands included immigration restrictions. Marxism undermined this basic feature of the struggle against international capital. The most extreme positions today on the issue are those of the anarchists and the Trotskyites, both of whom align themselves with international capitalism in their call for 'open borders.' For example, Latino communist Eduardo Martínez Zapata stated to the Freedom Socialist Party in the United States:

> Humanity needs to move to our next stage—not corporate globalization, but collective globalization, in which the needs of all will be met. We will have no use for national borders; people will not be forced to uproot their entire families from their homelands just to survive. Movement from place to place will be the free choice of free people.[22]

Zapata's statement is representative of the Left of many different types. Note that he calls for 'globalisation' in which the free movement of people across the world is advocated as a 'choice,' while paying a passing reference to the rootedness of homeland, presumably to appeal to the diehard nationalistic sentiments among Latinos while standing for something quite different: 'collective globalisation.' The difference between 'corporate globalisation' and 'collective globalisation' is that in the former CEOs rule in the name of shareholders, while in the latter commissars' rule in the name of 'the people.' The 'identity politics' of the Left are expressed in the statement of the Freedom Socialist Party in trying to appeal to sundry disaffected minorities: 'The

---

22 Eduardo Martínez Zapata, 'What Immigrants Need: Amnesty, Open Borders, and a Movement That Won't Back Down,' *Freedom Socialist Bulletin*, Winter–Spring 2006, http://www.socialism.com/drupal-6.8/?q=node/1502.

Freedom Socialist Party is a working class organization composed of women and men of many races, nationalities, sexual orientations and ages who are fighting for a new, just social order that will serve the majority of the human race.'[23]

The Freedom Socialist Party follows the Trotskyite line of Marxism.[24] The appeal for support is to 'Women, particularly working-class women of color,' 'The revolt of sexual minorities,' 'The struggles of oppressed minorities and immigrants.'[25] This is the line followed by Trotskyism throughout the world, as well as by anarchist factions. It is contrary to the original position of the Labour movement and how the pioneers of that movement understood capitalism.

Immigration restriction was and is a workers' cause. Real socialists, real anti-capitalists, before the labour movements were taken over by internationalist doctrines, recognised this. Old Labour would have spat on today's Left-wingers as lackeys of global capitalism. The absurd notion of the contemporary Left that racism and immigration restrictions are capitalist tools to divide the international working class is refuted by the fact that it was the Labor Party and trades unions which fought for the introduction of the 'White Australia Policy' against global capitalism. Now the Left, having become obsessively anti-White in the quest to lead what Spengler termed the 'coloured world-revolution,'[26] have identified the 'White working class' with White oligarchy, having common interests and privileges vis-à-vis 'coloured' peoples. The 'coloured' peoples thus enjoy a special position of esteem within the Left:

23 Freedom Socialist Party, 'About Us,' http://www.socialism.com/drupal-6.8/?q=node/2.

24 Freedom Socialist Party, Platform, 'For a Mass Workingclass Party,' http://www.socialism.com/drupal-6.8/?q=node/16.

25 Ibid.

26 Oswald Spengler, *The Hour of Decision* (New York: Alfred A. Knopf, 1934), 'The Coloured World-Revolution,' 204–30.

Non-ruling class white people are both oppressed and privileged. They are *oppressed* most significantly on the basis of class, gender and sexuality, and also on the basis of religion, culture, ethnicity, age, physical abilities and politics. At the same time, they are *privileged* in relation to peoples of color.[27]

White indentured servants enjoyed a privileged position over Black slaves, according to this mythology: 'English or "white" servants were granted specific forms of *privilege* or *preferential treatment* which was specifically denied to slaves, or "Negroes."'

In summary, the system of white privilege for non-ruling class whites reinforces the system of racial oppression against people of color. And the *complementary* systems of white privilege and racial oppression maintain the system of white power for ruling class whites.[28]

Hence, to the Left, and to liberal academics, the 'white race' is not a biological entity but a political construct created to perpetuate oppression, and the 'white' workers—including indentured servants sent to the colonies, children working down coal mines, and families separated and put into workhouses, etc.—enjoyed privileges as part of the 'white oppressor' construct. This is part of a post-colonial narrative that serves political and racial agendas in demonising the European heritage. Today, all Whites, whatever socio-economic class and whatever their deprivation, are regarded in the post-colonial narrative as beneficiaries of the colonial exploitation of coloureds. One can however redeem oneself by becoming a Communist and violently rejecting one's European heritage and identity. Before the days of post-colonial academic discourse, or what is commonly referred

---

27 Colours of Resistance, http://www.coloursofresistance.org/741/shinin-the-lite-on-white-part-one-white-privilege/.

28 Ibid.

to now as 'political correctness,' the pioneers of the Labour movement held different views.

There were no such illusions among the workers at the time as to their conditions, or feelings of guilt for supposedly being members by birth of an exploiting 'race.' In 1830, the Rev. Richard Oastler, a Methodist minister in York, protested the conditions in the Bradford woollen mills where little children laboured thirteen hours a day and were beaten if they fell asleep. Oastler attacked the hypocrisy of Yorkshire clergymen and politicians who zealously condemned the enslavement of Blacks in the West Indies while in England, 'thousands of our fellow creatures . . . are this very moment . . . in a state of slavery more horrid than are the victims of that hellish system of colonial slavery.' Oastler was publicly thanked by a delegation of English labourers at a meeting in York, '. . . for his manly letters to expose the conduct of those pretended philanthropists and canting hypocrites who travel to the West Indies in search of slavery, forgetting there is a more abominable and degrading system of slavery at home.'[29]

Moreover, the assumption that slavery was based on White privilege is a myth. Free Africans and American Indians were able to own White slaves, indicated by a proposal in South Carolina in 1717 that free Blacks could vote if they owned 'one white man.'[30]

As the Old Labour pioneers stated, the money-merchants had no loyalty to anything beyond profits. The same is true today. It is therefore nonsense to say that capitalism or even European colonialism were predicated on ideas of 'White supremacy,' and that the poorest classes of Whites

---

29 Cecil Herbert Driver, *Tory Radical: The Life of Richard Oastler* (Oxford: Oxford University Press, 1946), 36–55.

30 *Journals of the Commons House of Assembly of the Province of South Carolina: 1692–1775*, 5:294–95.

shared in the legacy of exploitation on the sole basis of 'White privilege' vis-à-vis non-White slaves. The system of mercantile economics that is again predominant in the world and has now become international (globalisation) saw—and sees—people only as economic units. Economists, businessmen, and politicians regarded poor Whites in England, Scotland, and Ireland as a burden that could be solved by enslaving them. Hence, in February 1652 in England it was enacted that

> . . . it may be lawful for . . . two or more justices of the peace within any country, citty or towne corporate belonging to this commonwealth to from tyme to tyme by warrant . . . cause to be apprehended, seized on and detained all and every person or persons that shall be found begging and vagrant . . . in any towne, parish or place to be conveyed into the port of London, or unto any other port . . . from where such person or persons may be shipped . . . into any forraign collonie or plantation . . .[31]

While one of the major complaints of present-day Leftist activists is that of the large numbers of Africans who died on board ship to the Americas, nothing much is said of the little vagabonds from England who were shipped to the colonies:

> From that time on little is known about them except that very few lived to become adults. When a 'muster' or census of the [Virginia] colony was taken in 1625, the names of only seven boys were listed [of the children kidnapped in 1619]. All the rest were dead . . . The statistics for the children sent in 1620 are equally grim . . . no more than five were alive in 1625.[32]

31 Egerton Manuscript, British Museum.
32 Hans L. Trefousse, *Andrew Johnson: A Biography* (New York: W. W. Norton & Co., 1989), 147.

The attitude of the international oligarchy[33] remains the same: people are here to be treated as economic units regardless of one's race, nation, culture, class, or ethnicity. It is therefore fallacious, and plays into the hands of oligarchy, for the Left to claim that all 'Whites' have a heritage of 'privilege' vis-à-vis everyone else. Another example is the oft-stated indignation that the Maori children of New Zealand were punished if they spoke Maori at school because of the system of White racist colonial oppression, which wanted to Anglicise the native subjects.

British imperialism did not act as a racial expression but as an economic expression. As indicated already, plutocrats did not owe allegiance to their own race a century and more ago, any more than they do today. Hence, Afrikaner children who spoke Afrikaans at school were also punished, and not only Afrikaans but also the Dutch language were suppressed. Indeed, the oligarchy in Britain, epitomised by the Rothschild family, looked down upon the Afrikaners just as much as they looked down on working-class Britons. For example: 'In 1906, the English Cape Town newspaper *The Cape Times* could condescendingly write that "Afrikaans is the confused utterance of half-articulated patois."'[34] When colonialism was transcended by internationalism and when the money centres focused on New York rather than the capitals of Europe, plutocrats who had been avid imperialists were just as eager to scuttle the empires in pursuit of a global economy, as will be shown in the next chapter.

---

33 'His sole obsession is to make money.' Plato, *The Republic*, 'The Oligarchic Character,' 9:5.

34 Kwesi Kwaa Prah, 'The Language Question. The Struggle between English and the Other Official and Unofficial Languages' (South Africa), p. 1, http://www.språkförsvaret.se/sf/fileadmin/PDF/The_Language_Question.pdf.

Babel, Inc.

Labour & the White Australia Policy

William Lane

Prior to 1878 there had been continuous but ad hoc opposition to Asian immigration by Australian workers. Chinese immigrants meant not only low wages but also strike breaking. The most eminent of Australia's Labour fathers was William Lane. He established the first union-owned newspaper in Australia, *The Worker*, and founded the Australian Labor Federation, which gave birth to the Australian Labor Party. Lane stated that the Labour movement's struggle was 'more than national or social. . . . It is a true racial struggle.' How different that outlook is from today's socialists. In contrast to the Marxist and anarchist notion that the working class has 'no nation, no nationality,' Lane declared in his labour newspaper, *The Boomerang*, bylined as 'A Live Newspaper Born of the Soil':

> We are for this Australia, for the nationality which is creeping to the verge of being, for the progressive people. . . . Whatever will benefit Australia: that we are for. Whatever will harm Australia: that we are against. While we plough our fields and measure our calico, and swing our hammers, history is being made and we ourselves are taking part in a stirring drama.

> Here we face the hordes of the east as our kinsmen faced them in the dim distant centuries, and here we must beat them back if we would keep intact all that can make our lives worth living. It does not matter that today it is an insidious invasion of peaceful aliens instead of warlike downpour of weaponed men. Monopolistic capitalism has no colour and no country.[35]

'*Monopolistic capitalism* has no colour and no country.' Lane

---

35   William Lane, *The Boomerang*, 18 February 1888.

is succinctly stating the precise opposite of Marx who said that the *working class* has no country, any more than the money-broker and the global oligarchy.

In 1889 Lane wrote a novel *White or Yellow? A Story of Race War 1908*. This work predicted an alliance between the pastoralists and wealthy of the Queensland Establishment and Asian capital. A treacherous Queensland Premier would place the colony in the hands of these alien capitalists. But trade union patriots led by an ordinary nationalist worker fought the enemy, expelling the Chinese 'invaders' and settling accounts with the local traitor class. Today, the trades union leaders would be in alliance with the oligarchy and Asian capital.

W. G. Spence

W. G. Spence, president of the Amalgamated Shearers' Union, which was the precursor of the Australian Workers' Union, stated: 'True patriotism should be racial.'[36] He explained:

Unionism came to the Australian bushman as a religion. It came, bringing salvation from years of tyranny. It had in it the feeling of mateship which he understood already, and which characterised the action of one 'white man' to another. Unionism extended the idea, so a man's character was gauged by whether he stood true to Union rules or scabbed it . . . Rough and unpolished many of them may be; but manly, true, and 'white' all the time and the Movement owes them much. . . . The exclusion of alien and coloured races gives a chance for the development of the Australian island continent of a great nation of the white race . . .[37]

---

36 William Guthrie Spence, *Australia's Awakening: Thirty Years in the Life of an Australian Agitator* (Sydney: Worker Trustees, 1909), 377.

37 Ibid., 53, 54, 243.

Opposition to Chinese labour galvanised the workers' movement, Spence writing of the successful resistance against the mine owners:

> The anti-Chinese movement was one of the early developments of democratic feeling in Australia. So strong was it that in 1861 it led to riot amongst the diggers at Lambing Flat, Burrangong, New South Wales. They drove the Chinese off the field, some of the pig-tailed heathens losing their lives. There were at that time 38,000 Chinese in the two colonies of New South Wales and Victoria—12,988 in the former, and 24,732 in the latter. But for the action of the gold diggers and restriction of Chinese immigration by a poll tax and otherwise, Australia would have been practically a Chinese possession. The same strong feeling that caused the Lambing Flat diggers to revolt actuated the miners of Clunes, Victoria, in 1876. The directors of the Lothair Gold Mining Company decided to introduce Chinese labor. The miners, who were all members of the A.M.A., determined to resist.[38]

Spence was one of the founders of the Australian Labor Party. He described the party doctrine in terms that would make him anathema to today's Labor party careerists:

> The party stands for racial purity and racial efficiency—industrially, mentally, morally and intellectually. It asks the people to set up a high standard of national character. . . . We want a people self-reliant in moral character and manhood able and willing to defend their hearths and homes in the advent of invasion. . . . Labor takes the home as the unit of the nation and works for all that is calculated to make it happy. . . . The present competitive struggle for existence will disappear . . . The Labor Party is dominated by two moral convictions—the Ethics of Usefulness and the Ethics of Fellowship.

---

38   Ibid., 34.

William Spence, president of the Amalgamated Shearers' Union (seated left)

> It holds that all work must have a social value to entitle
> to an income. . . . Governed by the Ethics of Fellowship
> there will only be one class, and that is the producing
> class. . . . Such a condition must come sooner in white
> Australia than in older lands.[39]

These early Australian socialists saw in Australia the
promise of a new White workers' paradise free of the
class war and exploitation of Europe at the time of the
industrial revolution. How far their cry is from the puerile
ideology of the liberals, Marxists, and anarchists. In
Australia in Spence's day it was the 'anti-Socialists' who
were unpatriotic, sooner employing non-European labour
rather than provide decent conditions for workers of their
own kind; while the labour movement was the herald of an
Australian nationalism:

> The Anti-Socialist is invariably the most unpatriotic
> person to be found. He belongs to the 'stinking fish'

---

39   Ibid., 377, 378, 381, 382.

party. If he cannot get his own stupid way he denounces the country in which he has done so well. The bedrock of the cry for a colour line across the continent, so that Anti-Socialists could boss niggers and yellow men, is found in the Anti-Socialist's nature. He is a born tyrant, and as the white Australian will not stand his tyranny he must have a nigger to order about. There is no patriotism in the Anti-Socialist press, hence it barracks for anything the capitalist crowd asks for.[40]

While the nature of capitalism has not changed, the character of the 'labour' and 'socialist' movements has, having long been in accord with the oligarchs.

The multicultural character of the British Empire saw a reluctance of the British Colonial Office to pursue policies that might undermine that character, as well as interfering with the 'rights' of business to utilise colonial subjects, whether White or coloured, as commercial circumstances required. Then as now, the doctrine of 'free trade' was dominant. Joseph Chamberlain, Britain's Colonial Secretary, stated that immigration restriction could not be condoned 'lest it offend Her Majesty's Indian subjects.' In 1896 Chamberlain informed the Intercolonial Conference that because Britain was seeking an alliance with Japan, Australia would have to moderate her immigration laws, but Australians resisted. Business interests were undermining Australia's immigration policy. In Northern Queensland sugar plantation owners imported several thousand Melanesians. In 1891 pastoral companies employed Chinese scab labour during the shearers' strike.

Ironically, less than a century later, it was the Australian Labor Prime Minister Gough Whitlam who jubilantly declared the 'White Australia Policy' to be 'dead' in 1973, having already pushed for the removal of the 'White

---

40   Ibid., 281.

Australia Policy' from Labor's platform in 1965, to the objections of the old guard led by Arthur Calwell. Liberal governments had already dealt more subtle blows to the White Australia Policy in the aftermath of World War II.[41] The fact that media magnate Rupert Murdoch, the perfect specimen of a globalist oligarch, backed the Labor Party under Whitlam indicates the direction of 'modern Labor' from this time. Among Whitlam's decisions was the vote of the Australian delegate for sanctions against South Africa at the United Nations Organization.

Joseph Chifley

Another great Labour statesman who championed the White Australia Policy was Joseph Chifley. In 1928 Chifley stood for the seat of Macquarie and won on the campaign that the government was undermining the White Australia Policy, although the incumbents were returned. In the rough and straight language of the pre-PC era, Chifley criticised the government for admitting 'so many Dagoes and Aliens into Australia.'

The Labour newspaper *The National Advocate* called on electors to vote for Chifley to protect White Australia. Chifley was a Labour nationalist who supported a centralised government to maintain national unity, and was a principal advocate for the nationalisation of banking.

In 1929 Labor assumed government. However, the Bank of England and the private banks forced the Scullin government to continue orthodox financial policies. From the backbenches Chifley opposed the government's financial orthodoxy. In 1931 the Scullin government was defeated. However in 1935 Chifley was appointed to the Royal Commission into the

---

41 'Abolition of the "White Australia" Policy,' Department of Immigration, Australian Government, http://www.immi.gov.au/media/fact-sheets/08abolition. htm.

banking system. Chifley disagreed with the commission's findings and submitted his own report calling for bank nationalisation. In 1941 he became Treasurer in the Curtin government, and served as Prime Minister from 1946–49. Chifley's Labor nationalism combined the need for economic freedom with that of White Australia, like Jack Lang and other stalwarts of the Old Labor movement.

Arthur Calwell—Last of Old Guard Labor

While communist elements in the Australian labor unions, and the Australian Confederation of Trades Unions, undermined the White Australia Policy of the Old Labor movement in favour of Marxist internationalism, it was under the Liberal governments of Robert Menzies (1949–66) and Harold Holt (Minister for Immigration 1949–56, Prime Minister 1966–67) that the first major cracks began to appear in the protective walls of the White Australia Policy which, as mentioned previously, was finished off by the Whitlam Labor government during the 1970s. The dictation test was abolished, skilled non-Europeans were allowed in, naturalisation was easier, and Australian citizens could bring in Asian spouses and their children.[42]

Harold Holt became Prime Minister in January 1966. Former Labor Immigration Minister and staunch defender of the White Australia Policy, Arthur Calwell wrote: 'Significantly, Mr Holt's first action as Prime Minister was to announce liberalisation of our immigration regulations regarding Asians . . . Those changes can yet be disastrous for Australia.'[43]

Academics and white-collar professionals who looked with disdain upon the White Australia Policy had undermined

---

42 'Abolition of the "White Australia" Policy,' Department of Immigration, op. cit.
43 Arthur Calwell, *Be Just and Fear Not* (Hawthorn, Victoria: Lloyd O'Neil, 1972).

Arthur Calwell, right, and his deputy Gough Whitlam in 1964

the Labor Party. The Old Guard was led by Arthur Calwell, leader of the Parliamentary Labor Party. The trades unions still had considerable power at executive level and ensured that the policy was maintained, whilst the opposition was forming behind Gough Whitlam and Don Dunstan. Attempts to have the policy dropped failed in 1959, 1961, and 1963.

Calwell wrote of the original Australian Labor tradition, which was more than just 'reformist,' and aimed at creating a new European civilisation in the South free of the class divides and exploitation of the Old World:

> . . . I still think that Australia needs the sort of revolution that will produce fundamental far-reaching changes. Every country needs such a revolution every now and then to make some beneficial changes in its social, political and economic affairs. . . . The last thing I want to do is shock native born reactionaries and kill them off prematurely by hinting at the word revolution in this country. Yet what else is there to talk about if man is

to survive in the mess that capitalism has made of our society with its wars, its pollution of the air, the sea and the land and its degradation of our moral, social and economic health? . . .

We need sweeping changes that will result in the creation of an Australian Socialist society. Unfortunately, the great majority of Australians are too smug, too greedy, too slothful to care about the benefits of Socialism.[44]

As for White Australia, Calwell was quoted in the Australian press in 1971:

Ninety percent of people of Australia support me in my attitude today. Australians are not going to turn Australia over to those inspired by an angry vocal minority of pseudo-intellectuals. These pseudo-intellectuals think they can promote the cause of a permissive society by flooding this country with people from all parts of the world. I have a tremendous respect for the Chinese who have yellow skins and have pride in their race. I have a tremendous regard to the coffee-coloured Indians who have a great respect for the colour of their race, and for both peoples because of their regard for their cultures, their histories and their achievements. However, Australia has got to be held by people who are predominantly Celtic, Anglo-Saxon, Germanic, Scandinavian and Southern European. These are the only people who can make an integrated community. Why should anyone be hurt by a recitation of the truth?[45]

The impetus for change came from a coterie of Melbourne University academics who formed the Immigration Reform

---

44 Ibid.
45 Cited by Alec Saunders, *The Social Revolutionary Nature of Australian Nationalism* (2001), Part III, http://home.alphalink.com.au/~radnat/sr-nature/partthree. html.

Group.[46] Support also came from university students, ever-ready to espouse any cliché-ridden cause that serves the Establishment they think they are opposing.

The 1963 ALP Conference was pressured into setting up an Immigration Review Committee, which was dominated by the Old Guard, but which eventually compromised by agreeing to recommend that the ALP drop the name of the White Australia Policy from the ALP Platform. This recommendation was adopted by the 1965 ALP Conference. The same Conference also lifted the party ban on the Immigration Reform Group.

When the Australian Workers' Union, which remained stalwart in its defence of the White Australia Policy, amalgamated with the internationalist Australian Confederation of Trades Unions, its influence was undermined. The ACTU itself had been filled with white-collar workers and professional administrators who did not identify with the legacy of Australian Old Labor. In 1971 the anti-White Australia faction gained enough influence at the ALP Conference to enable the policy to be removed. After the ALP government was elected in 1972, Whitlam and Immigration Minister Al Grassby set about destroying the White Australia Policy.[47]

---

46   Chris Anderson, 'Academia and the Immigration Reform Groups,' Section 6: *Demise of the White Australia Policy*, http://ausnatinfo.angelfire.com/demise3-06. htm.

47   Chris Anderson, ibid., Section 11: 'The Australian Labor Party and the Destruction of the White Australia Policy,' http://ausnatinfo.angelfire.com/ demise3-11.htm.

Babel, Inc.

Jack Lang Describes the White Australia Policy

Jack Lang, Labor Premier of New South Wales 1925–27 and 1930–32, is noted as having defied the Bank of England, which demanded repayment of loans at usurious interest during the Depression. In his autobiography *I Remember* (1956), Lang gives a history of the White Australia Policy, and exposes how British imperial interests conflicted with that policy:

> White Australia must not be regarded as a mere political shibboleth. It was Australia's Magna Carta. Without that policy, this country would have been lost long ere thus. It would have been engulfed in an Asian tidal wave. There would have been no need for the Japanese to invade this country. We would have been swallowed up by the rolling advance of a horde of coloured people, anxious to escape the privations of their own countries and prepared to impose their own standards on this country.

> It is necessary only to examine the racial composition of present-day Fiji, where the Hindus have elbowed the natives out of the picture, to visualise what could have happened in this country had the White Australia policy not been fought for doggedly at the end of the 19th Century. We were then fighting for our national survival. Had we weakened, the flood gates would have opened and the natural increase of population according to Asian standards would have done the rest. It would then have been too late. This country would have become a pushover for the Asiatics.

> The first Federal Platform for the Labor Party, adopted at an Interstate Conference held in Sydney on January 24, 1900, was a model of brevity. It was the platform on which the party fought its first Federal election in the

Jack Lang was the Premier of New South Wales
during 1925-1927 and 1930-1932.

following year. There were only three planks. They were (1) Electoral Reform, providing for one adult one vote. (2) Total Exclusion of coloured and other undesirable races, and (3) Old Age Pensions. . . .

But it was the question of White Australia that knit the first Federal Labor Party together. In 1908 when the party decided to draft a much more elaborate platform, the first plank agreed upon was 'Maintenance of White Australia.' It headed the list.

So the Australian Labor Party was actually brought together with White Australia as its primary objective. Later the word-spinners put it much more elegantly as 'The cultivation of an Australian sentiment, based on the maintenance of racial purity.'

That was not, however, the real reason for the development of the White Australia policy. It did not have its origin in any idea of racial superiority, or colour prejudice. From the start it was a simple bread-and-butter issue. Australian workers were trying to defend their own living standards. They were trying to save their jobs. They knew that unrestricted immigration of coloured races would mean the introduction of a kind of industrial Gresham's Law—the bad wages would put the fair wage out of circulation. The white Australian worker would soon be reduced to coolie levels. Having got rid of convict labour, they did not want to be reduced to the rice bowl. Yet that was the threat that was actually hovering over the people of this country. . . .

Trouble first started during the Gold Rush. It didn't take long for news of the strike to reach the gold merchants of Shanghai and Hong Kong. Chinese had flocked to the Californian fields in 1849, so that even today San Francisco has the largest Chinese settlement outside Asia. Then as the Californians pulled up their grub stakes and followed the trail to the new strikes in the Southern Hemisphere, the Chinese followed on. They were the fossickers of the gold.

Trouble broke out between the diggers and the Chinese on the Lambing Flat fields in July, 1861. The tough diggers attacked the Chinese and used strong-arm methods. There were all kinds of wild threats. The Government ordered troops into the fields, including artillery, and in the riots that followed one digger was killed. The miners then decided to take an interest in politics, with the elimination of the Chinese as their first objective. Lambing Flat is in fact just as significant in the history of the Labor Party in this State as Eureka Stockade was in Victoria.

Some of the mining companies had discovered that the Chinese were prepared to work longer hours for much lower wages than Australians. That was the chief reason why they were resented. Trouble spread to the shipping companies, and there were strikes brought about by the employment of Chinese on Australian ships.

Chinese were also coming into Australian ports, deserting and starting their own businesses. [Henry] Parkes[48] saw what was happening in Sydney. He announced that he was against further Chinese immigration. He was attacked by wealthy employers and accused of having a bias against the Chinese because they were colored they said he was treating them as an inferior race. Parkes retorted: 'They are not an inferior race. They are a superior set of people. A nation of an old, deep-rooted civilisation. It is because I believe the Chinese to be a powerful race, capable of taking a great hold upon this country, and because I want to preserve the type of my own nation, I am and always have been opposed to the influx of Chinese.'

The Cowper Government was the first to introduce a poll-tax on Chinese. After Lambing Flat it introduced a Chinese Immigration and Restriction Act . . . Parkes further tightened the Act, and made the poll-tax apply not only to those coming in by sea, but also to those entering from another State.

In 1888 Parkes imposed even more drastic restrictions. He limited the number to one Chinese passenger to every 300 tons, increased the poll-tax to £100, refused them naturalisation and stipulated that they could not work in the mining industry without a permit from the Minister for Mines.

The fight had only just started. It was one thing imposing a poll-tax, but it was another policing it. . . . Many slipped in without paying the head-tax. Gradually, they

---

48   Henry Parkes (1815–96) is considered the father of Australian Federation.

started to congregate in Chinese quarters in the city and take up their own occupations. Merchants indentured labour from Canton, and had the Chinese tied up with labour contracts that made them little better than slaves.

Furniture-making became one of the chief occupations. They were excellent cabinet makers. But instead of an eight-hour day, they were working twelve and fourteen hours, seven days a week. . . .

Urged on by the Labor Party, George Reid, in 1897, had a Bill for the Exclusion of Inferior Races passed through both Houses. When it reached the Governor, he decided to reserve it for Royal Assent. It was forwarded to Downing Street, and the British Government ruled that it would infringe on Britain's trading treaties with China, and might even endanger the holding of Hong Kong. So on the advice of her Government, Queen Victoria refused her Royal Assent. Reid returned to the attack, and passed another Bill which authorised the N.S.W. Immigration authorities to apply a dictation test to any intending immigrant, if they so decided. That was the origin of the Dictation Test device, which was later incorporated into the Commonwealth Immigration Act of 1901 . . .

In Queensland they had the Kanaka problem with the sugar cane industry. The sugar mills said they couldn't compete with sugar grown with coloured labour in the West Indies, or even Fiji. So they recruited island labour from the South Seas, who were called 'Kanakas.' Polynesians were indentured for five years at nominal wages. That led to the black-birding of labour in the islands by bullying captains. The Queensland Labor Party under Dawson and Fisher led the fight against Black Australia. Sir Samuel Griffiths, later Chief Justice, took up the cause and agreed to legislate to prohibit the importation of Kanakas from the islands. He won the elections and passed the Act. Then the sugar combine got to work. They told him that he would ruin the sugar industry. Griffiths then repudiated his election pledge, on which he had beaten McIlwraith and brought in a number of regulations regarding how the blacks should be employed. Labor kept up the fight in Queensland and eventually won, after agreeing to the proposition that the sugar industry should be subsidised by a bounty to keep it white. That was not until after Federation. . . .

. . . Had we listened to the do-gooders and the crusaders for international brotherhood and racial equality, the barriers would have come down long ago. Our living standard would have been destroyed. We would have had intermarriages of races, half-castes and quarter-castes with all the social dilemmas that invariably follow such racial mixtures. We would have had a Black, Brown and Brindle streak right through every strata of our society. Instead we risked the charge that we were drawing the colour line. We decided to keep this country as a citadel of the white peoples. Australia is still White Australia thanks to those who battled against those who wanted to exploit coloured labour for their own ends. We must keep it that way.[49]

The same situation pertained to New Zealand, Canada, and the United States. Today these aspects of the 'class struggle,' those of the White workers' revolt on the Rand in 1922, Canada in 1906, and elsewhere, have been put down the 'memory hole' by the Marxist and liberal bosses of the trades unions and socialist parties. The Left finds it opportune to cultivate the backing of ethnic minorities, feminists, and the so-called 'rainbow coalition,' since the 'working class' has been stubbornly resistant to Marxist overtures.

---

49   J. T. Lang, 'White Australia Saved Australia,' *I Remember* (Sydney: Invincible Press, 1956), cited by Kevin McCauley, *The Labor Party and White Australia*, Sydney, 2002, http://home.alphalink.com.au/~radnat/thelaborpartyandwhiteaustralia/labortwo.html.

Babel, Inc.

Although the first Act to restrict Asian immigration in Canada was passed in the colony of Victoria in 1855, this was not enforced and in 1883 coal miners went on strike for a wage increase.[50] Mine and railway magnate Robert Dunsmuir sacked the strikers and replaced them with Chinese coolie workers at $1 a day, compared to the White's $2. In response, 2,000 White workers marched on the waterfront at Vancouver and prevented 100 Chinese from disembarking.

Lieutenant Governor James Dunsmuir, son of Robert, had been premier of British Columbia. His administration was noted for its opposition to union labour and encouragement of Asian immigration. He had entered into a contract with the Japanese-Canadian Nippon Company of Vancouver to recruit 500 coolies to work the coal mines.[51] The Victoria Labour Congress declared its opposition to 'cheap labour.' On 27 March 1907 the Vancouver Trades Union issued a declaration deploring the women of wealthy families in British Columbia who wished to import Chinese servants, stating that 'the women of the working class do their own work; when they need help, they employ their own race.' If these women however preferred to play bridge and sip tea rather than working, they should decently remunerate 'girls of their own race.'

The early labour movement recognised the crux of the immigration problem: the necessity of dispensing with reliance on migrant labour, something that has contributed to the bringing down of civilisations from the Nubian labour of ancient Egypt to the reverse colonisation of Europe by the migrants of ex-colonies. It is a problem that segregation

50 Robert McIntosh, *Boys in the Pits: Child Labour in Coal Mines* (Quebec: McGill-Queen's University Press, 2000), 57–59.
51 'The 1907 Arrival of Many Low-Wage Labourers Precipitated the September, 1907 Vancouver Asiatic Riot, Immigration Watch Canada,' 14 August 2011, http://www.immigrationwatchcanada.org/2007/09/08/the-1907-arrival-of-many-low-wage-labourers-precipitated-the-september-1907-vancouver-asiatic-riot/.

in the Southern states of the United States could not resolve, nor even the bold doctrine of apartheid in South Africa with its aim of separate states. If a society wishes to maintain its cultural integrity, it must have a social and economic system that raises the standards of labour rather than relying on cheap migrant labour. This is something that the labour movement understood over a century ago, but which is now damned as 'racism' by the modern labour movement, in conjunction with global business.

Hence, in 1906 while the labour movement demanded immigration restrictions and the employment of White labour at decent remuneration, Alderman James Fox, representing the Canadian Manufacturers Association, called for two million Chinese immigrants to help develop Canada, stating: 'We must look at this from a practical and selfish point of view. To the material disadvantage of our workingmen it is intended to help. It is sad to see our laws prostituted to race prejudice.'

In 1905 coolie migrants started coming from places other than China. That year Japanese immigration companies began 'selling' workers from India. Dunsmuir's Canadian Pacific Railways and Steamship Line sent agents to Hong Kong to sell tickets to Indians, and 2,000 Indians came to replace unionised labour at Dunsmuir's saw mills.

1907 was a significant year. British Columbia passed two Acts to restrict Asian immigration, but these were blocked by the Federal Government. Dunsmuir's Wellington Colliery contracted to import thousands of Japanese workers over five years. Unionists and small businessmen formed the Asiatic Exclusion League, which also spread to U.S. cities. Dunsmuir's railroad company next contracted to import 12,000 Japanese to replace all of the White rail maintenance workers. On 26 July, 1,189 Japanese landed in Vancouver. Many were veterans of the 1905 Russo-Japanese War, and they marched into

Canada military style. Now also Sikhs were arriving, and most White mill workers had been replaced. On 7 September the now 20,000 member Asiatic Exclusion League called a 'Stand Up for White Canada' march, and 30,000 (almost half the population of Vancouver) joined the march.[52] Immigration restrictions were introduced, until in 1970 such measures were annulled by the Liberal government.

In the United States a similar situation developed, where 20,000 Chinese were introduced to work the mines and railroads in California.[53] In San Francisco the American Workingmen's Party, founded in 1877 and led by Denis Kearney, became a power in politics. Consequently, in 1882 the Chinese Exclusion Act was passed. One researcher, looking beyond the clichéd condemnations of Kearney and the Workingmen's Party, gets to the root of an exploitive system that worked against White Americans and Chinese alike:

> Indeed, most of the Chinese immigrants were indentured laborers who had been inveigled or impressed into decade or longer contracts by unscrupulous Chinese entrepreneurs, the notorious 'companies.' Indentured or contracted, free or unfree, the Chinese immigrants were formidable economic rivals: they worked hard, they worked cheap, and they gave no labor problems— the Chinese 'companies' which ruled the immigrants with an iron hand saw to that.[54]

From 1850 to 1877 there were many protests against Chinese immigration, but to no avail:

> All of them failed in the face of opposition from entrenched business interests—especially the railroads,

52 Ibid.
53 Kevin Jenks, 'Denis Kearney and the Chinese Exclusion Acts,' *The Social Contract Journal* 6, no. 3 (Spring 1996).
54 Ibid.

banks, and steamship lines—and reinforced by a vociferous strain of 'liberalism' led by ex-abolitionists and egalitarians, churchmen, and 'reformers' of various stripes. Then as now, the pro-immigration forces were well situated to influence public opinion from prestigious pulpits, editorships and professorial chairs.[55]

Hence the alignment of forces 150 years ago was similar to today's alignment: big business together with what today would be called the 'Left,' and the same types of liberal.

New Zealand workers likewise objected to coolie labour. Their primary champion was the iconic New Zealand statesman Premier Richard John Seddon, a former gold-digger himself, who was persistent in introducing restrictive measures that were aimed at circumventing the demands of the British Colonial Office that one could not discriminate against Chinese, Japanese, or Britain's colonial subjects. Seddon's Asiatic Restriction Bill of 1896 was blocked by Britain.[56]

The descendants of those first Chinese migrants—then often critiqued not only for their coolie labour, but also for their opium and gambling—acculturated successfully over the course of several generations. On that account, unfortunately, the apologists of multiculturalism and an 'Asian New Zealand' use their example to 'prove' that present-day objections by New Zealanders to Asian immigration are based on ignorance and xenophobia. Today, however the situation is quite different, especially insofar as Asian immigration is one, most visible, symptom of merging New Zealand (and Australia) into an Asian economic bloc as part of the globalisation process. A second factor is that China, unlike Seddon's time, has emerged

55 Ibid.
56 John E. Martin, 'Refusal of Assent—a Hidden Element of Constitutional History in New Zealand,' *Victoria University Law Review* 41, no. 1 (June 2010).

as a superpower and has geopolitical designs on this region. Again, Chinese immigration is a symptom of our relationship with China. Thirdly, it was thanks to Seddon and other statesmen, and the efforts of workers and small-scale merchants and tradesmen, that there were brakes put over a century ago on Asian immigration, without which New Zealand's demography and submergence into Asia might have proceeded well before the present.

Even in those times there were those within the labour movement who said that the answer was to unionise Asians workers and organise across racial lines, on the basis of class; that 'racism' and immigration restrictions serve capitalism in dividing the international working class. It is an example, yet again, of the Marxian and anarchist Left only being able to comprehend matters in terms of economics, without taking into account that ethnicities, cultures, and peoples are deeply rooted, innate, and not merely economic constructs that can be eliminated by changing economic and property relations, whether under socialism or capitalism.

The stalwarts of the old Labour movement, especially in the Anglophone world, including the United States, fought the consequences of alien immigration. Within the British Empire such immigration had the backing of the Colonial Office. The Empire had ceased to be living as an expression of the British spirit of Robert Clive, James Cook, and Francis Drake, and the heroism of Rorke's Drift. What the Empire had become, with the rise of the cosmopolitan oligarchs such as the Rothschilds and David Sassoon (whose opium trade was backed by the military might of the Empire), was an expression rather of moneyed interests, largely of non-British origin, as exemplified by the name Rothschild. Already the strained relations between Rothschild and Cecil Rhodes were symptomatic of the division that existed between the traditional, quintessential *British* merchant-explorer-statesman who had created the Empire, and the often alien oligarch who reaped the financial rewards. As we shall see in the next chapter, it was now an Empire that fought the Boers in the interests of new 'Britons' such as Alfred Beit whose loyalty to the Imperial idea, like the loyalty of today's oligarchs to any specific nation, lasts only as long as the interests of money are served.

As Karl Marx predicted—with satisfaction—capital would become increasingly internationalised, or what today is called globalised—and the old European colonial empires by World War I were restricting global profit maximisation. The empires required dismantling, and being replaced by international free trade. This latter became the official war aim of the new centre of international finance, the United States, and remains so in America's wars against 'terrorism' for 'democracy.' We shall now consider how the European empires were dismantled, with the purpose of allowing what the Left calls 'neo-colonialism' (generally without understanding its full implications) to fill the void.

Decolonisation as the Prelude
to Globalisation

The story of the eclipse of White rule in Africa, as with the European colonies of Indochina and elsewhere, is one of calculated world power-politics. Those who brought ruin to White Africa were not, as is commonly supposed among the Right, Moscow-trained communists and terrorists, but the 'Money Power' centred in Washington and New York. The reason for this is that the old empires had become too restrictive for capitalism that, as Karl Marx predicted gleefully, would become increasingly international. Additionally, the money market was becoming increasingly centred on Wall Street, New York, rather than in the old capitals of Europe. The empires had outlived their usefulness and had to be removed as impediments. The aim was to replace these old empires with a global empire, which is not loyal to any national tradition, people, culture, monarch, or state. The consequences of this have been for corporate interests to fill the void with the departure of the colonial powers, the competitors being the USSR and later Red China. China, while maintaining its own national interests, has nonetheless been willing to work in economic symbiosis with Western big business, which means that Russia remains more an obstacle to globalisation.[57]

The problem for the United States, after World War II, which had finally exhausted the old imperial powers through debt owed to the United States, and devastation, was how to push the colonial powers into divesting their empires, while (1) maintaining these ex-imperial states as allies in the Cold War, and (2) support so-called 'national liberation movements' that would not align with the USSR. The United States' opposition to European colonialism was therefore more cautious than it would otherwise have been

57   K. R. Bolton, *Geopolitics of the Indo-Pacific* (London: Black House Publishing, 2013).

had the USSR not emerged as a post-war rival rather than continuing her wartime alliance.

This was the policy pursued towards France in Indochina, where the United States aimed to eliminate French influence without alienating France as a Cold War ally or allowing a regime that would be aligned with the USSR.[58] *The Pentagon Papers* state of early U.S. policy on Indochina:

> Ambivalence characterized U.S. policy during World War II, and was the root of much subsequent misunderstanding. On the one hand, the U.S. repeatedly reassured the French that its colonial possessions would be returned to it after the war. On the other hand, the U.S. broadly committed itself in the Atlantic Charter to support national self-determination, and President Roosevelt personally and vehemently advocated independence for Indochina. F.D.R. regarded Indochina as a flagrant example of onerous colonialism which should be turned over to a trusteeship rather than returned to France. The President discussed this proposal with the Allies at the Cairo, Teheran, and Yalta Conferences and received the endorsement of Chiang Kai-shek and Stalin; Prime Minister Churchill demurred. At one point, Fall[59] reports, the President offered General de Gaulle Filipino advisers to help France establish a 'more progressive policy in Indochina'—which offer the General received in 'Pensive Silence.'[60]

Note that Stalin was among those agreeable to Roosevelt's proposition of trusteeship for Indochina in ousting the French after World War II, whereas Churchill, Prime Minister of the largest of imperial states, was to find himself

---

58 'U.S. Involvement in the Franco-Viet-Minh War 1950–1954,' *The Pentagon Papers* (Boston: Beacon Press, 1971), vol. 1, ch. I, pp. 53–75, https://www.mtholyoke. edu/acad/intrel/pentagon/pent5.htm.

59 Bernard Fall, *Last Reflections on a War* (1967).

60 *The Pentagon Papers*, vol. 1, ch. I, 'Background to the Crisis, 1940–50,' pp. 1–52.

Babel, Inc.

confronted with American anti-colonial policy. As is often the case, America played a duplicitous policy vis-à-vis its allies:

> U.S. commanders serving with the British and Chinese, while instructed to avoid ostensible alignment with the French, were permitted to conduct operations in Indochina which did not detract from the campaign against Japan. Consistent with F.D.R.'s guidance, the U.S. did provide modest aid to French—and Viet Minh—resistance forces in Vietnam after March, 1945, but refused to provide shipping to move Free French troops there. Pressed by both the British and the French for clarification U.S. intentions regarding the political status of Indochina, F.D.R maintained that 'it is a matter for postwar.'[61]

> . . . Through the fall and winter of 1945–1946, the U.S. received a series of requests from Ho Chi Minh for intervention in Vietnam; these were, on the record, unanswered. However, the U.S. steadfastly refused to assist the French military effort, e.g., forbidding American flag vessels to carry troops or war materiel to Vietnam.[62]

The problem for the globalist vision of a post-war 'new world order' was that Stalin, the United States' wartime ally, had rejected the prospect of the USSR serving as a junior partner with the United States to establish a Brave New World via the United Nations Organization. The USSR, moreover, pursued its own foreign policy that was more like the return of the old European colonialism that the United States was trying to undermine, than like comunist proclamations against imperialism.[63] Hence,

---

61   Ibid.
62   Ibid.
63   K. R. Bolton, *Stalin: The Enduring Legacy* (London: Black House Publishing,

the post-war policy pursued by the USSR that resulted in the Cold War required a more cautious approach by the United States in its anti-colonial agenda. In regard to Vietnam as elsewhere, especially in Africa right up until the withdrawal of Portugal from Africa in the 1970s, the United States enacted a policy of opposing colonialism while being cognisant of both losing its European allies and of allowing the Soviet Union to fill the void. In Indochina, while the United States had originally supported Ho's Viet Minh, there were suspicions of Soviet connections:

. . . However, the U.S., deterred by the history of Ho's communist affiliation, always stopped short of endorsing Ho Chi Minh or the Viet Minh. Accordingly, U.S. policy gravitated with that of France toward the Bao Dai solution. At no point was the U.S. prepared to adopt an openly interventionist course. To have done so would have clashed with the expressed British view that Indochina was an exclusively French concern, and played into the hands of France's extremist political parties of both the Right and the Left. The U.S. was particularly apprehensive lest by intervening it strengthen the political position of French Communists. Beginning in 1946 and 1947, France and Britain were moving toward an anti-Soviet alliance in Europe and the U.S. was reluctant to press a potentially divisive policy.[64]

. . . Increasingly, the U.S. sensed that French unwillingness to concede political power to Vietnamese heightened the possibility of the Franco-Viet Minh conflict being transformed into a struggle with Soviet imperialism. U.S. diplomats were instructed to 'apply such persuasion and/or pressure as is best calculated [to] produce desired result [of France's] unequivocally and promptly approving the principle of Viet independence.' France was notified that

2012), 125–39.

64 *The Pentagon Papers*, 'Background to the Crisis, 1940–50.'

the U.S. was willing to extend financial aid to a Vietnamese government not a French puppet . . .[65]

Interestingly, in 1948, the Office of Intelligence Research in the U.S. Department of State conducted a survey of communist influence in Southeast Asia, reporting that it was the French rather than the Viet Minh who were suspicious of U.S. motives:

> To date the Vietnam press and radio have not adopted an anti-American position. It is rather the French colonial press that has been strongly anti-American and has freely accused the U.S. of imperialism in Indochina to the point of approximating the official Moscow position.[66]

The same situation confronted the United States and the USSR in North Africa in regard to France. Both powers, as rival contenders to fill the power vacuum after European colonial scuttle, were obliged to take a softly-softly approach towards France in the Cold War. Yahia Zoubir writes of this:

> The decolonization of the Maghreb (Algeria, Morocco, and Tunisia) confronted the United States and the Soviet Union with challenging and similar dilemmas. The process of decolonization took place at the peak of the Cold War, a time of high tension in many places around the globe. The two superpowers' difficulties stemmed from the challenge not only of calculating how best to preserve their vital interests in the region and maintain their good relationship with France, the colonial power, but also of reconciling this need with winning over the colonial peoples seeking independence from France, thus preventing them from joining the rival's bloc.[67]

---

65 Ibid.
66 Ibid.
67 Yahia Zoubir, 'U.S. and Soviet Policies Towards France's Struggle with

Zoubir states that 'both superpowers pursued similar policies aimed at reconciling contradictory objectives to safeguard their own strategic, political, and economic interests. Owing to the importance they accorded to their respective relationships with France, they sought to appease the colonial power while simultaneously trying to gain the friendship of the nationalist movements opposed to it.' In fact, according to Zoubir, the USSR and the French Communist Party believed that the North African colonies should remain within the 'French Union.' Zoubir states that 'The Soviets mistrusted the political and ideological inclinations of the Maghrebi [French North Africa] nationalist leaders due to the latter's contacts with American officials whose support they solicited in their anticolonial struggle.'[68] The USSR, pursuing realpolitik rather than communism, saw France—which pursued an independent foreign policy—as a bulwark against U.S. influence. Zoubir states:

> This explains why Americans played a much more active role in the Maghreb than did the Soviets. But, it was this vigorous role assumed by the U.S. which compelled the Soviets and the French to be equally distrustful of American objectives in the Maghreb. Therefore, not surprisingly, Stalin's policy consisted in preserving the status quo in the French colonies and in preventing them from becoming part of the American sphere of influence.[69]

What temporarily thwarted the United States' anti-colonial intentions was the need to rebuild Europe in the aftermath of World War II, in face of Soviet expansion. This also necessitated rebuilding the economies of the colonial

---

Anticolonial Nationalism in North Africa,' *Canadian Journal of History* 30, no. 3 (December 1995).

68   Ibid.
69   Ibid.

powers. Hence, an ambiguous policy had to be pursued, which stated 'that in any given colonial issue, the United States must make a determination as to whether its security interests are best served by a support of the position of the colonial power or by the efforts to bring adjustments in the direction of the demands of nationalist groups.'[70]

As in Indochina, the French remained suspicious of U.S. objectives in North Africa, while U.S. diplomats and politicians tried to allay France's concerns. After the independence of Morocco and Tunisia, the U.S. granted economic support to these states. Following the discovery of oil in the Algerian Sahara, France's suspicions of the United States increased, and were aggravated by U.S. arms shipments to Tunisia following Franco-Tunisian clashes on the Algerian border.[71]

The consequences for the former colonial powers have included their own reverse 'colonisation' by migrants from their former colonies, while the former colonies, freed from the old European empires, have been integrated into a new world empire focused on Wall Street.

The Congress of Berlin (1884–85)

The Congress of Berlin showed how Europe could act collectively vis-à-vis non-Europeans. Although the Portuguese had established their colonies in Africa since the 16th century, the Congress brought the European colonial powers together to delineate spheres of interest to allow for the harmonious development of the Continent.[72] Even here, however, the United States was a signatory, showing that it had wider interests in the world than suggested by the

---

70 'The United States Attitude on the Colonial Question,' *Foreign Relations of the United States*, vol. III: United Nations Affairs (Washington, D.C., 1979), p. 1078. Cited by Zoubir.

71 Zoubir, op. cit.

72 Congress of Berlin, http://courses.wcupa.edu/jones/his312/misc/berlin.htm.

The Berlin Conference of 1884–85

Monroe Doctrine that supposedly focused U.S. interests over the Americas, and was intended to keep European powers out of the Americas.

Woodrow Wilson's Fourteen Points

The United States was born as a desire to become detached from Europe. The Anglo-Puritan origins of the United States are fundamentally a revolt against Western tradition. From another direction, the Masonic and Enlightenment ideals of the American Revolution made the United States the custodian of a messianic world revolutionary mission, the continuation of France's revolutionary Jacobinism which aimed to establish a 'universal republic' in the pursuit of free trade as a revolutionary doctrine. This neo-Jacobinism is the ideological basis for globalisation. The United States pursues the same revolutionary zeal in reconstructing the world in its image. Like the Jacobins, the United States has proclaimed itself the liberator of the world, guided by so-called 'American ideals.' Jefferson, who drafted the American Declaration of Independence, was supported by what were called 'Jacobin Clubs' in his bid for the American Presidency, Jefferson having written of the French Jacobin revolutionaries: 'The liberty of the whole earth was depending on the issue of the contest, and was ever such a prize won with so little innocent blood?' The huge amount of innocent blood that was indeed spilt during the 'Reign of Terror' was glossed over by Jefferson as justified.[73] As will be seen later, America was founded as a revolutionary state with a revolutionary mission—like Jacobin France, and the early years of Bolshevik Russia—to remake the world it its image, and that messianic revolutionary mission continues to motivate U.S. policies.

Alain de Benoist, the French philosopher and founder of the European 'New Right,' explained the character of the United States:

> The thought of the Founding Fathers was mainly inspired by Enlightenment philosophy,[74] which implies contractualism,[75] the 'language of rights,' and a belief in progress. With some justice, Christopher Lasch has said that the suppression of roots in the United States has always been seen as the main precondition of expanding freedoms.[76] This negative attitude towards the past is quite typical of liberal thought. The United States was born from a will to break with Europe. The

73   Thomas Jefferson, 'Letter to William Short' (3 January 1793), Thomas Jefferson Papers at the Library of Congress, Series 1, Reel 17, http://chnm.gmu.edu/revolution/d/592/.

74   The philosophy of the 18th-century intelligentsia which claimed that 'science'—generally their own drawing-room preconceptions of the world—would overthrow the 'tyranny of religious superstition' including the 'divine Right of Kings,' and establish a 'Universal Republic' of free peoples. These doctrines gave birth to the French Revolution and the American Revolution alike. The dogmas continue to dominate the Western world, and an increasing number of states that succumb to globalism.

75   The basis of a nation and of citizenship, being a legalistic 'social contract,' typically in the form of a written constitution, between individuals, defining their rights. Hence, nations are not defined in cultural or ethnic, organic terms, but in terms of a contractual agreement among individuals in a certain space.

76   'Roots' imply a collective identity, such a kinship bond with one's race, people, or culture.

first immigrant communities wanted to free themselves, which meant, in effect, freeing themselves from European rules and principles. On this basis, there arose a society which Ezra Pound[77] characterized as 'a purely commercial civilization.' Pound's characterization accords with that of Tocqueville, who claimed: 'The passions that animate Americans are commercial, not political ones, for they have carried into their politics the habits of trade.' The first immigrants wanted not only to break with Europe. They wanted to create a new society that would regenerate the whole world. They sought a new Promised Land which would become the model of a Universal Republic.'[78]

Benoist went on to explain this messianic globalism in terns of U.S. foreign policy:

Thomas Jefferson defined it as 'a universal nation in pursuit of indisputable universal ideas.' John Adams saw it as a pure and virtuous republic whose destiny was to govern the world and to perfect mankind. This messianic vocation later took the form of Manifest Destiny, which John O'Sullivan proclaimed in 1839; America's mission, he claimed, was to bring its way of life, the best conceivable, to the rest of the world. In 1823, James Monroe presented the country's first foreign policy doctrine as if it were a testament of Providence. Nearly all his successors have done likewise. . . . Foreign relations, then, are only conceived as a way of diffusing the American ideal to the whole Earth. Because they

---

77 American-born poet, and a founder of modern English literature, who spent most of his life in Europe and particularly in Italy, where he supported the Fascist regime during World War II with his radio broadcasts. Pound's foremost concern was to free culture from oligarchy, and towards this end he also avidly supported Social Credit economic theory. See K. R. Bolton, *Artists of the Right* (San Francisco: Counter-Currents Publishing, 2012), 97–119.

78 'French "New Right" Philosopher Alain de Benoist on America,' French Dissidents, 20 February 2012, http://frenchdissidents.wordpress.com/2012/02/20/french-new-right-philosopher-alain-de-benoist-on-america-2/.

see their society as better than any other, the Americans feel not the slightest need to learn about others, and feel it's up to others to adopt their way of life.[79]

This is the messianic globalist spirit that animates America whether under administrations that are Republican or Democratic, or supposedly 'Left' or 'Right.' Hence, when President George W. Bush announced the U.S. and United Nations' war against Iraq in 1990, he did so in the name of a 'new world order,' in the name of the universalistic 'Enlightenment' principles that the United Nations had been founded upon:

> This is an historic moment. We have in this past year made great progress in ending the long era of conflict and cold war. We have before us the opportunity to forge for ourselves and for future generations a new world order—a world where the rule of law, not the law of the jungle, governs the conduct of nations. When we are successful—and we will be—we have a real chance at this new world order, an order in which a credible United Nations can use its peacekeeping role to fulfil the promise and vision of the UN's founders.[80]

Bush's announcement reflected the founding principals of the American Republic as the herald of a 'Universal Republic' based on contractual agreements, as though peoples, nations, states, races, and cultures can be remoulded in the same manner as commercial and trades agreements, by a global 'rule of law,' as Bush referred to it.

President Woodrow Wilson's 'Fourteen Points'[81] for the reconstitution of the world in the aftermath of World War

---

79   Ibid.

80   President George W. Bush to U.S. Congress, 16 January 1991.

81   Woodrow Wilson, 'Fourteen Points,' 1918, http://www.fordham.edu/halsall/mod/1918wilson.html.

I expressed the same globalising tendency of capitalism by the early 20th century. Crucially, World War I showed the 'coloured world' the weaknesses in the White world, on which the German conservative philosopher-historian Oswald Spengler wrote:

> This war was a defeat of the white races, and the Peace of 1918 was the first great triumph of the coloured world: symbolized by the fact that today it is allowed to have a say in the disputes of the white states among themselves in the Geneva League of Nations—which is nothing but a miserable symbol of shameful things.[82]

This was a harbinger of the more acute crisis of the White world wrought by World War II and the rise of the coloured world.

Wilson's manifesto was Bolshevik—and Jacobin—in spirit. His doctrine has remained the basis of U.S. policy, as indicated by the example of President Bush's 1991 declaration of war against Iraq. Wilson, speaking on behalf of Wall Street, clearly had a pro-Bolshevik attitude towards Russia. He was addressing himself on the world stage in the first instance to assure the precarious Bolshevik regime the goodwill of the United States where business interests were keen to sign contracts with their supposed deadly enemies,[83] and secondly to the colonial peoples in representing the United States as the leader of anti-imperialism. The new world order Wilson outlined was based on global free trade that would necessitate the elimination of the old European empires, to be replaced by a new 'empire' of money ruled from Wall Street and Washington:

> III. The removal, so far as possible, of all economic barriers and the establishment of an equality of trade

---

82 Oswald Spengler, *The Hour of Decision* (New York: Alfred A. Knopf, 1934), 209.

83 The 'intervention' in Russia by American troops supposedly to help the White armies against the Bolsheviks is one of the great myths of history. See K. R. Bolton, *Revolution from Above* (London: Arktos Media, 2011), 66–97.

conditions among all the nations consenting to the peace and associating themselves for its maintenance.

V. A free, open-minded, and absolutely impartial adjustment of all colonial claims, based upon a strict observance of the principle that in determining all such questions of sovereignty the interests of the populations concerned must have equal weight with the equitable claims of the government whose title is to be determined.

XIV. A general association of nations must be formed under specific covenants for the purpose of affording mutual guarantees of political independence and territorial integrity to great and small states alike.[84]

Although the specifics allude to the Central Powers, as far as the 'Fourteen Points' go for the *reorganisation of the post-war world*, they are unequivocally directed against all traditional Empires:

In regard to these essential rectifications of wrong and assertions of right we feel ourselves to be intimate partners of all the governments and peoples associated together against the Imperialists. We cannot be separated in interest or divided in purpose. We stand together until the end.[85]

Wilson's declaration gave the coloured world the assurance of American support. It is from this time that a misconception arises, especially among the American Right, that British imperialists from the 'Round Table' network, and the internationalists around Wilson, who formed the Council on Foreign Relations, established an Anglo-American conspiratorial network to rule the world.

---

84 Wilson, 'Fourteen Points.' This 'general association of nations' was a reference to Wilson's plan for a League of Nations, precursor to the United Nations Organization. Ironically, the Senate voted against U.S. membership.

85 Wilson, 'Fourteen Points.'

This misconception came from a conspiratorial rendering[86] of several dozen pages from American historian Dr. Carroll Quigley's *Tragedy and Hope*.[87] Quigley however got the facts uncharacteristically wrong, and they have since spawned a lot of theorising.

Anglo-American Breach

Far from there being a longstanding accord between Anglophile elitists in the United States and Britain to rule the world, when the Empires had become too restrictive for High Finance, an anti-imperialist, internationalist agenda centred on Washington and New York became the new paradigm. As Quigley stated, this did indeed centre around the think tank, the Council on Foreign Relations (CFR), but the mooted alliance between the Americans and British did not eventuate.

In fact the British imperialists of the Round Table Group and the Wall Street internationalists represented by 'Colonel' Edward Mandell House's think tank 'The Inquiry,'[88] had a falling out over post-war aims. Thom Burnett explains that the identification of what Quigley (and subsequent conspiracy writers) call an 'Anglophile' network for world domination is a misinterpretation.

The intentions of these internationalist bankers, industrialists, and intellectuals were to unite with the British Round Table Group, the latter becoming the Royal Institute of International Affairs. This had been agreed upon at the Versailles Peace Conference in 1918. The aim

---

86   W. Cleon Skousen, *The Naked Capitalist: A Review and Commentary on Dr Carroll Quigley's Book Tragedy and Hope* (Salt Lake City: the author, 1971).

87   Carroll Quigley, *Tragedy and Hope: A History of the World in Our Time* (New York: Macmillan, 1966).

88   After World War I, 'The Inquiry' became the Council on Foreign Relations, originating for the purposes of advising President Wilson on post-war foreign policy. See Bolton, *Revolution from Above*, 30–47.

had been to create an American Institute of International Affairs. However it soon transpired that neither the British nor the Americans were eager to continue with a joint project.[89]

Peter Grose confirms this breach in his official history of the CFR, *Continuing The Inquiry: The Council on Foreign Relations from 1921 to 1996*:

> To Shepardson fell the task of informing the British colleagues of this unfortunate reality. Crossing to London, he recalled thinking that 'it might be quite unpleasant to have to say for the first time that the Paris Group of British colleagues could not be members' of the American branch. The explanation to the British was begun (shall we say?) haltingly. However, instead of the frigid look which had been feared, the faces of the British governing body showed slightly red and very happy. They had reached the same conclusion in reverse, but had not yet found a good way of getting word to the other side of the Atlantic!'[90]

Burnett[91] shows that after World War II the globalists around the CFR were willing to cooperate with the USSR in establishing a post-war new world order, but they would concede nothing to British imperial interests. These American-based globalists working along the same anti-imperialist direction as the USSR, sought to undermine and replace the British and all other European empires. However U.S.-Soviet post-war cooperation was rejected by the USSR, despite U.S. overtures.[92] As mentioned

89 Thom Burnett and Alex Games, *Who Really Runs the World?* (London: Collins and Brown, 2005), 102.

90 Peter Grose, *Continuing The Inquiry: The Council on Foreign Relations from 1921 to 1996* (New York: Council on Foreign Relations, 2006). The entire book can be read online at: Council on Foreign Relations: http://www.cfr.org/about/history/cfr/index.html.

91 Burnett, *Who Really Runs the World?*, 106–7.

92 Bolton, *Revolution from Above*, 24–25. Also, Bolton, *Stalin: The Enduring Legacy*.

previously, the breach between the United States and the USSR in the aftermath of World War II, resulting in the Cold War, meant that American foreign policy had to tread a careful balance between destroying the old European empires while keeping those imperial powers within the anti-Soviet orbit.

The Atlantic Charter

World War II had brought most of the imperial powers to exhaustion, and the United States and the USSR emerged as the dominant powers in the midst of European ruin.

The 'Atlantic Charter' established the U.S. vision for the post-World War II era with the same internationalist, anti-imperial agenda as Wilson's 'Fourteen Points' after World War I. Point three of the Charter states that the United States and Britain guarantee to 'respect the right of all peoples to choose the form of government under which they will live . . .' As with the 'Fourteen Points,' the focus for the post-war era was on international free trade, which would necessarily undermine imperial trade preferences. Point four stated that Britain and the United States would 'endeavor, with due respect for their existing obligations, to further the enjoyment by all States, great or small, victor or vanquished, of access, on equal terms, to the trade and to the raw materials of the world which are needed for their economic prosperity.'[93]

British Prime Minister Winston Churchill was alarmed by Roosevelt's intentions, as evident from the account of proceedings given by the President's son, Elliott. The United States' post-war agenda would include the dismantling of the Empires for the purpose of creating an American neo-colonialism under the guise of free trade.

---

93   Franklin D. Roosevelt and Winston S. Churchill, The Atlantic Charter, 14 August 1941, http://usinfo.org/docs/democracy/53.htm.

President Franklin D. Roosevelt and Winston Churchill

Roosevelt said to Churchill: 'Of course, after the war, one of the preconditions of any lasting peace will have to be the greatest possible freedom of trade. No artificial barriers. As few favoured economic agreements as possible. Opportunities for expansion. Markets open for healthy competition.'[94]

When Churchill raised the question of Empire trade agreements Roosevelt interjected:

> Those Empire trade agreements are a case in point. . . . The peace cannot include any continued despotism. The structure of the peace demands and will get equality of peoples. Equality of peoples involves the utmost freedom of competitive trade. Will anyone suggest that Germany's attempt to dominate trade in central Europe was not a major contributing factor to war?[95]

Note that Roosevelt states a major factor in the war

---

94   Elliott Roosevelt, *As He Saw It* (New York: Duell, Sloan and Pearce, 1946), 35.
95   Ibid.

against Germany was the Reich's success in negotiating what was becoming a self-sufficient trading bloc based on barter; thereby taking states out of the international trade and financial system.[96] Roosevelt wanted the predatory economic system to prevail over the world by the elimination not only of the Reich, but also of all the Allied empires that he equated with the Reich. Today this is called 'globalisation,' and we are having ever more wars—against Serbia, Iraq, Afghanistan, Libya, and so on—to impose this system while the so-called 'colour revolutions' funded and instigated by the Soros network, the National Endowment for Democracy, USAID, Freedom House, and a myriad of other globalist organisations, subvert and topple regimes that are reticent about opening up to globalisation.[97]

The following day, Churchill spoke in despair, knowing that Britain could not survive the war without U.S. support: 'Mr. President, I believe you are trying to do away with the British Empire. Every idea you entertain about the structure of the post-war world demonstrates it.'[98]

Decolonisation of Africa

While the United States pursued a decolonisation agenda throughout the world, being able to point to its own relinquishing of the Philippines as evidence of its good faith, it is in Africa that the White peoples were left to their fate with the Mau Mau in Kenya, Holden Roberto's butchers in Angola, and the gutless antics of subhumans that continue today in former Rhodesia and South Africa. When conservatives throughout the world looked with alarm at the prospect of the USSR controlling the former colonies and especially the mineral wealth, this served as

---

96   For a description of Axis Germany, Italy, Japan economic policies, see Bolton, *The Banking Swindle*, 103–20.

97   Cf. Bolton, *Revolution from Above*, 213–44.

98   Roosevelt, *As He Saw It*, 31.

a convenient red-herring for the United States to advance its neo-colonialist agenda on the pretext of thwarting communism by handing power over to 'moderate Blacks.' Hence while the USSR trained Black leaders at Patrice Lumumba University,[99] the United States was training and funding its own Black cadres to establish and run puppet governments.

The first imperial powers to be targeted by the United States were France and Britain in West Africa. The United States gave $94.7 million to West Africa.[100] The intention of such aid in displacing the European administrations was clear. In 1955, the U.S. House of Representatives stated 'that the United States should administer its foreign policies and programs and exercise its influence so as to support other peoples in their efforts to achieve self-government or independence.'[101] 'Self-government or independence' was a euphemism—or doublethink—for Wall Street control of the ex-colonial territories.

Creating the Post-Colonial Bureaucracy

In 1953 the Africa-America Institute (AAI) was established to fund and train the Black leadership and bureaucracy of decolonised Africa. The purpose was stated to be to enable the United States to 'build relationships with the new African leadership,' as the White administrators were ousted. Debbie Meyer, an AAI director, stated that over the course of fifty years 22,000 Africans have received their postgraduate education in the United States, many having returned to Africa 'to play leading roles in developing their

99 C. Germani, 'Moscow's academic nightmare, University in decline: Patrice Lumumba University,' *The Baltimore Sun*, 5 November 1995, http://articles. baltimoresun.com/1995-11-05/news/1995309007_1_patrice-lumumba-dream-school-moscow.

100 Frederick Pedler, *Main Currents of West African History, 1940–1978* (New York: Barnes & Noble, 1979), 96.

101 Ibid., 267.

countries and in *linking them to the global economy.*'[102] The stated aim of the United States has not changed since President Wilson: to establish a world order based on a single economic paradigm, that of the free market and the international finance system upon which it is hinged; a 'global economy.'

The AAI states that its 'work is made possible through funds provided by the U.S. government, African governments, private foundations, corporate donors, multilateral institutions and individuals.'[103]

Among its first major programmes was the establishment of the 'U.S.-South Africa Leader Exchange Program' in 1958.[104] The AAI's Guinea Scholarship Program (1960–69) provided the training for the new leadership of 'post-independence Guinea,' with funding from the American government agency, USAID.[105] The Southern African Student Program 1961–1983 was funded by the U.S. State Department, as 'an effort to provide educational training to students from South Africa, Namibia, Angola, Mozambique and Zimbabwe, to provide a cadre of leadership in these countries which were transitioning into independent nations.'[106] The African Training Program (1964–69) was directed toward Africans in the French colonies, with funding from USAID.

In what was presumably training for fleeing terrorists, the AAI operated programmes for 'refugees' including the East Africa Refugee Program (1962–71) and the Southern African Training Program (1971–76). The initial

---

102 Emphasis added.
103 The Africa-America Institute, 'About AAI,' http://www.aaionline.org/about-aai/.
104 http://www.aaionline.org/about-aai/history/1950s/.
105 The Africa-America Institute, http://www.aaionline.org/programs/past-programs/the-guinea-scholarship-program-gsp-1960-%E2%80%93-1969/.
106 The Africa-America Institute, http://www.aaionline.org/programs/past-programs/southern-african-student-program-sasp-1961-%E2%80%93-1983/.

programme was for the training of personnel 'in anticipation of independence.' The latter programme—once Portugal had scuttled from Africa—was then directed towards the remaining White states of Southern Africa: 'Namibia, South Africa and Zimbabwe, for employment in their countries of asylum with a later focus on the repatriation of trainees.'[107] This programme was continued through 1976–1981, with funds from USAID.[108]

While Portuguese fled Mozambique for their lives, the Money Power moved in, unperturbed by noises about 'nationalisation.' Millions in aid money came in from the West, and lucrative business deals were made regardless of nationalisation. Likewise, in Zambia, when Kaunda grabbed a 51 per cent share in the Anglo-American owned copper industry, Oppenheimer regarded 'government participation' as a welcome move.[109]

The AAI is not some Marxist lobby or a group of naïve, wealthy liberals who have been tricked into funding communistic causes. It has since its foundation been a nexus between the U.S. Government and Big Business in shaping post-colonial Africa and providing the personnel for the bureaucracies. The present Chair of the AAI Board, Kofi Appenteng, has been employed with Thacher Proffitt, corporate lawyers, is a lifetime member of the Council on Foreign Relations (CFR), and is on the board of the Ford Foundation.[110]

---

107 http://www.aaionline.org/programs/past-programs/southern-african-refugee-education-project-sarep-1976-%E2%80%93-1981/.

108 http://www.aaionline.org/programs/past-programs/southern-african-refugee-education-project-sarep-1976-%E2%80%93-1981/.

109 Ibid., 47.

110 The reader should not be confused into thinking that because the Ford family does not run the Ford Foundation, that it is a body that has been infiltrated and controlled by Leftists, rather than functioning in the service of plutocracy. Ford and other such Foundations are run by directors and trustees affiliated with Big Business, often with Rockefeller connections. See Bolton, *Revolution from Above*, 27–30.

The President and CEO of AAI is Mora McLean, who came from the Ford Foundation, and is a CFR member. Members of the Board include: William Asiko, President of the Coca-Cola Africa Foundation & Director of Public Affairs and Communications for the Coca-Cola Company in Africa; Rosalind Kainyah, ex-Director of Public Affairs, USA for the De Beers Group, part of the Oppenheimer mining conglomerate; George Kirkland, Executive Vice President, Chevron Corporation; Carlton Masters, President & CEO, GoodWorks International, a CFR member; Steven Pfeiffer, Chair, Executive Committee, Fulbright & Jaworski LLP, corporate law firm, a CFR member; Maurice Tempelsman, past Chairman AAI, Senior Partner, Leon Tempelsman & Son (involved with mining, investments and business development), and 'Chairman of the Board of Directors of Lazare Kaplan International Inc., the largest cutter and polisher of 'ideal cut diamonds in the United States,' member of the International Advisory Council of the American Stock Exchange, member of the CFR, etc.[111]

The AAI provides a few profiles of the 23,000 Africans they have trained, such as: Joy Phumaphi, Botswana, Vice President and Head of the World Bank Human Development Network; Dr. Mbuyamu I. Matungulu, Congo, Mission Chief to Benin, International Monetary Fund; Charles Boamah, Controller and Director, African Development Bank; H. E. Nahas Angula, Prime Minister, Republic of Namibia; Mamadou Dia (Senegal) Country Director for Côte d'Ivoire and Guinea, Africa Region, World Bank; Dr. Renosi Mokate, Deputy Governor, South African Reserve Bank, et al.[112]

It would be naive to think that the United States, in conjunction with the global financial powers, have trained

---

111 AAI, 'Board,' http://www.aaionline.org/about-aai/board/.
112 AAI, 'Alumni Profiles,' http://www.aaionline.org/alumni-network/alumni-profiles/.

Babel, Inc.

23,000 Africans to take over post-colonial Africa simply as a humanitarian gesture. Some of the sponsors of AAI include for 2008 (the latest available): Barrick Gold Corporation; Citibank; Coca-Cola Africa; Credit Suisse; Chevron; Coca-Cola Africa Foundation; De Beers Group; Exxon Mobil Corporation; Fulbright and Jaworski LLP; Global Aluminium; Goldman Sachs & Co.; H. J. Heinz Co.; J. P. Morgan Chase; Lazare Kaplan International Inc.; PepsiCo. Inc.; Shell International Limited; Thacher Proffitt & Wood LLP; H. J. Heinz Company Foundation; American Express Foundation; International Finance Corporation, etc.[113]

Note the involvement of the Council on Foreign Relations, and luminaries of the Money Power such as Goldman Sachs, Oppenheimer, and Rockefeller interests.

Belgian Congo

The former Belgian colony of the Congo represents a special story on the incursions of global neo-colonialism, the civil war between the central authority and the breakaway province of Katanga reflecting rivalry between two factions of monopoly capital. U.S. Congressman Donald Bruce exposed the forces at work in a speech before Congress in 1960.When Katanga attempted to secede, United Nations troops invaded it. Congressman Bruce showed that the reason for the UN invasion of Katanga was to secure for the American Anaconda group the copper mining interests owned by Union Minière du Haute Congo. A consortium had been formed by American and Swedish companies, and was directed by Bo Hammarskjöld, brother of the UN Secretary-General Dag Hammarskjöld. Sture Linner, UN representative in the Congo, had been the chief engineer of the Liberian-American Mining Company (LAMCO), one of the consortia. UN Congo 'experts' Sven Schwartz and Borj Hjortsberg-Nordlund, were both also part of LAMCO.

---

113 AAI, 'Supporters,' http://www.aaionline.org/support-aai/supporters/.

A UN Army carrier crosses a bridge in the Congo 1963.

From the U.S. Fowler Hamilton, the State Department official responsible for implementing U.S. policy through USAID in Africa, was part of the U.S.-Swedish consortium. Congressman Bruce's investigation found that prior to the UN invasion, Schwartz had been sent to the Congo by the UN to undertake a study on mining. His recommendation was that Union Minière interests should be nationalised.[114]

U.S. policy operated through the United Nations, with the aim of undermining the Katanga secessionist government of Tshombe, where Belgian mining interests were maintained and which had the support of Rhodesian and Belgian interests. The UN invasion of Katanga aroused much ill-will in Europe against the US-UN action.[115] The UN forces went on a rampage through Katanga, where ambulances were strafed and bombed and civilians were shot.[116]

114 Benson, *The Struggle for Africa*, 51–53.
115 U.S. Department of State, 'Congo Crisis,' *Foreign Relations*, 1961–63, vol. XX, 13 January 1995.
116 G. Edward Griffin, *The Fearful Master: A Second Look at the United Nations* (Boston: Western Islands, 1964), Part I, 'Katanga,' pp. 3–64.

In 1974 what is now called Zaire served notice on 50,000 non-Blacks that their properties and businesses had been nationalised.[117] Conversely, American Big Business was described as 'a financial power in the country.'[118]

Last Empire: America's Assault on Portuguese Africa

While the Portuguese armed forces were engaged in fighting Black guerrillas in Angola and Mozambique, in their rear they were being 'stabbed in the back' by a much more lethal enemy based in the United States. The Portuguese territories in Southern Africa were the last vestiges of European colonial power that not long ago had spanned the world.

Imperial Scuttle

While most of the European colonial powers had been engaged in a fratricidal war that left them materially and morally ravished, and in debt to international finance, Portugal was an exception, wisely having maintained her neutrality during World War II, and continued to develop her African territories. The Portuguese Empire administered by a Christian Corporatist[119] 'New State' inaugurated by Professor Salazar, was a major obstacle to the post-1945 new world order.

While the focus for superpower incursions into Africa and other decolonised territories was on the USSR, which trained

---

117 Benson, *The Struggle for Africa*, 49.
118 Ibid., citing *The Daily News* (Durban), 6 April 1974.
119 'Corporatism,' not to be confused with financial corporations, was a new method of government based on traditional Catholic social doctrine, that gained widespread support as an alternative to both Marxism and capitalism after World War I. Corporatist states, which aimed to integrate both capital and labour above class divisions, into a unified nation, where political representation was based on guilds, syndicates, unions or 'corporations,' rather than by political parties, were inaugurated around the world from Brazil to Austria.

its African puppets at Patrice Lumumba University, few realised that the major centre of subversion was the United States. While Patrice Lumumba University was established in 1960,[120] the United States had established the Africa-America Institute (AAI) in 1953 to train their Black puppets.

Although the Portuguese regular army had uprooted FRELIMO in Mozambique in 1970 with Operation Gordian Knot, that terrorist organisation continued receiving funds from the Ford Foundation via the Mozambique Institute.[121] Black terrorists were provided with a refuge and training under the AAI's East Africa Refugee Program (1962–71) and the Southern African Training Program (1971–76).

Fernando Andresen Guimarães, a director of the UN Department of Peace Keeping Operations, stated that the United States gave support at an early stage to the murderous Holden Roberto:

> The Kennedy administration also acted beyond the United Nations and sought directly to support an anti-colonial movement against the Portuguese. Holden Roberto, the U.P.A. (and later FNLA leader) had by the end of the 1950s established a wide range of contacts in the United States. Due to its prominent role in the anti-colonial uprising in northern Angola in 1961, the U.P.A. was the Angolan nationalist movement with the most international exposure. Washington authorized the C.I.A. to extend support to Roberto and U.P.A.[122]

In 1959 Roberto travelled to Washington where he met President Kennedy. U.S. support to Roberto included a university scholarship programme for African students from the Portuguese colonies.

---

120 http://www.rudn.ru/en/.

121 Ben Whitaker, *The Foundations: An Anatomy of Philanthropy and Society* (London: Eyre Methuen, 1974), 24.

122 F. A. Guimarães, The United State and Decolonisation of Angola, Lisbon, October 2003, http://www.ipri.pt/artigos/artigo.php?ida=5.

U.S. military assistance for Portugal was cut from $US25,000,000 to $3,000,000 and a ban on commercial sales of arms to Portugal was imposed in mid-1961. The United States supported the prohibition on the use of NATO war materiel in Africa.[123] From 1965 U.S. military aid to Portugal was reduced to $1,000,000 annually, and mostly consisted of spare parts.[124] That year the U.S. State Department advised its Embassy in Lisbon what its line should be towards Salazar:

> Basis for U.S. policies: . . . U.S. believes change fact of life in our era. Changes in Portuguese Africa as inevitable as elsewhere in world, though Portugal still has power to decide whether they will take place with her or against her. We believe failure to respond now to self-determination aspirations of Portuguese Africans will result in changes detrimental to interests of United States and West as well as to Portugal. This is why U.S. continually urges Portugal in its own interest become champion of political changes which will take place in her territories and, being based on pragmatic principles, it is why U.S. policies in respect this situation have not changed and should not be expected to change. . . .
>
> You should also tell Salazar U.S. gratified at indications certain African leaders interested in further talks with Portugal. We plan emphasise with Foreign Ministry importance these conversations and our concern that there be no prior conditions attached to them. We hope Portugal will adopt constructive attitude toward such meetings.[125]

---

123 Ibid.

124 U.S. briefing memorandum on military assistance to Portugal, from the Country Director for Kenya, Tanzania, Seychelles, and Uganda (Feld) to the Deputy Assistant Secretary of State for African Affairs (Moore), Washington, October 28, 1968. Department of State, Central Files, DEF 19–8 US–PORT. Secret.

125 Telegram from the U.S. Department of State to the Embassy in Portugal, Washington, April 16, 1964.

As we have seen previously in regard to U.S. policies towards the French in Indochina and Algeria, Washington feared alienating Portugal during the Cold War, but the United States' support for Roberto continued nonetheless. The policy was typically duplicitous, and a classic 'stab in the back.' Roberto's adviser was John Marcum, an adviser to Averell Harriman[126] on the Portuguese colonies. Already in 1964 there was a close association between Americans in Leopoldville linked to the U.S. Embassy, the CIA, Congolese political circles and Holden Roberto. 'Later in 1975, this triangle was to be instrumental in formulating the context for the U.S. decision to provide covert support for the FNLA.'[127]

However, U.S. support to Roberto was more significant than indicated by Guimarães. Since 1969, Roberto had been on a $10,000-a-year retainer from the CIA.[128] Yet, despite the U.S. support for the FNLA to supposedly counter the Soviet-backed MPLA, the official policy was *not* to discourage the MPLA.[129] What is not stated in such analyses is that international power politics and Cold War rivalries were being played out over the corpses of White settlers. Roberto, as the 'moderate' option to the Soviet-backed MPLA, was later to recall that when his gang invaded from their base in the Congo in 1961, overrunning farms, government outposts, and trading centres, 'this time the slaves did not cower. They massacred everything.'[130] The subsequent 27-year civil war between the FNLA and the MPLA resulted in 500,000 deaths.

---

126 Harriman was a U.S. Establishment luminary, serving in numerous ambassadorial roles, and as assistant and under secretary of state, chairman of the Business Council, member of the internationalist Club of Rome, and the Council on Foreign Relations, and an initiate of the powerful, crypto-Masonic, Yale-based secret society Lodge 322.

127 Guimarães, op. cit.

128 *New York Times*, 25 September 1975.

129 State Department Circular 92, 16 July 1963.

130 'Holden Roberto Dies at 84, Fought to Free Angola from Portuguese Rule,' *New York Times*, 4 August 2007.

Recolonisation

The AAI's initial programme for 'refugees' (i.e., fleeing terrorists) from Portuguese Africa was for the training of personnel 'in anticipation of independence.' After Portugal's departure from Africa the program was directed towards 'Namibia, South Africa and Zimbabwe, for employment in their countries of asylum with a later focus on the repatriation of trainees.'[131] This programme was continued through 1976–1981, with funds from USAID.[132]

In 1975, soon after the Portuguese departure from Africa, the AAI established the Development Training Program for Portuguese-Speaking Africa (DTPSA) to train the post-colonial leadership for the former colonies of Angola, Mozambique, Guinea-Bissau, Cape Verde, São Tomé, and Príncipe. This programme was also funded by USAID,[133] which serves as a means by which U.S. influence is extended worldwide via foreign aid.

As the European colonial administrators moved out of Africa, international corporations extended their own form of colonialism by entering into partnerships with the new African leaders. Behind the façade of nationalisation, global capital embarked on lucrative business arrangements under the protection of the post-colonial tyrannies. For example, the day that Mozambique's President Samora Machel announced his nationalisation programme General Mining, linked with the Oppenheimer dynasty's Anglo-American Corporation, negotiated with the new regime a deal for bulk-handling chrome loading equipment.[134]

---

131 http://www.aaionline.org/programs/past-programs/southern-african-refugee-education-project-sarep-1976-%E2%80%93-1981/.

132 http://www.aaionline.org/programs/past-programs/southern-african-refugee-education-project-sarep-1976-%E2%80%93-1981/.

133 http://www.aaionline.org/programs/past-programs/development-training-program-for-portuguese-speaking-africa-dtpsa-1975-%E2%80%93-1985/.

134 Ivor Benson, *The Struggle for Africa* (Perth: Australian League of Rights, 1978), 54.

The Portuguese 'New State' that had outlived all other such experiments from Europe to South America, was an anomaly in a world that was being prepared for 'globalisation' and the 'new world order.' Salazar's 'New State' subordinated economics to High Policy, which in turn was based on traditional Christian European values. Such a state could not be allowed to endure in a world that had to be reshaped on economic principles. Journalist and author Ivor Benson, who lived in Africa and knew the situation well, having been an adviser to the Rhodesian government of Ian Smith, commented that 'in Portugal politics has remained in power and has not become subordinate to economics . . . they have not made the Gross National Product their God. Therefore in Portugal economics is the servant, not the master.'[135]

Unlike most politicians then or since, the Portuguese statesmen were conscious of what they were up against. Dr. Franco Noguieira, Portuguese Foreign Minister, stated of the subterranean forces at work in Africa:

> Africa has been subjected to a regime that excludes European interests and African interests as well, neither being sufficiently strong to impose themselves. A form of autonomy and independence has been created which ensures the destruction of the old forms of sovereignty and permits the setting up of new forms of sovereignty so precarious and so artificial that it is an easy matter to dominate them. The result has been that the real autonomy and the real control are to be found outside the frontiers of the new political units. The aim is to dominate Angola and Mozambique and to include them in the spheres of foreign influences, to utilise their economic and strategic positions for the benefit of other Powers.[136]

---

135 Ivor Benson, *This Worldwide Conspiracy* (Melbourne: New Times, 1972), 73.
136 Quoted by Benson, *This Worldwide Conspiracy*, 70–73.

The scuttling of Portuguese Africa followed soon after the 'Carnation Revolution,' the leftist army coup of junior officers in 1974 that toppled the New State; a revolution moreover that had been precipitated by years of economic strain as Portugal fought to hold her empire. The war against the Soviet and U.S. backed terrorists had accounted for 42 per cent of Portugal's annual budget.[137] However, the new leader of Portugal, General Spinola, had nonetheless aimed to establish a Portuguese federation and keep the African territories within the Portuguese sphere, but Spinola was soon passé. The way was opened for the continuation of the onslaught against the final bastions of European rule in Africa: Rhodesia and South Africa.

Rhodesia and South Africa

The destruction of White rule in the Portuguese Territories was the beginning of the end for the White geopolitical bloc of Southern Africa. Rhodesia was targeted next. In 1965 R. D. McClelland, U.S. Consul-General in Rhodesia, gave the American green light to the terrorists when he stated that,

> there is as much legitimacy in revolution as there is in government. To be other than a revolutionary is to defend the status quo, and the status quo was colonialism. It is the innate role of the revolutionary, and this applies *a fortiori* to the still white-dominated southern part of the Continent, to change an existing and unsatisfactory order.[138]

Pressure began to be applied on Rhodesia when U.S. Secretary of State Henry Kissinger met with South Africa's Vorster to lay down the law on the northern neighbour,

137 Marvine Howe, 'Portuguese Find the Spirit of Salazar Still Dominant,' *The New York Times*, 20 August 1972, 16.
138 Quoted by Benson, *This Worldwide Conspiracy*, 69.

Rhodesia's Prime Minister Ian Smith signing
Declaration of Independence in 1965.

while simultaneously 'South Africa suddenly found the money taps of America and Europe inexplicably turned off,' according to G. Sutton, editor of the *South African Financial Mail*. The strategy to destroy White rule in Rhodesia followed a familiar tactic: a pincer movement of terrorism from below and economic pressure from above. These names stand out in the elimination of White rule:

• Lord Soames, last Governor of Rhodesia, installed for the purpose of handing over political power, was a director of N. M. Rothschilds and the National Westminster Bank;

• 'Tiny' Rowland, CEO of Lonhro, involved in brokering the Lancaster House talks of 1979, which settled the political future of Rhodesia;

• British Foreign Minister Lord Carrington, a director of Hambros Bank, Chairman of ANZ Bank, and a member of the Trilateral Commission, a globalist think tank founded by David Rockefeller; chairman of the globalist Bilderberg Group, and later a member of Kissinger Associates, the global consultancy firm of omnipresent former U.S. Secretary of State Henry Kissinger.

South Africa, the final redoubt of White rule anywhere in the world, lost its vision after the assassination of Verwoerd.[139] Like Portugal under Salazar and Caetano, Verwoerd knew precisely what the forces were at work against European authority, stating of Harry Oppenheimer's economic empire: 'With all that money power and with his powerful machine which is spread over the whole country, he can, if he so chooses, exercise enormous interference against the Government and against the state.'[140]

Oppenheimer for his part explained precisely why the Money Power opposed White authority in Africa, and it has nothing to do with humanitarian ideals: 'Nationalist politics have made it impossible to make use of Black labour.'[141]

Legacy

In 1959 J. G. van der Meersch of the international banks J. H. Whitney and Dillon Reed & Co. formed the American-Eurafrican Development Corporation 'with the object of meeting the financial needs of emerging African nations when the former colonial powers left.'[142] Mr. van der Meersch stated with exactitude what lay behind the façade of 'human rights,' 'equality,' decolonisation,' 'opposition to apartheid,' and the other facile slogans that were used to remove White rule from Africa and replace it with cosmopolitan finance.

---

139 K. R. Bolton, 'Apartheid: Lest We Forget (Or Never Knew),' Counter-Currents Publishing, http://www.counter-currents.com/2011/09/apartheid-lest-we-forget-or-never-knew/.

140 D. Pallister, S. Stewart, and I. Lepper, *South Africa Inc.: The Oppenheimer Empire* (London: Corgi Books, 1988), 98.

141 Pallister et al., quoting Oppenheimer, ibid., 80.

142 Cited by A. K. Chesterton, *Candour*, 22 July 1960.

Saint Nelson Mandela's 'long road to freedom' established a privatised economy, in place of the Afrikaner's interventionist economy, and has set about selling off the state-owned corporations, the *parastatals*, as a legacy of apartheid.[143] In 1996 Mandela affirmed that 'privatisation is the fundamental policy of the ANC and will remain so.'[144]

Since 'liberation' in 1994 over 3,000 White farmers have been killed.[145] The old ANC slogans are again popular: 'One settler, one bullet!,' 'Kill the Boer, kill the farmer!,' *'Maak dood die wit man'* (Kill the White man).

In former Rhodesia, 4,000 farmers have been driven from their land.[146] However, it would be an error to think that the Blacks are the biggest benefactors of Robert Mugabe's lunatic land policy. The biggest landowner in Zimbabwe is Nicholas Hoogstraten. Along with the late 'Tiny' Rowland of Lohnro Corporation, mentioned previously, they were the main patrons of rival terrorist leaders Mugabe and Joshua Nkomo respectively. Hoogstraten first purchased land in Rhodesia in 1963, where he met Rowland, and they agreed to each back the two terrorist leaders, but Hoogstraten, 'like any canny businessman did a bit of betting on both sides.'[147]

At the time when Hoogstraten was serving a ten-year jail sentence for the alleged contract killing of a debtor (overturned on Appeal),[148] Claire Davies wrote that he is 'one of Britain's richest sons . . . best known as an unscrupulous landlord':

---

143 See following chapter: 'Apartheid: Lest We Forget.'

144 N. R. Mandela, *Financial Mail*, June 7, 1996.

145 D. McDougall, 'White Farmers "Being Wiped Out,"' *Times* (London), 28 March 2010, reproduced on AmericanRenaissance.com, http://www.amren.com/mtnews/archives/2010/03/white_farmers_b.php.

146 Ibid.

147 D. Black, 'An Aristocrat of Africa,' *Daily Mail & Guardian*, 26 November 1999.

148 Hoogstraten nonetheless was ordered to pay the victim's family £6,000,000 after the family bought a civil case in 2005.

In his property business, Hoogstraten was always clear that it was the buildings that concerned him not the people in them; he was well known for hounding out sitting tenants by whatever means possible. He once said: 'Tenants are filth, by their very nature. What kind of person is a tenant? A person with no self-respect. I don't look after tenants. Why should I look after tenants? One looks after the building, looks after one's asset.'[149]

I suspect that this view on the common folk is widely held by the globalist oligarchy who, unlike feudal lords, or the old rural gentry, have no concept of *noblesse oblige*, no sense of honour or ethos beyond making money, and cannot see others as fellow Americans, Britons, French, et al., but only in terms of how one might be of use in the global economy. If Hoogstraten's attitude seems reminiscent to that of a gangster then perhaps it is not surprising that in addition to the former suspicion for a contract killing, in 1968 he was jailed for contracting a gang to throw a grenade into the house of a rabbi whose son owed him £2,000. He was again jailed in 1972 on eight counts of handling stolen goods, and was given a further 15 months for bribing prison officers to smuggle him luxuries, commenting on his time: 'I ran Wormwood Scrubs when I was in there.'[150]

Hoogstraten's view of British tenants as 'filth' echoes his opinion on Zimbabwe farmers as 'White trash.'[151] In 2006 Hoogstraten, indicative of his political clout in Zimbabwe, had a British TV crew from Channel 4 put under house arrest when he learnt they were to make a documentary critical of Mugabe, and retorted that 'if they stepped out

149 Claire Davies, 'Downfall of the Devil's Dandy Landlord,' *Camden New Journal*, 20 February 2003, http://www.camdennewjournal.co.uk/archive/r200203_3. htm.

150 'Jane Kelly meets Nicholas van Hoogstraten,' *The Times* (London), 1 August 2006.

151 B. Peta, 'Van Hoogstraten to take over top bank and colliery in Zimbabwe,' 14 July 2005, Democraticunderground.com, http://www.democraticunderground. com/discuss/duboard.php?az=view_all&address=102x1627138.

Convicted killer, thug and Mugabe henchman : Nicholas Hoogstraten

of line I would deal with them personally.' A 2006 report stated that he had become 'Mugabe's most prominent friend in international business,' after John Bredenkamp fled the country after having backed a losing Zanu-PF faction. 'Mr van Hoogstraten, who has a vast ranch in central Zimbabwe which has not been seized by the president's supporters, has spoken frequently of his friendship with Mr Mugabe, and said recently that he had lent him $10 million, although Mr Mugabe's spokesman later denied it,' according to a report in *The Guardian*.[152]

In 2005 Hoogstraten, following the same path as Big Money in other African 'socialist' states, became 'the majority shareholder in Zimbabwe's leading coal producing company . . . and has a controlling stake in the National Merchant Bank.'[153] He is now the second biggest shareholder in

152 A. Meldrum, 'Tycoon Flees Zimbabwe After Falling Foul of Mugabe,' *The Guardian*, 9 June 2006, http://www.guardian.co.uk/world/2006/jun/09/zimbabwe.topstories3.

153 Peta, op. cit.

Hwange Colliery Company Limited, and has numerous other important investments.[154]

Such was the predictable ineptitude of Comrade Mugabe's African socialist regime that, with inflation running at 20,000 per cent, the Zimbabwe Dollar (at one point printed as a denomination of Z$100 trillion, seized being legal currency and was replaced by foreign currencies in 2009. Once a food exporter, Zimbabwe, having driven the White farmers from their land, now has to import food and at a colossal debt.[155] Behind the mask of 'Black Power' stands 'Money Power' and the much heralded creation of Zimbabwe on the ruins of a prosperous, farm-based Rhodesia, continues to benefit global capitalism.

While conservatives feared the encroaching spectre of communism and the USSR over the Dark Continent, and hence the capture of the mineral resources and strategic positions, they were blind-sided. The 'Soviet menace' was a red-herring that allowed the Money Power to establish its hegemony over Africa on the pretext of 'stopping communism,' and in so doing eliminated the White settlers, often with bloody consequences that have not yet concluded.

154 D. Ndlela, 'Hwange Crisis—Gratifying Van Hoogstraten's Rancour,' AllAfrica. com, 17 August 2011, http://allafrica.com/stories/201108191237.html.
155 Oana, 'Zimbabwe Dollar,' http://www.oanda.com/currency/iso-currency-codes/ZWD.

Apartheid: Lest We Forget (Or Never Knew)

Again turning to Professor Noam Chomsky, in relation to his previously quoted views on capitalism as 'anti-racist,' and desiring to homogenise humanity as economic cogs, he also made some comments on the question of apartheid and its opponents.

Question: Professor Chomsky, one issue where I've noticed that activists get kind of a good press in the United States—and it seems out of sync with what we usually see—is coverage of people protesting South African apartheid. I'm wondering if you have any ideas why coverage of that might be a bit more positive?

Chomsky: I think you're right: anti-apartheid movements in the United States do get a pretty good press—so when some mayor or something demonstrates against South Africa, there's usually kind of a favorable report on it. And I think the main reason is that Western corporations themselves are basically anti-apartheid by this point, so that's going to tend to be reflected in the media coverage.

See, South Africa had been going through an internal economic transformation, from a society based on extractive industry to one based on industrial production—and that transformation has changed the nature of international interests in South Africa. As long as South Africa was primarily a society whose wealth was based on extracting diamonds, gold, uranium and so on, what you needed were large numbers of slaves, basically—people who would go down into the mines and work for a couple years, then die and be replaced by others. So you needed an illiterate, subdued population of workers, with families getting just enough income to produce more slaves, but not much more than that—

then either you sent them down in to the mines, or you turned them into mercenaries in the army and so on to help them control others. That was traditional South Africa. But as South Africa changes to an industrial society, those needs also are beginning to change: now you don't need slaves primarily, what you need is a docile, partially educated workforce.

Something similar happened in the United States during our industrial revolution, actually. Mass public education was introduced in the United States in the nineteenth century as a way of training the largely rural workforce here for industry—in fact, the general population in the United States largely was opposed to public education, because it meant taking kids off the farms where they belonged and where they worked with their families, and forcing them into this setting in which they were basically trained to become industrial workers. That was a part of the whole transformation of American society in the nineteenth century, and that transformation is now taking place for the black population in South Africa—which means for about 85 percent of the people there. So the white South African elites, and international investors generally, now need a workforce that is trained for industry, not just slaves for the mines. And that means they need people who can follow instructions, and read diagrams, and be managers and foremen, things like that—so slavery is just not the right system for the country anymore, they need to move towards something more like what we have in the United States. And it's pretty much for that reason that the West has become anti-apartheid, and that the media will therefore tend to give anti-apartheid movements a decent press.

I mean, usually political demonstrations get very negative reporting in the United States, not matter what they're for, because they show that people can do things, that they don't just have to be passive and isolated—and you're not supposed to have that lesson, you're supposed to think that you're powerless and can't do anything. So any kind of public protest typically won't be covered here, except maybe locally, and usually it will get very negative reporting; when it's protest against the policies of a favored U.S. ally, it always will. But in the case of South Africa, the reporting is quite supportive: so if people go into corporate shareholder meetings and make a fuss about disinvestment, generally they'll get a favorable press these days.

Of course, it's not that what they're doing is wrong—what they're doing is right. But they should understand that the reason they're getting a reasonably favorable press right now is that, by this point, business regards them as its troops—corporate executives don't really want apartheid in South Africa anymore. It's like the reason that business was willing to support the Civil Rights Movement in the United States. American business had no use for Southern apartheid, in fact it was bad for business.[156]

Chomsky pointed out that a socio-economic-political system that maintains ethnic lines to preserve traditions and identities, especially in a complex mosaic of races such as South Africa, was a barrier to the construction of a nebulous mass of producers and consumers. As a Leftist intellectual although he recognised that opposition to apartheid was serving globalisation, he still could not accept that apartheid was perhaps a more viable system for South Africa than any other. Hence, even as the anti-apartheid demonstrators were serving the interests of the globalist corporations, they were nonetheless 'right' (*sic*) to do so, regardless of the outcome being a 'docile, partially educated workforce.' Chomsky seems to have been overcome with 'doublethink.'

---

156 Chomsky, *Understanding Power*, op. loc.

Chomsky also errs in describing the old mining-based economy as related to 'traditional South Africa.' This was never the case. The mainly Jewish mining magnates, especially the Oppenheimer dynasty, which has long owned much of the industry and the press in South Africa, are the implacable enemies of 'traditional South Africa.' As will be explained below, apartheid was founded in the aftermath of Afrikaner conflict with these mining interests, which sought to use cheap Black labour against the White miners. As with moneyed interests in Australia, New Zealand, Canada, the United States, and elsewhere, cheap labour was sought via immigration. 'Traditional South Africa' was fully cognisant of who their real enemies within were.

In 1962 Dr. Hendrik Verwoerd, Prime Minister of South Africa and generally recognised as the 'architect of apartheid,' stated of these anti-Afrikaner forces in a speech before Parliament:

> The directors, when they meet, hold private discussions. In the case of such a powerful body there is also a central body which lays down basic policy. The influence of that central body, to say the least, must be great in our economic life. Nobody knows, however, what they discuss there. In the course of his speeches, Mr. Oppenheimer, the leader, makes political statements; he discusses political policy, he tries to exercise political influence. He even supports a political party. . . . In other words he has political aims; he wants to steer things in a certain direction. He can secretly cause a great many things to happen. In other words, he can pull strings. With all that money power and with his powerful machine which is spread over the whole country, he can, if he so chooses, exercise enormous interference against the Government and against the state.[157]

---

157 Pallister et al., 98.

The Oppenheimer dynasty was the Nationalist Party's primary opponent; it was and is the 'South African Establishment,' which has always been the implacable enemy of Afrikanerdom.

Chomsky also errs in believing that Leftist protest movements show that 'the people' can 'do something.' As with the anti-apartheid movement, other Leftist and liberal causes, such as feminism, psychedelia, and the New Left, have generally served business interests and have often received CIA funding to move the 'centre' of society leftward under the guise of 'progress.'[158]

Anglo-Boer War Justified by 'Uitlander Rights'

It is of note that the distinctly non-Afrikaner capitalists who coveted the gold of the Transvaal Republic attempted to seize control on the pretext of defending the rights of the *Uitlanders* (non-Afrikaners) who then outnumbered the Afrikaners in their own land. The Republic denied these *Uitlanders*, who had no attachment or loyalty to the Boer Republic beyond making money, the right to vote, in order to try to preserve the Boer heritage. The British economist John A. Hobson (after a three month investigation) commented that there was a strong prima facie case for the view that the franchise was entirely a sham grievance. He noted that a 'larger number of non-British Outlanders [were] mostly Russian, Polish and German Jews, with roving propensities and no strongly rooted attachment to an old country.'[159] Hobson wrote further:

> We are fighting in order to place a small international oligarchy of mine-owners and speculators in power at Pretoria. Englishmen will surely do well to recognize

---

158 Bolton, *Revolution from Above*.

159 J. A. Hobson, *The War in South Africa: Its Causes and Effects* (London: Nisbet, 1900), 66–70; cited by Stephen Mitford Goodson, *General Jan Christian Smuts: The Debunking of a Myth* (Pretoria: Bienedell Uitgewers, 2012), 8.

that the economic and political destinies of South Africa are, and seem likely to remain, in the hands of men most of whom are foreigners by origin, whose trade is finance, and whose trade interests are not chiefly British.[160]

The initial attempt to overthrow the Afrikaner Republic was the Jameson Raid of 600 soldiers who, in 1895, planned to support an *Uitlander* uprising. The uprising did not eventuate and the soldiers were captured.[161] While the Jameson Raid was abortive, the contrived issue of *Uitlander* voting rights was used as a pretext for the Second Anglo-Boer War (1899–1902). The financial interests that were using the British Empire were determined to subjugate the Afrikaners on the pretext of defending the *Uitlanders*. Transvaal President Kruger had already offered to lower the residency requirement for voting down to a mere five years, but the position of British officialdom was intransigent.[162]

What is of relevance is that the cosmopolitan money-grabbers who coveted the gold of the Transvaal used a contrived issue of what would today be called 'human rights' and 'majority rights' to justify attacking the Afrikaners. Decades later, after the Afrikaners had gained their independence and sought to maintain their identity through apartheid, the same type of rhetoric was used, this time not in the name of the *Uitlanders* but in the name of 'Black majority rule.'

A similar situation can be seen in the globalist war to dislodge the Serbs from mineral rich Kosovo, in the name of assisting the Kosovo Albanians against Serb 'ethnic cleansing.' Up until that time, it was the Albanian drug-running gangsters of the Kosovo Liberation Army who had

---

160 Hobson, *The War in South Africa*, 197.
161 Goodson, *General Jan Christian Smuts*, 8.
162 Ibid., 10.

undertaken attacks on the Serb community in Kosovo. In the globalist war against Iraq the claim was that the Kurd minority had to be saved from 'ethnic cleansing.' In all cases—South Africa, Serbia, Iraq—the globalist grab for wealth was involved.

'White Workers of the World Unite for a White South Africa'

How many of those who were committed to the dispossession of the Afrikaner 'exploiters' have heard of the epochal 1922 revolt on the Rand? This Afrikaner revolt against the mining interests was the catalyst for the victory of a Nationalist-Labour alliance that inaugurated the first steps towards apartheid.

In late 1921 the Chamber of Mines announced that 25 semi-skilled job levels reserved for Whites would be given to Blacks, and that there would be thousands of White redundancies. At the same time coal mine owners announced wage cuts. The Mineworkers Union called a general strike. While the Communist Party was involved, the main influences were the Afrikaner Mynwerkersbond; mostly former Boer farmers and war veterans who had been left destitute by the British scorched earth policy during the Anglo-Boer War, and allied Labour Party supporters. When the mineworkers raised their banners proclaiming 'Keep South Africa White' and 'White Workers of the World Unite for a White South Africa,' the Communists were in no position to object. The coal miners, gold miners, engineers, and power workers on the Rand voted to strike and had the backing of both the Labour Party and the National Party. Prime Minister Jan Smuts urged the Chamber of Mines to negotiate, but they refused, and instead arrogantly announced a new labour ratio of 2 Whites to 21 Blacks, meaning many more redundancies. The Labour Party-backed South African

Industrial Federation created a 'strike commando' to resist Black scab labour, although resisting calls for a General Strike. Smuts caved in to the demands of the monopolists and ordered the miners back to work. In response, the Miner Councils of Action deployed commandos throughout the Rand. Smuts responded with force and three Whites were killed by police at Boksburg. The National Party demanded a Parliamentary enquiry. The South African Industrial Federation wanted to negotiate but the Chamber refused. Only then was a general strike proclaimed. Armed commandos seized Johannesburg and proclaimed a 'White Workers' Republic.' Mine officials, bosses, and Black scabs were executed. Government forces attacked and the air force levelled the miners' quarters. On 14 March 1922 the strike headquarters was overtaken and the strike leaders were killed. The last resistance was put down on 16 March.[163]

Such was the outrage against Smuts that in 1924 the Afrikaner Nationalists, in alliance with the Labour Party, assumed office and, starting with labour laws, the foundations of apartheid were laid.[164]

Plutocratic Crusade Against Afrikaners

As in 1922, the primary enemy of the Afrikaner was the Oppenheimer mining, industrial, and media empire, which includes the Anglo-American and De Beers corporations. There was no more persistent enemy of the Afrikaner than the Oppenheimer dynasty, routinely referred to in the early Afrikaner Nationalist press as the 'Hoggenheimers.'[165]

---

163 John Jewell, 'White Revolt on the Rand 1922,' in *A Salute to Dr Hendrik Verwoerd & the Boer Folk*, ed. K. R. Bolton (Paraparaumu Beach, New Zealand: Renaissance Press, n.d.), 6–10.

164 Ibid., 9–10.

165 'Max Hoggenheimer' was invented circa 1906 as a character by the South African cartoonist and arts patron Daniël Cornelis Boonzaier as the archetypal Rand magnate, often featured in Boonzaier's cartoons.

Babel, Inc.

The labour movement in Britain was very aware of the actual forces that were trying to control South Africa—to the detriment of the Afrikaners. *Justice*, the newspaper of the Social Democratic Federation of H. M. Hyndman, stated in 1896 that of the foreign interests, 'Beit, Barnato and their fellow-Jews [aimed for] an Anglo-Hebraic Empire in Africa stretching from Egypt to Cape Colony.'[166] No member of the House of Commons spoke out more vigorously against the war than John Burns, Labour Member of Parliament for Battersea, who stated in the House in 1900 that, 'Wherever we examine, there is the financial Jew operating, directing, inspiring the agencies that have led to this war.' The British Trades Union Congress even passed a resolution in September 1900 condemning the Anglo-Boer war as designed 'to secure the gold fields of South Africa for cosmopolitan Jews, most of whom had no patriotism and no country.'[167] As in Australia, the labour movement was acutely aware that cosmopolitan finance, whether one calls it Jewish or not, has 'no patriotism and no country.' Again, one might be struck by the awareness of the labour movement in identifying capitalism as intrinsically anti-national, unlike today's labour movement that is itself anti-national.

Labour Leader, organ of the Independent Labour Party, described the character of what had become of imperialism as being 'run by half a dozen financial houses, many of them Jewish, to whom politics is a counter in the game of buying and selling securities.'[168] We might see here a gulf between the Empire that had been built by merchant-warriors and privateers such as Robert Clive of India and Sir Francis Drake, and the conniving new lords of the empire, who run operations from counting houses and city mansions.

---

166 C. Hirshfield, 'The British Left and the "Jewish Conspiracy": A Case Study of Modern Antisemitism,' *Jewish Social Studies* 43, no. 2 (Spring 1981), 105–7.
167 Ibid.
168 Ibid., 13, 23.

Oppenheimer

The head of the Oppenheimer dynasty during most of the apartheid era was Harry F. Oppenheimer. He became a Member of Parliament for the United Party when that party was the main opposition to the Nationalists. When anti-Nationalist veterans founded the militant Torch Commando in 1950, Oppenheimer provided the funding.[169] When the Progressive Party was formed by a breakaway from the United Party in 1959, Oppenheimer became its financial patron. When the Progressives first contested the Coloured seats in 1965, he funded all the campaigns then and subsequently, with 40,000 Rand annually. In 1966 he funded the Progressive general election campaign with 50,000 Rand.[170]

Something of Oppenheimer's motives can be discerned from his statement on the formation of the liberal think tank, the South Africa Foundation, in 1960:

> In effect the advent of the South Africa Foundation reflects the return of big business to active politics. Picture the industrial revolution that will take place in Africa if the Black Man's economic fetters are struck from him! Think of the millions of skilled men who will enter the labour market. Think of the vast new consuming public! I think I can claim the main credit for this exciting vision of the new Africa, yet all that I have done really is to allow myself to be guided by the best interests of Anglo-American.[171]

Nearly two decades later Oppenheimer was explaining: 'Nationalist politics have made it impossible to make use of Black labour.'[172]

---

169 David Pallister, Sarah Stewart, and Ian Lepper, *South Africa Inc.: The Oppenheimer Empire* (London: Corgi Books, 1988), 78–80.

170 Ibid., p. 91.

171 H. F. Oppenheimer, *Africa South* (1960), cited by Ivor Benson, *Behind Communism in Africa* (Pinetown, South Africa: Dolphin Press, 1975), 14.

172 Harry F. Oppenheimer interviewed by Brian Hackland, Johannesburg, 30

Perhaps the good and the righteous should contemplate that, the next time they pontificate about how they 'marched against apartheid'?

Up until the assassination of South African Prime Minister Dr. Hendrik Verwoerd on 6 September 1966, the Nationalists remained acutely aware of the identity of their real adversaries, Prime Minister Daniel F. Malan stating: 'What we have against us is money power, principally under the leadership of Oppenheimer.'[173]

Dr. Verwoerd, regarded as the 'architect of apartheid,' and a statesman of immense stature who had the respect of Black Africa, provided the philosophical basis for separate development and the defence of the European in Africa.[174] After his assassination in 1966 his successors lacked the ideological coherence and a comprehension of the forces working against them, and adopted a defensive and inadequate—even apologetic—position.

In 1953 even Nelson Mandela stated of the Oppenheimer empire: 'Rather than attempt the costly, dubious and dangerous task of crushing the non-European mass movements by force, they would seek to divert it with fine words and promises and divide it by giving concessions and bribes to a privileged minority.'[175] Yet when Oppenheimer died in 2000 Mandela eulogised:

'His contribution to building a partnership between Big Business and the new democratic government in the first period of democratic rule can never be appreciated too much.'[176]

October 1978, cited in Pallister et al., 87.

173 Pallister et al., 80.

174 For example, read: H. F. Verwoerd, 'The Rights of the White Man in Africa,' Parliamentary speech, 9 March 1960, reprinted in *A Salute to Dr Hendrik Verwoerd & the Boer Folk*, 18–24.

175 N. R. Mandela, 'The Shifting Sands of Illusion,' *Liberation*, June 1953, http://www.africawithin.com/mandela/shifting_sands_0653.htm.

176 N. R. Mandela, 'Eulogy: Harry Oppenheimer,' 4 September 2000, *Time*, http://

Predictably, Saint Nelson had prostituted himself to plutocracy, and has received the worshipful accolades of the world ever since, his conviction as a key member of a terrorist plot having been put down the memory hole. It was the pattern that was followed all over post-colonial Africa, where a cosmopolitan, oligarchic neo-colonialism, with the backing of the U.S. military, arose over the ruins of the European empires.

Helen Suzman and the Progressive Party

While the Afrikaners fought the ANC and Spear of the Nation terrorists, the Progressive Party assumed the Parliamentary opposition in the political jungle. Founded in 1959 by Helen Suzman, who was its sole MP for 13 years, Oppenheimer became the primary source of funds for the Progressive Party. After the betrayal of the Afrikaners by their compromising leaders, Suzman and her colleagues redirected their efforts to the inauguration of a post-apartheid South Africa that would be opened up to globalism, a direction, as will be seen below, that has from the start been followed by the ANC regime. For this purpose, Suzman et al. established the Helen Suzman Foundation in 1993 to promote 'liberal democratic values,'[177] a euphemism for globalisation and privatisation.

The character of the 'liberal democratic' South Africa for which she worked can be discerned from the Trustees of the Foundation which, like other such think tanks around the world, combine business with academia in refashioning society according to business interests. Among the trustees are: Doug Band, a board director of companies such as Standard Bank Group, and Bidvest Group; Temba Nolutshungu, director of the Free Market Foundation;

---

www.time.com/time/magazine/article/0,9171,997869,00.html.

177 Helen Suzman Foundation, 'What We Do,' http://www.hsf.org.za/what-we-do/what-we-do.

Krishna Patel, Chief Executive of Global Private Banking; Gary Ralfe, who served for most of his career with the Anglo-American and De Beers corporations; Richard Steyn, currently a director of Editors Inc., and formerly director of corporate affairs and communications at Standard Bank; David Unterhalter, chairman of the Appellate Body of the World Trade Organization.[178] The director of the Foundation is Francis Antonie, who was senior economist at Standard Bank (1996–2006) and founder of Strauss & Co.[179]

The financial patrons of the Foundation include Oppenheimer, Soros, and Rothschild interests. Among them are:

- German-based Friedrich Naumann Foundation for Freedom, founded in 1991, focusing on 'advocating liberal reform concepts that further the democratic and economic development of countries' in Black Africa, training public officials and political party leaders.[180]

- Open Society Foundation for South Africa, founded in 1993 as part of the global revolutionary network of currency speculator George Soros.[181]

- Oppenheimer Memorial Trust.

- HSBC global investment bank.

- Investec 'specialist bank and asset manager.'

- Hollard, insurance and finance.

- Webber Wentzel, corporate and commercial law firm.

- E. Oppenheimer & Son.

- ABSA Bank.

- Standard Bank South Africa, an international bank and one of South Africa's largest. This bank was established

---

178 Helen Suzman Foundation, 'Trustees,' http://www.hsf.org.za/about-us/trustees.
179 Helen Suzman Foundation, 'Staff,' http://www.hsf.org.za/about-us/staff.
180 Friedrich Naumann Foundation for Freedom, http://www.africa.fnst-freiheit. org/overview/.
181 Open Society Foundation of South Africa, http://osf.org.za/.

in 1862 as a subsidiary of Standard Bank in Britain. In 2002, Standard Bank acquired 90 per cent of Uganda Commercial Bank, the new bank being called Stanbic Bank (Uganda) Limited, Uganda's largest commercial bank. In 2007 Standard Bank Group acquired controlling interest in IBTC Chartered Bank forming, StanbicIBTC Bank Nigeria Limited. It is indicative of the global economic nexus that now welds power over post-colonial Black Africa. The Standard Bank has particularly close relations with China.

- Deloitte, global financial consultants.
- N. M. Rothschild & Sons Ltd.[182]

What the 'Progressives' fought for, with Big Business backing, was a post-apartheid South Africa which could more readily utilise and create a vast Black labour and consumer market. Again, the mental gymnastics of doublethink are required to enable the anti-apartheid zealot to believe that in opposing the Afrikaner he was 'fighting capitalism.'

The Long Walk to Slavery [183]

While journalists, politicians, clerics, academics and other mental retards of sundry types worship Mandela as the Risen Christ, even getting tearful when they speak His name, South Africa has descended into a hell on earth.[184]

What has been the result of post-apartheid South Africa? The answer is that the 'anti-apartheid struggle' ushered in a regime of privatisation and globalisation on the ruins of the state-directed economic structure that the Afrikaners had created. Far from being exploitive capitalists, whipping

---

182 Helen Suzman Foundation, Donors, http://www.hsf.org.za/about-us/partners.
183 Paraphrasing Mandela's autobiography, *The Long Walk to Freedom*.
184 See for example: 'Why we are White Refugees,' http://why-we-are-white-refugees. blogspot.co.nz/.

old Darkie with the *sjambok*, as stereotyped by Marxist propaganda and the Western news media, the Afrikaners were an anomaly in the world economy: the last of a traditional European peasantry bonded to faith, blood and land. The industrial structure included the *parastatals*, corporations fully or partly owned by the state. With the advent of Saint Nelson's ANC/Communist Party coalition, as one would expect, the 'comrades' have set about delivering South Africa to international capitalism. In 1996 Saint Nelson, despite once having supported nationalization, stated: 'Privatisation is the fundamental policy of the ANC and will remain so.'[185]

ANC economics adviser C. Mostert has detailed the history and ideology of privatisation in South Africa, stating that the Nationalists introduced state supervision of the economy in 1948, a policy which began to be dismantled by the corrupted National Party in 1987, which has been continued by the ANC government.[186] Mostert states that the ANC has embarked on a policy recommended by the International Monetary Fund. He states that the word 'privatisation' is not generally used, but rather the phrase 'restructuring of state assets,' which is widely associated with privatisation. The Government Communication and Information Service (GCIS) uses the two phrases interchangeably when it describes economic developments and policy.[187]

These privatisation initiatives have taken different forms and include:

185 N. R. Mandela, *Financial Mail*, 7 June 1996. Cited by Clive Barnett, "The Limits of Media Democratisation in South Africa: Politics, Privatisation and Regulation," *Media, Culture & Society* (London: Sage Publications), 655, http://rcirib.ir/articles/pdfs/cd1%5CIngenta_Sage_Articles_on_194_225_11_89/Ingenta751.pdf.

186 C. Mostert, 'Economic Policy Co-Coordinator for the Economic Transformation Committee of the NEC of the African National Congress,' *Reflections on South Africa's Restructuring of State-Owned Enterprises*, Occasional Papers No. 5 (Johannesburg: Friedrich Ebert Stiftung, March 2002), http://library.fes.de/pdf-files/bueros/suedafrika/07164.pdf Ibid., p. 13.

187 Ibid., 18.

- The complete sale of companies, like Sun Air and seven radio stations to consortiums;

- Build, Operate and Transfer arrangements for the building of roads;

- The opening of private-public partnerships at local government level for the provision of services like water;

- Selling a partial stake (30 per cent) in Telkom to combined American-Malaysian consortium; and

- The proposed sale of a 25–30 per cent stake of South African Airways.

The ANC has stated: 'Eskom is one of a host of government owned *parastatals* created during the apartheid era which the democratically elected government has set out to privatise in a bid to raise money.'[188]

Why does a country that had hitherto been so prosperous now need to raise capital by selling off its assets? The answer lies in South Africa having been quickly reduced to a basket case, a bottomless economic sinkhole, like every other 'decolonised' state on the Dark Continent. The plutocrats who pushed for the destruction of so prosperous a nation apparently had a long-term *dialectical* plan that seemed, in the short-term, to undermine their profitability. In the long term, however, the impoverishment of South Africa by the incompetence that *invariably* results from 'majority rule' has obliged South Africa to become an open economy operating an ongoing garage sale. But so long as South Africa now has universal franchise and has put the redundant Boer in his place, it matters not to most of the useful idiots of the Left who were merely performing their historic role as lickspittles of Money.[189]

In the next several chapters we shall consider the

---

188 ANC Daily News Briefing, June 27, 2001.
189 For the historical alliance between Marxism and capitalism, see Bolton, *Revolution from Above*, inter alia.

multicultural doctrines of international capitalism that are used to rationalise and intellectualise the creation of a new slave race in the service of a global economic order, a process that apartheid had blocked.

'One World, One Race'

Our species is an African one . . .
—The Geographic Project[190]

While atheists and agnostics ridicule the Biblical story of Adam and Eve, which is normally interpreted as meaning a common ancestor-couple for all humanity, we are simultaneously asked to believe in a Darwinian version. Indeed, the scientific literature often refers to the 'African Eve.' This common human origin is then used for propagandistic purposes to promote internationalism, multiculturalism, and the idea of 'one world, one race.'

In 2008, *60 Minutes* ran a story on Spenser Wells, Explorer in Residence for the National Geographic Society, who is mapping the genetic linkages of the world population. The media are naturally eager to promote Wells' genetic mapping because it supports the 'Out of Africa' or 'African Eve' hypothesis. The liberal Establishment is eager to proclaim that we are all part of a nebulous mass of humanity without any differences other than what can be learned. The interviewer, a blond woman, was pleased to state that she was 'once an African' (*sic*). It is symptomatic of those Europeans who yearn to be anything other than what they are—Europeans—and are oblivious to their own heritage, yearning for the exotic, like the 18th-century literati and their debased wealthy patrons and matrons who enthused and were titillated by the theoretical construct of the 'Noble Savage' dwelling in peaceful communistic utopias in the South Seas, Africa, and the Americas.[191] Our 'moderns' and 'progressives' of today are no different from

---

190 The Geographic Project, National Geographic, https://genographic. nationalgeographic.com/human-journey/.

191 On the doctrinal and poetic origins of the 'Noble Savage' in the 18th century, which continues to inform Western politics and academia, see 'The Myth of the Noble Savage' in K. R. Bolton, *The Parihaka Cult* (London: Black House Publishing, 2012), 23–27.

their ignorant ideological forebears of several centuries ago. Hence multiculturalism has become a cult, and is lauded as the wave of the future by those who have no appreciation for the past, and exploited by those who see it as a means of obliterating barriers to global profit maximization and political control.

In 1992 Wilson and Cann proposed the 'Out of Africa' hypothesis of human migrations 200,000 years ago.[192] While this 'Out of Africa' is the new orthodoxy, contrary evidence is ignored by the popular media. Those geneticists advocating the 'African Eve' hypothesis are not in agreement with another branch of science—paleoanthropology, the examination of fossil remains. On the basis of the fossil remains paleoanthropologists maintain that there is a wide divergence of humanity going well back prior to the mere 200,000 years ascribed to different populations by the 'African Eve' protagonists. Human divergence occurred one to two million years ago, when the features that today mark Europeans, Australian Aborigines, Chinese, et al. were already present.

Multi-Regional Evolution

What paleoanthropologists now call 'multiregional evolution' on the other hand postulates divergence far beyond that time. Alan G. Thorne and Milford H. Wolpoff maintain the polygenic or multiregional basis of modern human origins. They state that there is no single recent dispersal for modern humans, that humans originated in Africa and then slowly developed their modern forms in every area of the Old World. Therefore stating that all humanoids originated in Africa means very little, but gives the false impression that all of humanity is an undifferentiated African globule.

---

192   Allan C. Wilson and Rebecca L. Cann, 'The Recent African Genesis of Humans,' *Scientific American*, no. 266, 1992, 68–73.

According to the multiregional view, mitochondrial DNA is not our only source of evidence. Fossil remains and artefacts represent more reliable evidence. Multiregional evolution traces all populations to humans first leaving Africa 1.8 million years ago. Distinctive populations have maintained physical differences. The features that distinguish Asians, Australian Aborigines, and Europeans are said to have evolved over a long period where these peoples are found today. The hominid fossils from Australasia show a continuous anatomic sequence, with the earliest Australians displaying features seen in Indonesia 100,000 years ago. Similar evidence is seen in northern Asia where one million year old Chinese fossils differ from Javanese fossils in ways that parallel the differences between north Asians and Australians today.[193]

In a typically biased account by Pat Shipman in *The New Scientist* the hypothesis of Thorne and Wolpoff was nonetheless succinctly described among misleading comments about how genetic differences among races play no role in their relationship to society. Some of the relevant descriptions of the Thorne, Wolpoff hypothesis follow:

> The main battle centers on the attempts of a small band of researchers to prove that human races are hundreds of thousands of years older than conventional theories would have us believe. Milford Wolpoff of the University of Michigan and his colleagues maintain that the principal human races— Negroids, Caucasoids, Mongoloids, Australian aboriginal peoples and southern African Bushmen—began to evolve well before the appearance of anatomically modern humans, *Homo sapiens.* Contrary to mainstream thinking, races did not evolve as a result of modern humans leaving Africa to colonize the rest of the world some 100,000 to 200,000 years ago. Or so Wolpoff argues.

---

193 Alan G. Thorne and Milford H. Wolpoff, 'The Multiregional Evolution of Humans,' *Scientific American* 1992, no. 266, 76–83.

. . . Wolpoff, Alan Thorne of the Australian National University and their colleagues would trace racial characteristics as far back as 2 million years ago, to the extinct human species *Homo erectus*. According to their so-called multiregional hypothesis (see 'The case against Eve,' *New Scientist*, 22 June 1991), anatomically modern humans evolved from this more ancient form simultaneously in different parts of the world, and it was during this period of simultaneous evolution that the racial characteristics of *Homo sapiens* first emerged . . .[194]

Parallel Evolution

Thorne and Wolpoff are not the first to state the antiquity of human divergence. Carlton S. Coon, head of the American Association of Physical Anthropologists, one of the most eminent of physical anthropologists, was one of the more well-known proponents of what is today called 'multiregional evolution,' and what was then called 'parallel evolution.' Like Thorne, Wolpoff, and other sceptics of the 'African Eve' hypothesis, Coon stated that today's races evolved separately, in different continents, over different time periods.

Writing in 1962, Coon stated of the origin and early divergence of humankind:

Wherever *homo sapiens* arose, and Africa is at present the likeliest continent, he soon dispersed, in a very primitive form, throughout the warm regions of the Old World. Three of the five human subspecies crossed the sapiens line elsewhere. If Africa was the cradle of mankind, it was only an indifferent kindergarten. Europe and Asia were our principal schools.

As far as we know, the Congoid line started on the same

---

194 Pat Shipman, *The New Scientist*, 16 January 1993.

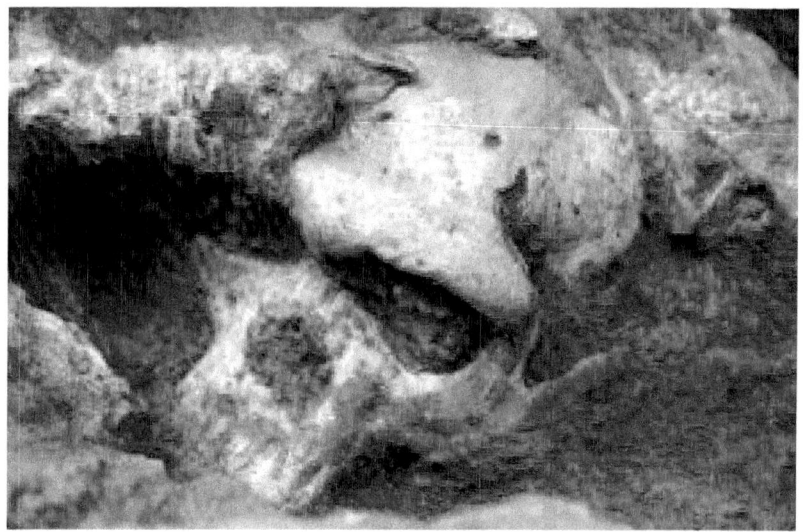

1.8-million-year-old Homo erectus skull from Dmanisi, Georgia.

evolutionary level as the Eurasiatic ones in the Middle Pleistocene and then stood still for a half a million years, after which Negroes and Pygmies appeared as if out of nowhere . . .[195]

R. Ruggles Gates, at the time the most experienced geneticist, had earlier said: 'Isolation has been the great factor, or at any rate, an essential factor, in the differentiation of races.'[196]

The multi-regional evolution of separate races almost two million years ago, was the commonly held theory among both geneticists and physical anthropologists until recent times. The fossil evidence accords with the very early divergence and separate evolution of the primary races.

---

195 Carleton S. Coon, *The Origin of the Races* (New York: Alfred A. Knopf, 1962), 108–9.

196 R. R. Gates, *Heredity in Man* (London: Constable, 1929), 295. Gates was the founder of chromosome genetics.

All Chimps Now?

A major tactic of the 'one world, one race' scientists and their Left-wing street and media shock troops is to pompously declare that there is only 'one race—the human race' on the basis that all subspecies of man share 99.9 per cent of their genes.

This argument purports to establish moral and political equality on the basis of genetic similarity. But similarity is not identity or equality. If our rights and obligations to one another are based on genetic similarity, and genetic similarity is a matter of degree, then so too must be rights and obligations. We would have greater obligations to closer kin than to distant ones. But this is not the sort of egalitarianism desired by the 'one world, one race' crowd.

Furthermore, the 'genetic similarity equals moral equality' position begins to look absurd when applied to non-humans as well. After all, the genetic relationship between chimpanzees and humans is 98.5 per cent. Some scientists are now contending on that basis that chimps and humans should now be classified as belonging to the same genus. Writing in *National Geographic News*, John Pickrell states:

> A new report argues that chimpanzees are so closely related to humans that they should be included in our branch of the tree of life. Chimpanzees and other apes have historically been separated from humans in classification schemes, with humans deemed the only living members of the hominid family of species.

> Now, biologists at Wayne State University School of Medicine in Detroit, Michigan, provide new genetic evidence that lineages of chimps (currently *Pan troglodytes*) and humans (*Homo sapiens*) diverged so recently that chimps should be reclassed as *Homo troglodytes*. The move would make chimps full members of our genus *Homo*,

along with Neanderthals, and all other human-like fossil species. 'We humans appear as only slightly remodelled chimpanzee-like apes,' says the study . . .

Studies indicate that humans and chimps are between 95 and 98.5 percent genetically identical. . . .

Derek E. Wildman, Goodman, and other co-authors at Wayne State argue in their new study, published today in the journal *Proceedings of the National Academy of Sciences*, that given the evidence, it's somewhat surprising that humans and chimps are still classified into different genera. Other mammalian genera often contain groups of species that diverged much earlier than chimps and humans did, said Goodman. 'To be consistent, we need to revise our definition of the human branch of the tree of life,' he said.[197]

But if chimps belong to the human genus, does it mean that it is racist not to give them the right to vote, the right to drive, the right to mate with one's daughter? Is it racist if we do not allow chimps to go to school? Will White people be blamed when chimps cannot pass the first grade? Will the President of the United States demand that 'no chimp be left behind'? I am all for the humane treatment of chimps, and every other living thing, but that does not require that we treat them as human beings. In fact, in such instances, equal treatment would be horribly unjust.

Behind the 'One World, One Race' Propaganda

What has brought about the widespread belief in the 'African Eve' hypothesis? Clearly it suits the political agenda of today, and has become a new article of faith among orthodox academe.

---

197 John Pickrell, 'Chimps Belong on Human Branch of Family Tree, Study Says,' *National Geographic News*, 20 May 2003.

Just like the myth of the 'Noble Savage,' the notion of an Edenic idyll existing among the primitive races untouched by the corrupting influences of European civilization, became the vogue among the so-called educated and cultivated classes of the 18th century and provided the ideological impetus for the French Revolution, so the new myth of the 'African Eve' is now serving similar interests.

The 'African Eve,' 'All Africans' dogma provides pseudo-scholarly impetus for the levelling of humankind into a nebulous mass, without identity, easily malleable in the hands of those who seek to establish a 'new world order.' There is a convergence of interests among the Left and Big Business[198] that both aim for 'one world, one race.'

The *New Scientist* article quoted above started with the obligatory references to 'neo-Nazism' and 'racism,' an implied conspiracy of a system that was militarily defeated and is politically suppressed, but which is convenient to silence any critic of multiculturalism, or any proponent of nationalism for that matter, with the spectre of Auschwitz.[199] Yet what we have arising from the dogma of 'one world, one race' is something vastly more totalitarian than even the spectre of Nazism. The egalitarian fallacy has wrought more evil—from the guillotine of Jacobin France to the 'killing fields' of Pol Pot, to the mass suicides of Jonestown—in the name of 'democracy' and 'human rights,'[200] than any system of the Right, no matter how totalitarian.

In looking for distant, primitive origins, we might just as well go back beyond the 'African Eve' to the primal slime

---

198 For such convergences, see K. R. Bolton, *Revolution from Above* (London: Arktos Media, 2011).

199 K. R. Bolton, '*Reductio ad Hitlerum* as a Social Evil,' *Journal of Inconvenient History* 5, no. 2 (Summer 2013), http://inconvenienthistory.com/archive/2013/volume_5/number_2/reductio_ad_hitlerum_as_a_social_evil.php.

200 K. R. Bolton, *The Psychotic Left: From Jacobin France to the Occupy Movement* (London: Black House Publishing, 2013).

of undifferentiated existence from which all life ultimately emerged, for it is just such a characterless, indistinct blob of humankind that our new slave masters seek to impose through the dysgenic reversal of evolution, in repudiation of the differentiation that is the basis of evolution. This— what we might call 'genetic discrimination'—to ensure the continuation of one's genetic lineage, has long been recognised by geneticists and physical anthropologists,[201] and has been reaffirmed by the latest evidence in the new scientific synthesis of sociobiology.[202] This innate loyalty to one's genetic kin manifests in social manners such as customs, laws, and taboos.[203] It is the broadening of family kinship to wider social kinships, forming the foundations of tribes and nations, which the Marxist globalists seek to replace with an economic kinship based on class, and the capitalist globalists seek to replace with a kinship with one's job and shopping mall. Now we think that we have overridden nature with technology. It is the modern-day *hubris*.

The use of genetics and anthropology for globalist propaganda can be seen from the comments on migrations from ancient to present times. The focus is not only on all of 'humanity' supposedly being one 'African' race, but that the 'human race' through its multiplicity of subgroups (presumably what one might now call Afro-Caucasoids, Afro-Mongoloids, Afro-Australoids, et al.) has always migrated over the Earth. Hence humans, we are now told, are inherently globalisers. Present-day globalisation and immigration are merely the continuation of a primeval instinct that has always taken place and always will, according to the globalist advocates. A DNA mapping

---

201 Arthur Keith, *The Place of Prejudice in Modern Civilisation* (London: Williams & Norgate, 1931).

202 See, for example, Richard Dawkins, *The Selfish Gene* (London: Granada Publishing, 1983).

203 A. James Gregor, 'On the Nature of Prejudice,' *The Eugenics Review* 52, no. 4 (January 1961).

project focusing on the Pacific region, which is intended to promote the globalist line, states:

> Waves of migration from China into and across the Pacific have taken place throughout China's history. The most recent emigration of Chinese, known as the Chinese Diaspora, occurred between the 19th and mid twentieth centuries. It was caused by war, starvation, European interventions and political instability in China. Most of the migrants in this diaspora were illiterate and poorly educated peasants or manual laborers. They were often called 'coolies' (Chinese: translation: hard labor). They left China to work in the Americas, Australia, Southeast Asia and other part of the world.[204]

> Human history has involved globalization for thousands of years. The peopling of this planet has been called the first great historical act of our species. We all have the same original ancestors. Our first homeland was Africa. Our species has 'globalized' the planet by migration and colonization.[205]

Note that the globalist propagandists using genetics as a scientific justification for multiracial migrations, emphasise that we are all one race, without biological variations that might account for differences in culture, temperament, and creativity, and that this single species of humanity has from its origins been 'globalisers.' Therefore, we are assured, there is nothing unique or troubling about present day globalisation and concomitant immigration. It should be embraced as the continuation of a globalising process that has existed since the dawn of the humanoid species. Weaved in with this is the attention given to Chinese migrations across the Pacific.

204 Transpacific Migrations, http://www.transpacificproject.com/index.php/transpacific-migrations/
205 Ibid.

Babel, Inc.

Globalisation, according to this narrative, becomes an essential and inherent part of what it is to be human, with genetics manipulated for propagandistic purposes. Hitler was accused of manipulating genetics to create a 'Master Race' supposedly to justify German world conquest. However, genetics is now being manipulated into promoting the concept of a 'Global Race' to justify a 'new world order' dominated by a corporate elite and involving family dynasties such as the Rothschilds and Rockefellers.

The Transpacific Migrations Project assures present-day White Americans that 'the first Americans were migrants from Asia.' 'This process is still taking place.'[206] Hence, present-day Asian immigration is part of a continuum that has always existed, and therefore Asian immigration should be accepted without concern as to the changing demographics of the United States. It is all part of a natural human process.

The pitch for multiculturalism and indeed 'hybridisation,' since we are all part of the same African genus anyway, is related to 'globalization' which, the Project states, 'belongs to a deep dynamic in which shifting civilizational centers are but the front stage of history,' while an ongoing process of intercultural interchange forms the often unperceived backdrop.[207]

> The evolutionary backdrop of our common origins in Africa confirms that humanity is a hybrid species. The species' subsequent 'clustering' in different regions of the world has not precluded large-scale contact and population movements across and between continents.[208]

---

206 Ibid.
207 'Paradigm   Shift,'   http://www.transpacificproject.com/index.php/paradigm-shift/.
208 Ibid.

Since humanity is nothing but one nebulous mass differentiated only by transient customs and languages, the ongoing process of migrations cannot be objectionable from a scientific, historical or any other viewpoint, other than that of blind xenophobia, according to this line. One example of the evolutionary impact of 'hybridisation' on culture is that of music.

> According to Portia Maultsby at Indiana University, the intercultural crossings and blendings of musical products produce both new interpretations of traditional forms and the creation of new musical styles. This process of cross-fertilization has been conceptualized in various disciplines as 'diffusion,' 'creolization,' 'syncretism,' 'hybridization,' 'transculturalism,' 'transnationalism' and 'globalization' and it has been applied in particular to music.[209]

Hence, new forms of hybridised culture are impelled by 'transnationalism,' 'transculturalism,' and 'globalization.' Again, this is presented as a natural development. While the apologists for this 'cultural hybridisation' declare it to be expressed in localised forms that somehow become 'indigenous,' the main impulsion towards hybridisation of culture today is for the purpose of global profit maximisation by manufacturing the arts as part of a mass production process with planned obsolescence: what in fashion and the arts are called 'trends.' During the 1950s and 1960s the music companies began introducing African rhythms into popular music in order to widen the appeal. While the globalist apologists for hybridisation might laud such processes as a natural part of human development, the motive is one of profit and the result is the dumbing down of the arts to appeal to the widest possible market. In a subsequent chapter we shall look at the way music and concomitant fashions are being used as part of a globalist strategy, promoted by the U.S. State Department.

---

209 Ibid.

The Transpacific Project states of itself: 'This project focuses on the history and contemporary significance of the transpacific relations between the peoples of the Pacific Basin . . .'[210] It is directed by Dr. Richard L. Harris, Professor Emeritus of Global Studies, California State University Monterey Bay and Managing Editor of the *Journal of Developing Societies*. It has a significant Chinese input in yet another example of how China and Western globalists work in tandem even while shadow-boxing on the world stage.[211]

The Pacific basin is of major importance to global capitalism, and the Transpacific Project makes its interests clear:

> The Pacific Ocean is a major contributor to the world economy and particularly to those nations it directly touches. It provides low-cost sea transportation between the countries around it and within it as well as extensive fishing grounds, offshore oil and gas fields, minerals, and sand and gravel for construction. A majority of the world's fish catch comes from the Pacific Ocean. And the exploitation of offshore oil and gas reserves is an ever-increasing source of energy for Australia, Indonesia, New Zealand, China, Peru and the USA.[212]

The prior sales pitch for hybridisation and transglobal migrations is presented as a prelude for the ultimate aim: economic globalisation. Finally one gets to the gist of the Project: the Pacific Basin as a very important trading region. Having introduced the reader to the mono-racial and hybrid character of humans and their tendency to having migrated over the Earth as a fluid entity since times immemorial, it is trade that is described as 'the most important form of

---

210 'Welcome to the Transpacific Project,' http://www.transpacificproject.com/index.php/2011/06/05/enricos-test/.

211 K. R. Bolton, Geopolitics of the Indo-Pacific, op. cit.

212 Transpacific Project, http://www.transpacificproject.com/.

social relations': 'Trade has been the *most important form of social relations* that has connected the peoples of the Pacific Basin since humans first migrated into and settled this vast area of the earth.'[213]

The closing paragraphs of the introduction to the Transpacific Project describe what is the purpose behind the science-laden rhetoric about the 'African Eve,' 'one race,' ancient migrations, and hybrid cultures: The next stage in this pseudo-evolutionary history of mankind, starting in Africa 150,000 years ago, is none other than economic and trade globalisation, specially with trade and economic relations extended over the past few decades between the United States and Asia. Since we have already seen how China was the cradle of the 'First Americans,' this modern symbiosis between the United States and Asia in the Pacific Basin, as part of a regional economic bloc, is the supposed product of millennia of history:

> Over the past two decades, there has been a significant increase in free trade agreements (FTAs) and international investments, which have expanded the economic relations and connections between the Americas and Asia. In addition to bilateral free trade agreements between individual Asian and American countries there is increasing regional and inter-regional economic integration within the Pacific Basin. The Asia-Pacific Economic Cooperation (APEC) forum, for example, is an association of 21 Pacific Basin countries that seeks to promote inter-regional trade as well as economic and technical cooperation within the so-called Asia-Pacific region.[214]

After an allusion to the proportion of world trade accounted for within the Pacific Basin region, the reader

---

213 Ibid., 'The Importance of Transpacific Trade.'
214 Ibid.

is directed to the APEC website. The reader is advised that 'APEC's stated goal is the economic integration of the Asia-Pacific area.'[215] The reader, by going through the Transpacific Project's history of human migrations over the course of 100,000 years should then come to the realisation that 'Asia-Pacific' 'economic integration' is part of an inexorable historical process. Advertising is then given to the primary globalist organisation promoting this Pacific Basin economic bloc, the Pacific Basin Economic Council (PBEC), which is quoted as being an '"apolitical and pro-business association that brings together business leaders across Asia Pacific." PBEC is an influential voice for businessmen and organizations in the Asia Pacific area.'[216] The PBEC description of itself makes it clear that the organisation is one of a number of globalist organisations that meet as a cabal, sometimes secretively, to discuss globalist agendas among businessmen, politicians, academics and policy advisers. Others of the ilk include the Trilateral Commission and the Asia Society, both formed at the behest of the Rockefeller dynasty to focus on Asia-Pacific issues; the Bilderberg Group, which has an international focus; the Council on Foreign Relations, a U.S. foreign policy think tank founded by bankers in the aftermath of World War I to promote a World State via the abortive League of Nations; and in more recent years the Open Society Institute and its myriad front groups, founded by currency speculator George Soros. All of these organisations, and hundreds of others, many associated with the U.S. governmental agencies such as USAID, are working in every corner of the world to establish a 'new world order.'[217]

The Transpacific Project makes the intentions for the use of the hypothesis clear by the focus the Project gives to

---

215 Ibid.
216 Ibid.
217 K. R. Bolton, *Revolution from Above* (London: Arktos Media, 2011).

explaining how today's globalisation is a development of the 'one race' hypothesis. Then it explains how genetic and cultural hybridisation are parts of this ongoing process, which is today impelled by global trade. Hence humans are presented as a migratory species without any biological imperative for a fixed territory (i.e., 'nations') or permanent abode established in time and space, and should be free to wander the Earth; or at least as 'free' as economic considerations allow or demand. Therefore, what is demanded is a constant state of flux that allows humans to be uprooted and transplanted around the world and anyone who objects is damned as a 'xenophobe,' a 'racist' and an anomaly. As the Transpacific Migrations Project explains, trade generally facilitated migrations; and the process of globalisation today is just the modern version of this perennial phenomenon. Globalisation is hence 'evolutionary,' 'progressive,' and natural. Cultural anthropology, sociology, and even genetics—once the abode of scientists who asserted that 'race' is biologically determined, rather than just a 'social' or 'cultural' construct that can be deconstructed and reconstructed at will—have been harnessed to the service of globalisation, as the above example of the Transpacific Migrations Project indicates.

As will be seen in a later chapter, transnational corporations have for several decades been heralded by philosophers of globalisation such as Professor Howard Perlmutter as the modern agents for 'one world,' and what has been called 'hybrid capitalism.' Recent DNA mapping and the 'Africa Eve' hypothesis have been enlisted into the globalist ranks to give global slavery a 'scientific' façade, reminiscent of the way certain biblical quotes were cited to justify the slavery of Africans. This time the aim is a world plantation, with 'hybrid' 'overseers' and CEOs and lordship by family business dynasties.

Multiculturalism as a Process of Globalisation

> The movement of people across borders is essential in today's globalised world. International business depends on an international labour force, and the ability of people to move around the world with ease.
>
> —Brunson McKinley[218]

Multicultural agendas, including those concerned with immigration, are methods of social engineering. Whoever raises a voice in public in opposition or even merely of caution is pilloried as a 'racist' and a 'reactionary.' Conversely, those who champion multiculturalism are upheld as the paragons of 'progress' and 'humanitarianism.' Yet behind the moral façade multiculturalism is a cynical stratagem, an important part of the process of globalisation in the interests of an oligarchy.

Ironically, as we have already seen in the chapter 'No colour, no country', an iconic intellectual of the contemporary Left, Professor Noam Chomsky, provided one of the most cogent explanations on the character of international capitalism visà-vis race and immigration, echoing sentiments that, as seen previously, were once common among the Left, before being taken over by Marxists and other internationalists. The reader is referred again to the Chomsky passage quoted in the previous chapter, 'No colour, no country.'

In terms of globalisation, Chomsky explains alot in one paragraph. He repudiates the now prevalent notion among the Left that capitalism is inherently racist. As seen previously, the Left now generally explains capitalism as a means of exploitation by 'White' oligarchs in a system of

---

218 Brunson McKinley, director general of the International Organization for Migration, 'Viewpoints: Should borders be open?,' BBC News 13 April 2004, http://news.bbc.co.uk/2/hi/3512992.stm#Khadria.

supposed 'White supremacy' that places even the White indentured servants of prior centuries in a 'privileged position' vis-à-vis coloured slaves and coloured colonial subjects. The Left completely fails to understand the nature of capitalism. this is not surprising because Marxism and other forms of Leftism derive from the same 19th-century economic outlook as their supposed enemy—free-trade capitalism. We have previously noted Marx's endorsement of free trade as a dialectical phase. As for Chomsky's statement, what we can note further on this is that:

• Chomsky states a heresy in saying that 'race is in fact a human characteristic.'

• Chomsky states that 'race' interferes with the aim of recreating humans as 'consumers and producers, interchangeable cogs.'

However, most of the Left has precisely the same aim as capitalism, and that is to refashion humans as cogs in an economic process.

Chomsky was answering a question on anti-apartheid demonstrations and the good press they received. The rest of Chomsky's statement that deals with apartheid was discussed in the previous chapter, 'Apartheid: Lest we forget (or never knew).

Despite the veneration that Dr. Chomsky receives from extreme Leftists, such as the cowardly 'anarchists' who wear black balaclavas (the 'Black Blocs') and riot against any manifestation of nationalism, you will not hear Chomsky's views on race and capitalism from such people because they are at root children of the Establishment they think they are fighting.[219] Also, you are not likely to hear the statements on Marxism, capitalism, and race by one of the

---

219 Bolton, 'New Left from Old,' *Revolution from Above*, 144–200.

original founders of anarchism, Marx's arch-rival Mikhail Bakunin who, unlike Marx, was a real revolutionary:

> Likewise, Marx completely ignores a most important element in the historic development of humanity, that is, the temperament and particular character of each race and each people, a temperament and a character which are themselves the natural product of a multitude of ethnological, climatological, economic and historic causes . . .[220]

For example, in semi-literate agonising over the 'racism' of Bakunin and the anarchist theorist Proudhon on an 'anarchist' website, one reads among others:

> What they wrote and how they lived their lives were as progressives, free-thinkers and libertarians, and any racist/prejudiced elements to their character were small in comparison to their overall philosophy. We'd all quickly reject such prejudices as incomptable [*sic*] with anarchism.[221]

'. . . Incompatible with anarchism' because 'anarchists' today are just another Left-wing reflection of the Establishment they think they are opposing, but can more often be seen opposing genuine opposition to globalisation led by the Right. The Right opposes globalisation regardless of its being undertaken in the name of the 'proletariat' or in the name of business efficiency. Both lead to the convergence of humanity as a singular glob without identity and a real sense of community. Hence once distinctions are broken down, whether by socialism or by free trade, the social engineers in the service of the 'World Socialist State' or the 'New International Economic Order,' are able to reconstruct humanity into what Chomsky calls an 'economic cog.'

---

220 Sam Dolgoff, ed., *Bakunin on Anarchy* (New York: Alfred A. Knopf, 1972), 282–83.

221 Volin, 'What Had people Got Against Bakunin?,' libcom.org, 5 April 2005, http://libcom.org/forums/thought/what-have-people-got-against-bakunin.

McDonald's sign in Shanghai, China.

Global Capitalism and Cultural Identity

... both CEOs and Ph.D.s insist more and more that it is no longer possible to speak in terms of the United States as some fixed, sovereign entity. The world has moved on; capital and labor are mobile; and with each passing year, national borders, not to speak of national identities, become less relevant either to consciousness or to commerce.

—David Rief[222]

It is with the aim of destroying national, cultural and ethnic boundaries that global capitalism promotes open immigration. As seen above, the Left believe in the same aims.

In their study of global corporations based on interviews with members of the corporate elite, Richard J. Barnet and Ronald E. Muller state that both Adam Smith and Karl Marx predicted that capitalism would become international.[223] Barnet and Muller wrote that, 'The world managers are the most active promoters of this Marxist prediction' of globalisation.[224]

222 David Rief, 'Multiculturalism's Silent Partner, It's the Newly Globalized Consumer Economy, Stupid,' *Harper's Magazine*, August 1993.

223 Richard J. Barnet and Ronald E. Muller, *Global Reach: The Power of the Multinational Corporations* (New York: Simon & Schuster, 1974), 77.

224 Ibid.

Barnet and Muller stated that the previously cited Jacques Maisonrouge, president of the IBM World Trade Corporation 'likes to point out that "Down with borders," a revolutionary student slogan of the 1968 Paris university uprising—in which some of his children were involved—is also a welcome slogan at IBM.'[225] Maisonrouge stated that the 'World Managers' (as Barnet and Muller called the corporate executives) believe they are making the world 'smaller and more homogeneous'; that the 'global corporation is "the great leveller."'[226] Maisonrouge approvingly describes the global corporate executive as 'the detribalised, international career men.'[227] It is this 'detribalisation' that is the basis of a world consumer culture, and is described with such terms as 'hybrid capitalism,' and the 'interchangeable cog' is heralded as the next stage in human evolution. These 'detribalised, international career men' have been described by financial journalist G. Pascal Zachary as being an 'informal global aristocracy,' recruited over the world by the corporations, depending totally on their companies and 'little upon the larger public,'[228] a new class unhindered by national, cultural, or ethnic bonds. They are without nationality, and are quite literally 'interchangeable cogs.' We will return to Zachary in the next chapter.

Creating the World Consumer

National, cultural, and ethnic boundaries hinder global marketing. Barnet and Muller quoted Pfizer's John J. Powers as stating that global corporations are 'agents for change, socially, economically and culturally.'[229] Barnet and Muller state that global executives see 'irrational nationalism' as inhibiting 'the free flow of finance capital,

---

225 Ibid., 19.
226 Ibid., 62.
227 Ibid.
228 G. Pascal Zachary, *The Global Me* (New South Wales: Allen & Unwin, 2000).
229 Barnet and Muller, *Global Reach*, 31.

technology and goods on a global scale.' A crucial aspect of nationalism is 'differences in psychological and cultural attitudes, that complicate the task of homogenising the earth into an integrated unit. . . . Cultural nationalism is also a serious problem because it threatens the concept of the Global Shopping Center.'[230]

Multiculturalism is used as a battering ram against this 'cultural nationalism' that 'complicates the task of homogenisation.' This is where the technique of dialectics comes in, of using multiculturalism, which implies literally a multiplicity of cultures that are being maintained, to deconstruct cohesive, culturally homogeneous societies in the name of 'diversity,' with the aim of reconstructing society by using the common denominator of money. Culture, citizenship, and nationality therefore become questions of how one fits into a consumer society. The culture that results is bland because everything is reduced to being a commodity to be mass-produced for quick profits. New mass markets are formed by reconstructing individuals as cogs in the mass consumption society, which does not have cultural, linguistic, or ethnic barriers. The point is most readily illustrated by observing that McDonald's, for example, is much the same whether in Europe, Asia, Africa, the United States, or Latin America. Coca-Cola is a global beverage, 'pop' a form of music that can be marketed to youth in any part of the world. This is the meaning of globalisation and the purpose of multiculturalism, as a prelude to world *monoculturalism*. In order to operate such a global market there must be globalised workers, executives, and technicians: the purpose of multiculturalism is to destroy the ethnic, national and other organic and historic boundaries that hinder the development and mobility of human cogs in a world economy. Hence, when the Left demands 'open borders' and states that the 'working class has no country,' they serve the aims of international

---

230 Ibid., 58.

capitalism, which also wants open borders to move labour, technology, and capital across the world as marketing requires.

Barnet and Muller cite A. W. Clausen when he was the head of the Bank of America, as stating that national, cultural, and racial differences create 'marketing problems,' lamenting that there is 'no such thing as a uniform, global market.'[231] It is this 'uniform global market' that is being pushed ahead at speed through what is now call globalisation. Harry Heltzer, the CEO of 3M, stated that global corporations are a 'powerful voice for world peace because their allegiance is not to any nation, tongue, race or creed but to one of the finer aspirations of mankind, that the people of the world may be united in common economic purpose.'[232] The globalist elitists back movements for 'human rights,' civil rights' 'open borders,' 'anti-racism,' 'immigrants rights,' etc., with the type of moral posturing referred to by Heltzer, and they view the noblest aspiration of humanity to be nothing other than a 'common economic purpose,' whereby all sense of organic identity and community can be obliterated and a new form of identity can emerge on the basis of buying and selling.

Global Cities

In the 1970s Howard Perlmutter and Hasan Ozekhan of the University of Pennsylvania's Wharton School of Finance Worldwide Institutions Programme prepared a plan for a 'global city.' Professor Perlmutter is a consultant to global corporations. His plan was commissioned by the French government planning agency on how best to make Paris a 'global city.' Perlmutter predicted that cities would become 'global cities' during the 1980s. For Paris this required 'becoming less French' and undergoing 'denationalisation.'

231 Ibid.
232 Ibid., 106.

This, he said, requires a 'psycho-cultural change of image with respect to the traditional impression of "xenophobia" that the French seem to exclude.' Perlmutter suggested that the best way of ridding France of its nationalism was to introduce multiculturalism. He advocated 'the globalisation of cultural events' such as international rock festivals, as an antidote to 'overly national and sometimes nationalistic culture.'[233]

Such modernist music has from the start been a means by which a 'global culture' can be imposed from above, whilst simultaneously making large profits, and breaking down cultural and ethnic barriers among the generations of youth, until everyone has become 'detribalised.' In more recent years we have witnessed the phenomenon of the young, right down to toddlers, being targeted by corporate advertising as consumers in their own right. Masses of youth since around the rock 'n' roll era of the 1960s—when Negro rhythms started being introduced to White youth—gyrate to discordant beats like some African tribal frenzy, and a nebulous global youth has been formed largely around the promotion of subcultures that have been made not only mainstream but predominant by the global music corporations. This is the 'globalisation of culture' recommended by Perlmutter to undermine 'nationalistic culture.' As will be seen below, the United States has a strategy of using multiculturalism to undermine the national identities of Europe.

Professor Perlmutter, who became director of Wharton School's Emerging Global Civilization Project,[234] had since the 1970s worked on an ideological basis for globalisation. Note that the programme he directed refers to a 'Global Civilization.' Since Perlmutter has been concerned

---

233 Ibid., 113–14.
234 'Howard V. Perlmutter, The Wharton School, http://www.wharton.upenn. edu/125anniversaryissue/perlmutter.html.

Babel, Inc.

throughout his professional career with the role of the global corporations as agents for change, the 'global civilisation' for which he works can be none other than the cultural prop for the global shop and the global factory.

The Global Me

Perlmutter taught that in order for business to expand it must act and think globally, and this means rejecting national and ethnic bonds as outdated, and the old idea that a corporation is part of the home country, whether 'American,' 'British,' 'French' . . . As alluded to above, the answer to national cultures and states is a 'global civilisation,' according to this doctrine. In a paper published in 2001, Perlmutter cites the previously quoted Jacques Maisonrouge of IBM in regard to what is called a 'geocentric company':

> The first step to a geocentric organization is when a corporation, faced with a choice of whether to grow and expand or decline, realizes the need to organize its resources on a world scale. It will soon or later have to face the issue that the home country does not have a monopoly of either men or ideas . . .

> I strongly believe that the future belongs to geocentric companies . . . what is of fundamental importance is their attitude of the company's top management. If it is dedicated to 'geocentricism,' good international management will be possible. If not, the best men of different nations will soon understand that they do not belong to the 'race de seigneurs' and will leave the business.[235]

One of the key elements of a 'geocentric' company is that its employees can be shifted about anywhere in the world in the interests of the company.[236] One's loyalty is therefore

235 Jacques Maisonrouge, 'The Education of International Managers,' *The Quarterly Journal of AIESEC International*, February 1967, quoted by H. V. Perlmutter, 'The Tortuous Evolution of the Multinational Corporation,' *Columbia Journal of World Business* (January–February 1969), 15–16, http://www.vcc.columbia.edu/files/vale/content/Howard_V_Perlmutter_-_The_tortuous_evolution_of_the_multinational_enterprise.pdf.
236 Perlmutter, ibid., 12.

first to one's corporation, without roots to any locale or ethnos; a modern type of global freebooter. Perlmutter cited a Unilever chairman's board statement as an example of this trans-national, trans-ethnic, trans-cultural new corporate man: 'We want to Unileverize our Indians and Indianize our Unileverans.'[237] The employees have even been given a new identity as 'Unileverans.'

The obstacles towards the 'geocentric' corporation, according to Perlmutter, include:

- Political and economic nationalism,
- Lack of an international money system,
- The interference of the state in corporate decisions,
- 'Nationalistic tendencies in staff,'
- Linguistic and cultural differences.

What can be seen from the above is that globalism, which transcends the 'geocentric corporation' today, is pushing for the development of nothing less than a new form of humanity: where anyone can be uprooted and placed around the world, without the bonds or boundaries of language, culture, and nation. Ideally, family bonds could be eliminated as an impediment to such a globalised humanity also, which might be why such U.S. agencies as the CIA, and the tax-exempt foundations of global corporations have long avidly funded and promoted feminism and the role of women as corporate employees rather than as mothers.[238] The ideal *Homo globicus* will be raceless, sexless, and stateless.

Perlmutter states of such a corporate figure:

> The geocentric enterprise depends on having an adequate supply of men [and women] who are

---

237 Cited by Perlmutter, ibid., 13.
238 Bolton, 'Feminism,' *Revolution from Above*, 160–200.

geocentrically oriented. It would be a mistake to underestimate the human stresses which a geocentric career creates. Moving where the companies need an executive involves major adjustments for families, wives and children. The sacrifices are often great and, for some families, outweigh the reward forthcoming—at least in personal terms. Many executive find it difficult to learn new languages and to overcome their cultural superiority complexes, national pride and discomfort with foreigners.[239]

Perlmutter stated that corporations had not yet solved the difficulties of relocating humans as corporate needs dictate; what he called 'the human costs of international mobility.'[240] Furthermore, a major obstacle is 'building trust between men of different nationality.' Perlmutter ends by describing the corporate executives as likely to be 'the most important social architects' for the creation of 'our evolving world community.' He sees global commerce as the key to peace.[241] Peace might indeed ensue when—in the name of globalised humanity—everyone surrenders all concepts of identity other than to the one-world economic and political system. Whether this is 'good' or 'bad' depends on what price one puts upon the higher things in life than the strictly economic. Others, including this writer, believe that economics should serve rather than enslave humanity. So far, the pursuit of the 'peace' of a globalised humanity has seen the bombing into submission of every regime and every state that resists some aspect of globalisation, such as Serbia's reluctance to privatise and globalise the mineral wealth of Kosovo. As will be considered in due course, bombs and debt are not the primary means of maintaining the globalist hold over humanity. The primary means is to change the ways of living—the culture—of every

239 Perlmutter, op. cit., 17.
240 Ibid.
241 Ibid.

individual. The way this is being done is via immigration and consequently multiculturalism, as a dialectical stepping-stone to a global monoculture in the service of commerce.

The transnational corporation serves as the primary agent of social and cultural change, or as Howard Perlmutter stated it, corporate executives become the 'most important social architects' of our time, reforging their employees to become what are often called 'world citizens,' lauded with the usual smokescreen of idealism that generally hides schemes for exploitation and domination.

An ideology of the globalised, rootless corporate employee has been developed, arguing that such a being is actually the next step in human evolution, and by implication all those who oppose this 'progress' are reactionary and have malign intent toward 'humanity.' Those who object that herding humanity into a 'one world, one race' nebulous mass at the behest of money-shufflers might not be such a benign objective, are quickly silenced by the corporate media and lackey politicians as 'racists' and 'xenophobes' and 'Nazis'; as nothing other than human anomalies—like the Afrikaners—in the modern world. The 'global me,' as G. Pascal Zachary termed the corporate model for the next stage of humanity, is the employee who has no roots of family, race, nation, or culture that world prevent him form relocating anywhere in the world that his corporation requires. Zachary, a financial journalist, has taken up the reigns of Professor Perlmutter whose qualifications were—interestingly—in both engineering and psychology—as the intellectual advocate for this new corporate humanity, although Zachary is pitching to a wider audience.

In a book review of *The Global Me* for *The Atlantic Monthly*, Alex Soojung-Kim Pang wrote of his and his family's own hybridity as the ideal of corporate globalism, referring to the multicultural character of a playground at Silicon Valley; 'just what one would expect in Silicon Valley, which is a magnet for engineers, designers, managers, and other professionals from all over the world.'[242] While many of the families of these different nationalities maintain ties to their homelands and cultures, there is 'no commonly accepted term' for Mr. Pang and his family and others of mixed descent. Mr. Pang proceeded to laud the merits of rootlessness for the global economy; the theme of Zachary's *Global Me*:

> ... our lives cross too many boundaries—racial, ethnic, national—that are usually (and erroneously) regarded as fixed and all-important. Call us hybrids—or, a cruder term, mongrels. Hybrids today are growing in numbers, public prominence, and economic importance: they jump-start regional and national economies, give industries a critical edge, strengthen states, and diversify the intellectual capital of corporations. Indeed, according to G. Pascal Zachary's new book, *The Global Me,* hybridity is the modern philosopher's stone, the key to economic vitality among global corporations and advanced nations.[243]

Mr. Pang alludes to such cross-ethnic, cross-cultural interchanges as not being unique in history, especially in terms of trade, and the benefits migrants bring to London and other financial capitals. It might be added that Jews have been a catalyst for globalisation in the past due to their unique international connections; a factor emphasised by the Amsterdam rabbi Menasseh ben Israel to Oliver Cromwell in seeking the readmittance of the Jews to England. Appealing to 'profit as the most powerful motive, and which all the World preferres [*sic*] before all

---

242 Alex Soojung-Kim Pang, 'Mongrel Capitalism,' *The Atlantic Monthly,* digital edition, November 2000, http://www.theatlantic.com/past/docs/issues/2000/11/pang.htm.

243 Ibid.

other things,' the Rabbi recommended the Jews as agents of global economic expansion because,

> the Nation of the Jews is dispersed throughout the whole world . . . Now this dispersion of our Fore-fathers flying from the Spanish Inquisition, some of them came to Holland, others got into Italy, and others broke themselves in to Asia; and so easily they credit one another; and by that means they draw the Negotiation wherever they are, with all of them marchandizing and having perfect knowledge of all the kinds of Moneys, Diamants, Cochinil, Indigo, Wines, Oyle, and other Commodities, that serve from place to place; especially holding correspondence with their friends and kins-folk, whose language they understand . . .[244]

It is with remarkable clarity and without recourse to 'anti-Semitism' that we can see the beginnings of what has become globalisation and the globalist ideal of a new race of 'hybrid,' sojourning the world without the restraints of nationality, tradition, religion, or language, in this letter from a 17th-century rabbi.

Today 'We Are All Jews Now' can be an added dimension to the 'We Are All Africans Now' in the pursuit of a globalised humanity. Whether the usury and new business practices that broke free from the ethical restrictions of the Church by these cross-cultural exchanges with Amsterdam, London, Paris, and New York have been a blessing or a curse to humanity is a matter of opinion, but it is from here that the road to our present globalisation has proceeded. However to proceed with Mr. Pang's review of Zachary's *Global Me*, in regard to the cross-cultural exchanges of prior centuries:

---

244 Menasseh ben Israel, 'How Profitable the Nation of the Jews Are,' letter to Oliver Cromwell, 'Lord Protector of the Commonwealth of England, Scotland and Ireland' (1655), in *The Jew in the Modern World: A Documentary History*, ed. Paul R. Mendes-Flohr and Jehuda Reinharz (Oxford: Oxford University Press, 1980), 9–12.

What's different today is the degree to which such mixing produces a new kind of people, and to which hybridity's benefits translate into significant economic advantages. Many factors now favor hybrids, who are more numerous and visible than ever: transnational, interracial, and multi-ethnic marriages are at an all-time high. Civil-rights activism over decades has created an atmosphere in many advanced nations in which discrimination is discouraged (if it hasn't been eliminated) and mixed social identities are possible. Transoceanic telephone service, e-mail, and international flights have made it easier to maintain strong, real-time ties around the world. Disney and Nike are global commodities, but so are Hong Kong action films, African music, and Brazilian soap operas (this kind of globalization has been accelerated by the Web). Transnational careers and reverse migration are more common. Finally, a greater consciousness of the 'invention of tradition' has made it easier for people to see conventional ethnic and racial categories as resources, not restrictions, and to define themselves not just by what they 'are,' or what others say they are, but by work, passionate interests, and experiences. Such people aren't rootless cosmopolitans or eternal outsiders, Zachary argues; it's now possible to have both 'roots' and 'wings'—to develop meaningful affiliations without renouncing one's origins.[245]

Other than bankrupt and indebted English aristocrats intermarrying with the scions of wealthy Jewish merchants[246] and, later, American heiresses over the past one to two hundred years, hybridity was limited and there were few of any class who intermarried with what were once colonial subjects. Since decolonisation, the former colonial subjects have been welcomed into former imperial states as

---

245 Pang, 'Mongrel Capitalism.'
246 See 'Hereditary Title-holders Who Married Jewish Women,' in Arnold S. Leese, *Our Jewish Aristocracy* (reprinted by Sons of Liberty, California, n.d.), 5–6.

'citizens,' the result being mass immigration of the former colonial races into England, France, Spain, Netherlands, Portugal, etc., while the European Union has facilitated further migrations across the Occident. The ex-colonial subjects have become the occupiers of their former master-states.

Mr. Pang alludes to 'civil rights activism' as a factor in assisting with globalisation. Such 'activism' has, like much else served malign interests while posturing with benign aims, like 'human rights' and 'equality.' The same situation pertains to the destruction of apartheid South Africa, which will be considered specifically in a subsequent chapter. Few 'civil rights activists' would realise that what they were marching for and screeching about, was not 'human rights' but the corporate rights for an integrated mass labour force; what Professor Chomsky, previously quoted, refers to as 'interchangeable cogs' in the economy.

Mr. Pang lauds the new world culture that is emerging; a culture that he accurately describes as consisting of 'global commodities.' Concomitant with this is what he calls the 'invention of tradition' where elements of culture are seen as economic 'resources.' Supposedly one can become part of a nebulous mass of producers and consumers without 'renouncing one's origins.' It is the old canard used by corporate apologists that it is the shareholders who run a company, not the executives. The apologists for corporate globalism are claiming that it is the new citizens of the world who shape their own future, and who are now free to pick and choose from an international ragbag of cultures, to recreate themselves as whoever they wish to be. It is the myth of what is also called 'consumer choice.' On the other hand, perhaps there is no real 'consumer choice,' no real opportunities to reinvent oneself by becoming whatever one wishes to be: once we are detached from out traditions life becomes transient and shallow, and what emerges is a mass

Babel, Inc.

global monoculture that opens up better opportunities for mass marketing throughout the world. Hence, culture becomes a commodity like any manufactured goods. The best way to gain quick profits is to have a quick turnover of goods with a very limited lifespan. Hence, 'pop' music, 'rap,' etc., can be churned out and sold at speed in comparison to Classical or Baroque. The impulsion of this mass global consumer culture is to market the ever-new of mediocrity rather than the enduring and great. This is what Pang and Zachary brazenly call 'global commodities' without any indication that they feel uncomfortable with calling the arts 'commodities.' The result of commoditising and globalising culture is to drag it down to the lowest denominator for the sake of gaining the largest number of consumers. The corporation is after all in the business of profits, not artistic excellence. The best way to optimise profits is to create global consumer with the same tastes by breaking down traditional cultures. The most efficient way of creating this global monoculture is via the stepping-stone of multiculturalism, leading to the 'invention of tradition,' not by the individual, with a bogus 'freedom,' but by the corporations that dictate trends whether in fashion, music or food, etc.

This commoditisation of the arts is lauded by Zachary for its levelling, egalitarian outcomes, where one might say that the arts are becoming increasing democratic and international, seeking the basest level. Of course, anything that can be called 'democratic' is *ipso facto* regarded as the greatest good by the great mass of the befuddled who formulate their opinions on the basis of sound-bites or the current wisdom handed down from on high from Ellen DeGeneres or Oprah Winfrey. One of the reasons so many of the great artists of the epochal post-War War I era—Ezra Pound, D. H. Lawrence, W. B. Yeats, T. S. Eliot, Knut Hamsun, Roy Campbell, et al.[247]—rejected democracy and

247 K. R. Bolton, *Artists of the Right* (San Francisco: Counter-Currents Publications,

131

capitalism in favour of the Right and even of Fascism was that they saw capitalism and industrialism as the dumbing down of the arts in the service of profits, and 'democracy' as the political means of manipulating the masses in the service of money. Zachary upholds global capitalism as the means by which culture becomes a question of quantity over quality for the sake of global mass production and consumption.

> Big corporations are champions of diversity, not just in their hiring practices but in what they sell. They revel in differences because, more so than other institutions, they suspend judgement about quality, or the distinctive attributes about a thing or activity. To multinationals all qualities are equal. The only attributes that matter are size of markets and the prospects of profit.[248]

That is the reality behind clichéd slogans such as 'cultural enrichment' through diversity. As T. S. Eliot explained, High Culture requires a fixity of place and a rootedness in tradition.[249] The impermanence and rootlessness of modern culture based on profit, has given us instead of a new Beethoven, Vivaldi, Leonardo, or Shakespeare, 'pop' culture 'celebrities' of usually fleeting fame. Such fleetingness of the 'pop culture' serves profit maximisation the same way as the planned obsolescence of automobiles, refrigerators, televisions, ad infinitum.

However, the apologists for this 'global me' come back to what it all means at base; identity based on work:

> Indeed, work emerges as one of the new critical sources of identity: in many of the case studies of individuals that are scattered throughout *The Global Me* (some first

---

2012).

248 Zachary, *The Global Me*, 208.

249 T. S. Eliot, *Notes Towards the Definition of Culture*.

Babel, Inc.

US rap singer Justin Timberlake adorns Afro 'dreadlock' hairstyle.

written about by Zachary in his capacity as a *Wall Street Journal* reporter), professional ability or devotion to work is as defining as nationality.[250]

The African slaves on the Southern plantations had more opportunities to maintain their identity than the produce-and-consume global mass that is being welded by globalisation. African slaves who knew who they were, had their own culture and their own kinship. The rootless masses especially of Europeans, both on the Continent and overseas, have no identity beyond their place on the economic treadmill. Furthermore, multiculturalism has interfered with the culture-building process of new nations, such as New Zealand and Australia. In terms of culture, there is everything in general and nothing in particular, and it is lauded a 'cultural enrichment' through 'diversity.'

However, according to the apologists of globalisation, such as Perlmutter, Zachary, and Pang, people are now 'free' from the limiting boundaries of kinship, to reinvent themselves

---

250 Alex Soojung-Kim Pang, op. cit.

'by how they work.' Such 'freedom' seems very convenient for the international oligarchs who want to move capital, technology, labour and expertise across the world without the hindrances of 'cultural nationalism,' as Perlmutter put it. Therefore 'cultural nationalism'—especially European culture and ethnicities—is condemned as 'xenophobic' and 'racist,' because it is European technology and European inventiveness that must be uprooted and placed in the cheap labour regions of the world. Meanwhile, the European states that provided the expertise and technology must open their borders to the imports that are produced in the cheap labour regions. Additionally, cheap labour must be free to be uprooted and placed in the European states; hence the call for 'open borders' from big business and its useful idiots on the Left.

Multiculturalism is the high-sounding social control mechanism with which to reshape societies and people to accept 'mongrel capitalism' and globalisation as the waves of the future.

The Jewish Factor

The first Negro organisation founded to promote racial integration in the United States was the National Association for the Advancement of Colored People (NAACP), established in 1909. This has served as the prototype for other minority lobbies such as the Hispanic organisation MALDEF.[251] The idea did not originate with a Black but with the leading Jewish banker of the time Jacob H. Schiff, senior partner in the Wall Street international bank, Kuhn, Loeb and Company. Schiff was to become one of the primary financial backers of the revolutionary movement in Russia to overthrow the Czar.[252]

Schiff floated the idea of the NAACP at the Henry Street Settlement, a socialist project founded by wealthy Jews, that assisted poor Jewish immigrants in New York City. 'The NAACP evolved from meetings at Henry Street, at one of which Schiff made a fervent speech on behalf of the guest of honor, W. E. B. Du Bois.'[253] Du Bois, a founder of the NAACP, has become an iconic figure in the United States as a Black sociologist. Du Bois was a long-time communist, although he did not join the Communist Party USA until 1961, at the age of 93. Interestingly, Du Bois had resigned from the NAACP in 1934 because he opposed the movement's total opposition to segregation, whereas he saw the benefits of voluntary Black segregation as a means of 'self-dependence.'[254]

Other luminaries of the Jewish banking fraternity who were founders of the 'Negro' organisation included Herbert H. Lehman, head of Lehman Brothers, who also became

---

251 Refer to the chapter, 'Purse Strings.'
252 Bolton, *Revolution from Above*, 57–60.
253 Leo Trachtenberg, 'Philanthropy That Worked,' *City Journal* (Winter 1998), http://www.city-journal.org/html/8_1_urbanities-philanthropy.html.
254 Peter Kihss, 'Dr. W. E. B. Du Bois Joins Communist Party at 93,' *New York Times*, 23 November 1961.

Governor and Senator of New York. Among Lehman's other achievements was as one of the leaders of the Big Business coterie that pursued and destroyed Senator Joseph McCarthy, who erroneously thought that the main enemies of the United States were communists and Soviet agents.[255] The NAACP Legal Defense Fund, responsible for the court cases that destroyed separate institutions, and especially separate schools, for Black and White children, rendering U.S. education dysfunctional and schools as perpetually violence ridden, includes a scholarship named after the Banker-Senator, the Herbert Lehman Educational Fund.

Although the ironically named Walter White, founding 'chief secretary' of the NAACP, was worried that non-Black funding of the NAACP would mean control of the organisation's policies by non-Negro patrons, during the Depression he sought out funding from these sources. He realised that the association would be 'more dependent on the contributions of "a few individuals or organizations which would control its policies."' During the Great Depression the NAACP became reliant on such donations. In 1930 Jacob Billikopf, director of the Federation of Jewish Charities in Philadelphia, and son-in-law of Louis Marshall, a luminary in Zionist circles and a leading legal counsel for the NAACP, introduced William Rosenwald, son of Julius Rosenwald, founder of Sears Roebuck to the NAACP, 'who helped initiate a series of financial pledges from Jewish benefactors, such as Herbert H. Lehman, Samuel Fels, and Felix and Frieda Schiff Warburg,[256] as well as non-Jews such as Edsel Ford,[257] that saved the NAACP from financial ruin and possible collapse.'[258]

255 Bolton, *Revolution from Above*, 40–41. Also see K. R. Bolton, 'Joe McCarthy's Real Enemies,' *The Occidental Quarterly* 10, no. 4 (Winter 2010–2011), http://toqonline.com/archives/v10n4/TOQv10n4Bolton.pdf.

256 Warburg banking dynasty. Frieda Schiff, daughter of Jacob H. Schiff.

257 Edsel Ford, Ford Motor Company.

258 Peter F. Lau, *Democracy Rising: South Carolina and the Fight for Black Equality*

Babel, Inc.

While we are primarily concerned about multiculturalism as part of a Big Business strategy for globalisation and a world economic system, the Jewish factor includes an added motive to that of the Gentile financial world. Jewish financial and Zionist interests have been avid promoters of multiculturalism for Gentile states, while vigorously opposing it not only for Israel but for the Jewish people.

Horace Kallen & 'Cultural Pluralism'

Zionism operates with a two-pronged strategy: (1) The exclusivity of Israel and the Jewish people are zealously maintained; (2) Any such ethno-nationalism on the part of non-Jews is as zealously opposed, and smeared as 'neo-Nazism,' 'xenophobia,' the prelude to another 'Holocaust,' etc. This is more than conjecture; the programme is explicitly stated.

Horace Kallen has been heralded as 'the first multiculturalist' and as the founder of 'cultural pluralism.' Cultural pluralism is designed as an attack on the cohesion of a nation-culture-people. It is an example of where the aims of Zionism and globalisation converge, albeit not always with the same intentions. It is erroneous to assume that plutocracy and globalisation are merely aspects of an 'international Jewish—or Zionist—conspiracy.' The Jewish-born oligarch George Soros is primarily a globalist rather than a Zionist, and has been critical of Israel. Soros reflects the attitude of many Jewish internationalists, both capitalists and socialists, when he fears the conspicuousness of Jews as a separate people, especially embodied in Zionism and Israel, having stated before an audience of the Jewish Fundraisers Network in New York in 2011:

> There is a resurgence of anti-Semitism in Europe. The policies of the Bush administration and the Sharon administration contribute to that. It's not

Since 1865 (University Press of Kentucky, 2006), 73–74.

137

specifically anti-Semitism, but it does manifest itself in anti-Semitism as well. I'm critical of those policies. If we change that direction, then anti-Semitism also will diminish. I can't see how one could confront it directly.[259]

Soros is also conscious of his own role in world politics and finance as encouraging beliefs that 'Jews rule the world,' stating: 'I'm also very concerned about my own role because the new anti-Semitism holds that the Jews rule the world. As an unintended consequence of my actions I also contribute to that image.'[260] Senior Zionist lobbyists were angered by Soros' frankness, and he was rebuked by Elan Steinberg, senior advisor at the World Jewish Congress; and Abraham Foxman, national director of the Anti-Defamation League, who called Soros' comments 'absolutely obscene.'[261]

Here we have within Soros' statements however, one of the aims of both the Jewish oligarchic and Zionist promotion of multiculturalism: that 'anti-Semitism cannot be confronted directly.' Rather the place of Jews in Gentile societies is secured through the destruction of national and cultural cohesion through 'cultural pluralism' or multiculturalism. The strategy is 'indirect' and the Soros 'Open Society' networks throughout the world expend billions in funding and directing programmes that are intended to destroy the traditional cultural, religious and moral fabric of societies, whether Muslim, Christian, or another. The promotion of feminism and liberalised abortion, or 'women's reproductive health rights,' as it is euphemistically called, is particularly useful, as are programmes for drug liberalisation (in which Soros is particularly active),[262] multiculturalism, immigrant and ethnic minority rights.

259 Uriel Heilman, 'Soros Says Jews and Israel Cause Anti-Semitism,' Jewish Telegraphic Agency, 3 August 2011, http://rense.com/general44/soros.htm.
260 Ibid.
261 Ibid.
262 Bolton, Revolution from Above, 125–29.

Babel, Inc.

The American Jewish Committee, Anti-Defamation League, and American Jewish Congress have supported simultaneously both 'cultural pluralism' for the United States (designed to militate against the emergence of an 'American Nationalism'), and Jewish nationalism. Horace Kallen as the founder of the theory of cultural pluralism and as a Zionist connected the two ideologically. Kallen was one of the first to advocate a multiplicity of cultures and peoples existing within the same land-mass as the American goal.[263] Kallen was also the head of the U.S. branch of a Zionist secret society called the *Parushim*, Hebrew for 'Pharisee' and 'separatist.'[264] Jewish separatism was legitimatised to Gentiles by promoting cultural pluralism in general, with the view to making Jewish separatism inconspicuous among a multiplicity of other cultures. Yet, this cultural pluralism does not reject the assimilationist ideal of the Melting-pot, other than for Jews. In some type of dialectic a society is supposed to function as a cultural plurality but still within the ideal of the Melting-pot of 'one world, one race.' The American Jewish Archive, which is a depository for Kallen's papers, states of Kallen: 'Kallen's concept of cultural pluralism affirmed that each ethnic and cultural group in the United States has a unique contribution to make to the variety and richness of American culture and thus provided a rationale for those Jews who wish to preserve their Jewish identity in the American melting pot.'[265]

The aim is suggestive of Coudenhove-Kalergi's prediction that the race of the future would be an African-Eurasian hybrid ruled by a 'new Jewish nobility.'

---

263 Horace M. Kallen, 'Democracy versus the Meltingpot: A Study of American Nationality,' *The Nation*, 25 February 1915, http://www.expo98.msu.edu/people/Kallen.htm.

264 Sarah Schmidt, 'The Parushim: A Secret Episode in American Zionist History,' The Council for the National Interest, http://www.councilforthenationalinterest.org/news/israellobby/item/1217-the-parushim-a-secret-episode-in-american-zionist-history.

265 Horace M. Kallen Papers, American Jewish Archives, http://americanjewisharchives.org/collections/ms0001/.

George Soros Hungarian-American business magnate.

As will be seen in the concluding chapter on 'multicultural dilemmas,' what emerges instead is not what is often called 'unity in diversity,' but rather voluntary resegregation, ranging from 'White flight' to the suburbs to self-segregation in prisons. Hence the politicians are faced with trying to make the unworkable work, and go from assimilation, to cultural pluralism, and back to assimilation, rather than question whether any of these ideas is sustainable. The globalists, as we have seen, aim to establish a global hybrid culture, whether through multiculturalism, assimilation, or a combination of both. These are transition phases towards the aim of 'one world, one race.'

The Melting-Pot, Israel Zangwill, and Emma Lazarus

The concept of the Melting-Pot strictly speaking stands in contrast to multiculturalism. One stands for assimilation into a mass, the other for the maintenance of separate cultures coexisting and inter-relating within the one state. The politicians seem to be trying one then the other without success. The term Melting-Pot was popularised by a play of that name by Israel Zangwill, a Jewish novelist and Zionist. In an appendix to the play, Zangwill explained:

> Meantime, however scrupulously and justifiably America avoids physical intermarriage with the negro, the comic spirit cannot fail to note the spiritual miscegenation which, while clothing, commercialising, and Christianising the ex-African, has given 'rag-time' and the sex-dances that go to it, first to white America and thence to the whole white world. . . . The action of the crucible is thus not exclusively physical—a consideration particularly important as regards the Jew. The Jew may be Americanised and the American Judaised without any gamic interaction.[266]

Zangwill was saying that it is not necessary for there to be physical integration between widely divergent races; their proximity is sufficient to allow for a permeation of cultures between them. This has certainly taken place on a rapid and global scale since Zangwill's time, and now encroaches on many peoples, states and cultures of the world, apart from the most isolated. It is what is now called 'globalisation,' and the cultural impact was foreseen with satisfaction by Zangwill. In his day he referred to 'rag-time' and 'sex-dances' as the means by which Negro culture was insinuating itself into 'white America.' Today, the African rhythms and dances, and not just the obvious types such as rap and hip hop, are the predominant styles of 'pop music,' however obscured by techno-beats. This 'Melting-Pot' culture that pervades the world is a primary means by which a global monoculture is being created at the service of mass marketing in the name of 'diversity.'

266 Israel Zangwill, *The Melting-Pot* (New York: The American Jewish Publishing Company, 1921 [1909]), Appendix III. http://www.gutenberg.org/files/23893/23893-h/23893-h.htm.

The Jewish Factor

David Quixano, the protagonist in Zangwill's play, sees America as being at root a rejection of European tradition, alluding to the Puritan founding fathers, and a secularised Puritanism has shaped the United States into its present character:

> David: Yes—Jew-immigrant! But a Jew who knows that your Pilgrim Fathers came straight out of his Old Testament, and that our Jew-immigrants are a greater factor in the glory of this great commonwealth than some of you sons of the soil. It is you, freak-fashionables, who are undoing the work of Washington and Lincoln, vulgarising your high heritage, and turning the last and noblest hope of humanity into a caricature.[267]

This rejection of Europe as the requirement for the new 'American crucible' is dramatised shortly later by David, exclaiming:

> I would not stand indebted to them. I know you meant it for my good, but what would these Europe-apers have understood of *my* America—the America of my music? They look back on Europe as a pleasure ground, a palace of art—but I know [*Getting hysterical*] it is sodden with blood, red with bestial massacre.[268]

The rejection of Europe would be the role that the Jewish immigrant would impart to the United States on the road to a Universal Republic where tradition was dead:

> David [*Struggling with himself*] Yes, I will calm myself— but how else shall I calm myself save by forgetting all that nightmare of religions and races, save by holding out my hands with prayer and music toward the Republic of Man and the Kingdom of God! The

267 Ibid, Act II.
268 Ibid.

Babel, Inc.

Past I cannot mend—its evil outlines are stamped in immortal rigidity. Take away the hope that I can mend the Future, and you make me mad. . . . I keep faith with America. I have faith America will keep faith with us. [*He raises his hands in religious rapture toward the flag over the door.*] Flag of our great Republic, guardian of our homes . . .²⁶⁹

With appeals to the American Flag and the greatness of the Republic, this is the type of facile 'patriotism' that today informs what it is to be 'American.' The American's patriotism is based on that of a Zionist playwright and novelist. He saw Europe through the lens of 'Jewish persecution.' He perceived the United States as it has been constituted since the Pilgrim Fathers, as having a messianic herald of a world 'Crucible' where all races, peoples, cultures, and tongues would be thrown together into a world Melting-Pot, from which will emerge a new breed.

Zangwill's call is for the creation of a new American nationality formed by the assimilation of Jews and various ethnic groups and races in the American 'Crucible.' In the final act Zangwill makes it clearer that he is not only talking of a crucible that will amalgamate Jews and sundry European ethnicities into a single American race, but all races:

David [*Prophetically exalted by the spectacle*] It is the fires of God round His Crucible. [*He drops her hand and points downward.*] There she lies, the great Melting Pot—listen! Can't you hear the roaring and the bubbling? There gapes her mouth [*He points east*]—the harbour where a thousand mammoth feeders come from the ends of the world to pour in their human freight. Ah, what a stirring and a seething! Celt and Latin, Slav and Teuton, Greek and Syrian,—black and yellow . . . Yes, East and West, and North and South, the palm and

---
269 Ibid.

143

the pine, the pole and the equator, the crescent and the cross—how the great Alchemist melts and fuses them with his purging flame! Here shall they all unite to build the Republic of Man and the Kingdom of God. Ah, Vera, what is the glory of Rome and Jerusalem where all nations and races come to worship and look back, compared with the glory of America, where all races and nations come to labour and look forward! [*He raises his hands in benediction over the shining city.*][270]

The play ends in a dramatic climax of what remains today the banal substance of 'American patriotism' defined by a Jewish universalist and Zionist:

An instant's solemn pause. The sunset is swiftly fading, and the vast panorama is suffused with a more restful twilight, to which the many-gleaming lights of the town add the tender poetry of the night. Far back, like a lonely, guiding star, twinkles over the darkening water the torch of the Statue of Liberty. From below comes up the softened sound of voices and instruments joining in 'My Country, 'tis of Thee.' The curtain falls slowly.[271]

Zangwill envisaged mankind in a universal brotherhood under the auspices of the League of Nations, predecessor of the United Nations Organization, with the world capital in Jerusalem, under tutelage of Jewish holy law. He wrote in 1914 on the impact of the play:

Played throughout the length and breadth of the States since its original production in 1908, given, moreover, in Universities and Women's Colleges, passing through edition after edition in book form, cited by preachers and journalists, politicians and Presidential candidates, even calling into existence a 'Melting Pot' Club in Boston,

---

270 Ibid., Act IV.
271 Ibid.

it has had the happy fortune to contribute its title to current thought, and, in the testimony of Jane Addams, to 'perform a great service to America by reminding us of the high hopes of the founders of the Republic.'[272]

Although Zangwill's assimilationist advocacy caused concern among the synagogues of the United States, as *The Melting-Pot* seems to be calling for the assimilation of Jews, Zangwill became 'one of the leading spirits of Zionism.' Where he differed from later mainstream Zionism was in his acceptance of possibilities of a Jewish Homeland somewhere other than Palestine. When the Zionists were offered British East Africa for a Jewish colony, but declined, Zangwill formed the Jewish Territorial Organisation.[273]

The other significant proponent of the Melting-Pot for all peoples other than Jews was the poetess Emma Lazarus. Zangwill ended his play *The Melting-Pot* with reference to the holy image of the Masonic Goddess, the Statue of Liberty,[274] that greeted all the new emigrants to the United States about to disembark on to Ellis Island. It is to Lazarus that the famous sonnet affixed to the statue owes its authorship. During the 1880s Lazarus wrote both of the need of Jews to establish themselves as a strong nation and in her book *The New Colossus* of the United States as the 'Mother of Exiles.' Hence the views of Lazarus and Zangwill were in accord. It is from here that the sonnet on the State of Liberty derives, which is heralded as the basis of the 'American Dream':

---

272 Israel Zangwill, ibid., Afterword VI, January 1914.

273 'Zangwill, Israel,' *Jewish Encyclopaedia*, 1906, http://www.jewishencyclopedia.com/articles/15162-zangwill-israel.

274 The architect of the statue was Frédéric-Auguste Bartholdi, and the designer of the structural framework, Gustave Eiffel, both Masons. The principal architect of the pedestal was Bro. Richard M. Hunt. The Ceremony of Consecration of the statue was organised by the New York State Grand Lodge.

. . . Give me your tired, your poor
Your huddled masses yearning to breath free
The wretched refuse of your teeming shore
Send these the homeless, tempest-tost to me
I lift my lamp beside the golden door![275]

The poem was written to raise funds for the pedestal of the Statue of Liberty.[276] On the other hand, to *The American Hebrew* she wrote:

Wake, Israel, wake! Recall to-day
The glorious Maccabean rage,
The sire heroic, hoary-gray,
His five-fold lion-lineage:
The Wise, the Elect, the Help-of-God,
The Burst-of-Spring, the Avenging Rod. . . .

With Moses' law and David's lyre
Your ancient strength remains unbent
Let but an Ezra rise anew
To lift the Banner of the Jew! . . .[277]

Lazarus held to Palestine as the homeland for the Jews, and 'promoted Zionism throughout the 1880s.'[278]

The Melting-Pot, or 'the Crucible,' as Zangwill called it, allows Jews to become inconspicuous among the multitude of other nationalities and races in a multicultural society, while their rabbinate and community organisations and ancient Law allow them to retain their identity as no other people have. Hence, we read for example of Isi Leibler, a former Chairman of the World Jewish Congress, when president of the Executive Council of Australian Jewry,

275 Emma Lazarus, *The New Colossus*, 1883.
276 Diane Lichtenstein, 'Emma Lazarus (1849–1887),' Jewish Virtual Library, http://www.jewishvirtuallibrary.org/jsource/biography/lazarus.html.
277 Emma Lazarus, 'The Banner of the Jew,' 1882.
278 Lichtenstein, op. cit.

stating to Australians: 'there is a need to sit together and establish a way in which Australians can recapture the spirit of multiculturalism which I think we are all proud of, and which is really under threat'; while stating to Jews: 'Multiculturalism has no place in Israel, created as a Jewish state for Jews.'[279]

In 1993, during the furore over the relative success of Pauline Hanson's One Nation Party, Leibler stated: 'There is a need to sit together and establish a way in which Australians can recapture that spirit of multiculturalism which I think we are all proud being part and parcel of, and which is really under threat.'[280]

Jewish intellectuals, bankers, and activists have provided the ideology and funding for assimilationist and multicultural doctrines that today converge, whether by accident or design or both, with the globalising demands of international capitalism. In Jewish nationalists such as Zangwill and Lazarus we find the duality of both Jewish separatism and universalism.[281]

279 John Masanauskas, 'Multiculturalism not for Israel—Leibler,' *Herald Sun* (Melbourne), 27 September 2000.

280 Ibid.

281 The reader is referred to Professor Kevin MacDonald, *The Culture of Critique: An Evolutionary Analysis of Jewish Involvement in Twentieth-Century Intellectual and Political Movements* (1998), http://www.kevinmacdonald.net/books.htm.

Cultural Imperialism

The way 'mongrel capitalism' is being propagated throughout the world is by creating a global culture based around production and consumption. The new identity of *Homo globicus* is to be based around one's loyalty to a corporation, one's identity is being shaped by consumption patterns, which are being standardised across the world. As we have seen anomalies such as 'cultural nationalism' are regarded as barriers to the spreading of this monoculture. In the following chapter we shall considered a specific example of how the United States uses Muslim immigration to break down the cultural identities of nations that are regarded as being still too 'xenophobic' and not sufficiently cosmopolitan. For the moment we shall consider how the destruction of traditional cultures in the pursuit of globalisation works in tandem with American military and foreign policies in the pursuit of a 'new world order.'

It becomes evident, when seeing what is behind the promotion of cosmopolitan trends in culture, from what one drinks and eats to the clothing one wears, what one watches on television or at the movies and the type of music one listens to, is shaped and directed by globalist corporations. In particular, youth subcultures are formed in the boardrooms and advertising agencies of global corporations that are shaping new generations of youth to be malleable consumers. Ironically, this is generally promoted as something 'rebellious' or 'nonconformist,' as a departure from outmoded and 'old-fashioned' ideas. No thought is given as to why such rebellion' or 'nonconformity' is being promoted by the biggest corporations in the world, and backed up by the military might of the United States. The cultural patterns of upcoming generations are as banal and phoney as the pseudo-rebels of the 1960s New Left. Their heirs today, like the 1960s generation of 'radicals,' are generously subsidised by the likes of the Ford Foundation,

USAID, the National Endowment for Democracy, the Open Society Institute, etc.[282]

The globalist aim is to deconstruct nations, cultures and ethnicities, and the reconstruction all of humanity as 'one world, one race,' undertaken in the name of novelty and progress. In so doing, the anchorage of tradition and custom is being swept away so that everyone is supposed to be kept in a state of flux. Roots are cut away leaving nothing but transience. Therefore, without roots, individuals and even masses can be moved about as marketing and labour needs dictate. Apologists for corporate globalism such as G. Paschal Zachary state that this is giving new generations broader options as what many call 'citizens of the world.' Culture, despite what is claimed by 'progressives,' does not grow without roots. While it is fashionable to now claim that 'culture' belongs to everyone, and that a Caucasian can appreciate the culture of Africa just as much as a Bantu or a Kalahari Bushman can immerse himself is a Beethoven symphony, that all people are culturally interchangeable, and nothing is fixed, this is just another marketing ploy to create a global consumer culture for an expanding market. Culture is nothing if not the development and transmission of lines of tradition. Luminaries of culture such as T. S. Eliot explained very precisely that there is an objective criterion for culture, for the arts,[283] and that it is not just a matter of subjective personal likes and dislikes, the transience of which again serves mass marketing aims. Eliot, and many others such as Pound and Knutson, et al., explained that the artist (including the musician, the writer, poet, painter, sculptor) does not just exist as a rootless individual entertaining a mass of other rootless individuals, but is part of a cultural tradition of which he is one link in a chain connecting the past with the future, with an audience that

---

282 Bolton, 'The Global Democratic Revolution,' *Revolution from Above*, 213–44.

283 T. S. Eliot, *Notes Towards the Definition of Culture* (London: Faber and Faber, 1948).

can appreciate his gifts because they too are part of that cultural chain.[284] That is why folk culture is enduring and timeless and thrives in societies that do not measure all things by profit and loss.

While state or aristocratic patronage of the arts is now disparaged as limiting 'artistic freedom,' what this artistic freedom actually means is *planned obsolescence*, since the arts are treated as commodities, like cars, washing machines, computers, or televisions. If something is made to last then there is no room for continuing profits as there is no need for continuous sales of new products *ad infinitum*. The arts as commodities must have a quick turnover to ensure profitability. Classical music, for example, endures for generations, and is therefore of limited profitability. 'Pop' music, and all other manifestations of 'pop' culture, on the other hand last for a relative five minutes, before being replaced by something else to be marketed by the millions— throughout the world. A new pop song hence is as enduring as eating a Big Mac, and is as likely to be marketed to the same generation around the world in the same manner as its counterpart in the global fast food industry.

The Puritan Factor: The Anti-Traditional Foundations of the United States

The United States is the globalist aim in the process of fulfilment. Hence, it is the centre from which globalisation emerges in its most developed form, which U.S. strategist Ralph Peters[285] approvingly refers to as 'culturally lethal.' The United States was born from a revolution not merely against the British Monarch but against the culture of traditional Europe. U.S. strategists such as Michael

---

284 T. S. Eliot, 'Tradition and the Individual Talent,' in *The Sacred Wood: Essays on Poetry and Criticism* (New York: Alfred A. Knopf, 1921), I:3.
285 See the section below, 'Culturally Lethal.'

Ledeen[286] laud the United States as having a 'revolutionary mission' from its beginnings. Israel Zangwill sang the praises of the United States as a 'Crucible' and a Melting-Pot out of which a hybrid would emerge as the focus of a universal republic. As we have seen, he alluded to the foundations of this messianic destiny being laid at the birth of the American Republic with the arrival of the Puritans to the colonies, severing their roots with the Occident. The culture that developed from Puritan origins was augmented by the egalitarian doctrines of the 18th century, and from the late 19th century by the 'Melting-Pot Crucible' that imbued a new 'American culture' with Negroid and Judaic influences. Despite the difference of these strands, what they all have in common is a rejection of a thousand years of Western Civilisation.

We have already seen something of the cosmopolitan culture that was being formed in the 'American Crucible,' described by Zangwill, which combined elements of the Jewish and the African, from which emerged the present cacophony that passes for 'culture' especially among the young throughout much of the world. How these Puritan foundations of the American Republic, alluded to by Zangwill, have shaped the United States into secular forms, is instructive for the present.

Puritanism is not conducive to the arts. Doctrinally it rejects leisure—the necessary milieu for the pursuit of High Culture—as ungodly.[287] For example, at the founding American Puritan colonies, the influence of music was minimal, and was excluded as a profession.[288] Puritan functionalism also worked against the development of a

---

286 Ibid.

287 F. J. Bremer, *The Puritan Experiment: New England Society from Bradford to Edwards* (New York: St. Martin's Press, 1976).

288 R. Crawford, ed., *America's Musical Life: A History* (New York: W. W. Norton, 2005).

significant Puritan visual art.[289] Work was a godly duty and should not be wasted on frivolous and distracting pursuits. This repudiation of the arts as an ungodly waste of work time metamorphosed into art as a profit-making commodity. Additionally, without a tradition of high art at America's founding, a culture of discernment such as found in the nobility of Europe, was not developed, and indeed, instead of a nobility based on ancient bloodlines, what emerged in the United States was an oligarchy. Hence, in secular America the arts became justified through profit, and remain so, not only in the United States but also now throughout much of the world through globalisation. The United States has also retained, again in secular form, the messianic sense of mission of both the Puritans and the Jews to remake the world on the type of universal principles enunciated poetically by Zangwill and Lazarus.

The genuine folk culture that emerged did so among Scots-Irish hillbillies and Southerners—both disparaged in popular entertainment—and in the ethnic enclaves of Irish, Italians, and other Europeans, while the corporations saw money to be made in peddling African rhythms to White youth in what has become an immense, worldwide market. Today, this is the America that is held up as a reachable dream for the youth of the entire world.

'Culturally Lethal'

Since the time of Woodrow Wilson's 'Fourteen Points' for a new world order in the aftermath of World War I, U.S. policymakers and certain sections of global Big Business have been motivated by a messianic sense of America's duty to impose its model of liberal-economic-democracy over the entire world. America has a doctrine that is for export and a desire to implement that on an international scale.

---

289 Bremer, op. cit.

Major Ralph Peters, a prominent military strategist who served with the Office of the Deputy Chief of Staff for Intelligence, and whose area of expertise is the former Soviet bloc and Eurasia, appears to have coined the term 'constant conflict,' an American strategy for keeping the world in a state of flux, off-balance, by means of what the Left called 'cultural imperialism.' Peters has written of this in an article by that name in a military strategy journal:

> We have entered an age of constant conflict. . . .

> We are entering a new American century, in which we will become still wealthier, culturally more lethal, and increasingly powerful. We will excite hatreds without precedent.

> Information destroys traditional jobs and traditional cultures; it seduces, betrays, yet remains invulnerable. How can you counterattack the information others have turned upon you? There is no effective option other than competitive performance. For those individuals and cultures that cannot join or compete with our information empire, there is only inevitable failure . . . The attempt of the Iranian mullahs to secede from modernity has failed, although a turbaned corpse still stumbles about the neighborhood. Information, from the internet to rock videos, will not be contained, and fundamentalism cannot control its children. Our victims volunteer.[290]

Peters is stating that this 'global information empire' led by the United States is 'historically inevitable.' This 'historical inevitability' is classic Marx, just as 'constant conflict' is classic Trotsky ('permanent revolution'). It is an example of how Marxism and global capitalism have come to intersect; something alluded to by Peters himself. This is a 'cultural revolution,' which is buttressed by American firepower.

---

290 Ralph Peters, 'Constant Conflict,' *Parameters* (Summer 1997), 4–14, http://www. usamhi.army.mil/USAWC/Parameters/97summer/peters.htm.

Babel, Inc.

Globalist hegemony is being imposed on the ruins of traditional cultures by a culture of 'comfort and convenience,' the *Brave New World* of Huxley's dystopia[291] of serfdom through pleasure, Peters writing in Huxleyan terms:

> It is fashionable among world intellectual elites to decry 'American culture,' with our domestic critics among the loudest in complaint. But traditional intellectual elites are of shrinking relevance, replaced by cognitive-practical elites—figures such as Bill Gates, Steven Spielberg, Madonna, or our most successful politicians—human beings who can recognize or create popular appetites, recreating themselves as necessary. Contemporary American culture is the most powerful in history, and the most destructive of competitor cultures. While some other cultures, such as those of East Asia, appear strong enough to survive the onslaught by adaptive behaviors, most are not. The genius, the secret weapon, of American culture is the essence that the elites despise: ours is the first genuine people's culture. It stresses comfort and convenience— ease—and it generates pleasure for the masses. We are Karl Marx's dream, and his nightmare.[292]

Here can be seen the Huxleyan 'addiction' (*sic*), to use Peters' own term, which now embraces much of the world, other than what the globalists consider to be the backward 'traditional elites' and cultures, the so-called 'Islamofascists,' and the resurgent orthodox religiosity and traditions of the nations of the former Soviet bloc on which George Soros has expended so much to thwart. Peters continues:

> Secular and religious revolutionaries in our century have made the identical mistake, imagining that the

---

291 Aldous Huxley, *Brave New World* (London: Chatto and Windus, 1969 [1932]). For a discussion of Huxley's concepts, see K. R. Bolton, 'Huxley's Brave New World,' *Revolution from Above*, 48–54.

292 Peters, 'Constant Conflict.'

workers of the world or the faithful just can't wait to go home at night to study Marx or the Koran. Well, Joe Sixpack, Ivan Tipichni, and Ali Quat would rather 'Baywatch.' America has figured it out, and we are brilliant at operationalizing our knowledge, and our cultural power will hinder even those cultures we do not undermine. There is no 'peer competitor' in the cultural (or military) department. Our cultural empire has the addicted—men and women everywhere— clamoring for more. And they pay for the privilege of their disillusionment.[293]

The 'constant conflict' is one of world cultural revolution, with the armed forces used as backup against any 'rejectionist states,' such as Serbia and Iraq. The world is therefore to be kept in a perpetual state of flux, with a lack of permanence, which Peters' calls America's 'strength,' as settled traditional modes of life do not accord with the aim of industrial, technical and economic 'progress' without end. Peters continues:

There will be no peace. At any given moment for the rest of our lifetimes, there will be multiple conflicts in mutating forms around the globe. Violent conflict will dominate the headlines, but cultural and economic struggles will be steadier and ultimately more decisive. The de facto role of the U.S. armed forces will be to keep the world safe for our economy and open to our cultural assault. To those ends, we will do a fair amount of killing.[294]

Note that Peters refers to the U.S. armed forces and the U.S. 'cultural assault' as working in tandem to maintain the United States' global economic domination, which more accurately means the domination of global corporations.

293 Ibid.
294 Ibid.

Peters has made 'American interests' synonymous with global corporate interests, although such corporations are not rooted to any specific nation-state, any more than the City of London branch of the Rothschild dynasty was rooted to the British Empire when it ceased serving its interests, or Rupert Murdoch was rooted to his Australian birthright when becoming an American citizen served his global business interests. Peters refers to certain cultures trying to reassert their traditions, and again emphasises that the globalist 'culture' that is being imposed primarily via U.S. influence is one of 'infectious pleasure.' Historical inevitability is re-emphasised, as the 'rejectionist' (*sic*) regimes will be consigned to what Trotsky called the 'dustbin of history':

> Yes, foreign cultures are reasserting their threatened identities—usually with marginal, if any, success—and yes, they are attempting to escape our influence. But American culture is infectious, a plague of pleasure, and you don't have to die of it to be hindered or crippled in your integrity or competitiveness. The very struggle of other cultures to resist American cultural intrusion fatefully diverts their energies from the pursuit of the future. We should not fear the advent of fundamentalist or rejectionist regimes. They are simply guaranteeing their peoples' failure, while further increasing our relative strength.[295]

Michael Ledeen[296] as one of the primary advocates of America's world revolutionary mission, in similar terms to that of Peters, calls on the United States to fulfil its 'historic mission' of 'exporting the democratic revolution'

---

295 Ibid.

296 Ledeen, consultant to the U.S. National Security Council, State Department and Defense Department, is currently a 'Freedom Scholar' with the Foundation for Defense of Democracies, which aims for 'regime change' throughout the world. See 'Michael Ledeen,' SourceWatch, http://www.sourcewatch.org/index. php?title=Michael_Ledeen.

throughout the world. Like Peters, Ledeen predicates this world revolution as a necessary part of the 'war on terrorism,' but emphasises also that 'world revolution' is the 'historic mission' of the United States and always has been. We have noted the origins of this in a confluence between two different currents in American history: its Puritan and Enlightenment foundations.[297] Writing in *National Review*, Ledeen states:

> . . . [W]e are the one truly revolutionary country in the world, as we have been for more than 200 years. Creative destruction is our middle name. We do it automatically, and that is precisely why the tyrants hate us, and are driven to attack us.

> Freedom is our most lethal weapon, and the oppressed peoples of the fanatic regimes are our greatest assets. They need to hear and see that we are with them, and that the Western mission is to set them free, under leaders who will respect them and preserve their freedom.

> . . . [I]t is time once again to export the democratic revolution. To those who say it cannot be done, we need only point to the 1980s, when we led a global democratic revolution that toppled tyrants from Moscow to Johannesburg. Then, too, the smart folks said it could not be done, and they laughed at Ronald Reagan's chutzpah when he said that the Soviet tyrants were done for, and called on the West to think hard about the post-Communist era. We destroyed the Soviet Empire, and then walked away from our great triumph in the Third World War of the Twentieth Century. As I sadly wrote at that time, when America abandons its historic mission, our enemies take heart, grow stronger,

---

297 For an examination of these two originally rival factions at America's founding, see Nicholas Hagger, *The Secret Founding of America: The Real Story of Freemasons, Puritans and the Battle for the New World* (London: Watkins Publishing, 2007).

and eventually begin to kill us again. And so they have, forcing us to take up our revolutionary burden, and bring down the despotic regimes that have made possible the hateful events of the 11th of September.[298]

Ledeen gives credit to the United States for bringing down not only the Soviet bloc, but also the Afrikaner, as part of the 'historic world revolutionary mission' that the United States has had since its founding. However, he states that the task of world revolution was left uncompleted, since the Third World has yet to be brought into the globalist orbit. There is also still a long way to go in regard to Eurasia and the former Soviet bloc, and in particular Russia, where there have been reversals in the process of the 'colour revolutions,' and where there is increasing resistance to what is being perceived as American ambitions towards global hegemony.

The United States has utilised globalist 'culture' since the 'Cold War,' when an entire operation under the auspices of the CIA, and funded by the Rockefellers,[299] was established to manipulate the arts and artists to subvert the Soviet bloc while enticing the world towards 'The American Dream.' The Congress of Cultural Freedom, as the front was called, was a collaboration between U.S. globalists, big business, the CIA, and the anti-Russian Left,[300] especially Trotskyite communists, who regarded the USSR since the purging of Trotsky by Stalin, as anathema.[301] Indeed, such was the hatred of these anti-Russian communists that many became the most avid of Cold Warriors on behalf of the United States, as exemplified by Trotsky's widow Natalya

298 Michael Ledeen, 'Creative Destruction: How to Wage a Revolutionary War,' *National Review*, 20 September 2001.

299 Particularly through the Rockefeller founded and funded Museum of Modern Art. See Bolton, 'The Congress for Cultural Freedom,' in *Revolution from Above*, 141–43.

300 Ibid., 138–43.

301 K. R. Bolton, 'Stalinism and the Art of Rootless Cosmopolitanism,' in *Stalin: The Enduring Legacy* (London: Black House Publishing, 2012), 28–54.

Sedova, who became a proponent of the war against North Korea.[302] These anti-Soviet Leftists morphed into what is now misnamed the 'neo-conservative movement' (more aptly termed 'neo-cons') who continue to herald the United States' 'world revolutionary mission.' The above-cited Ledeen and Peters are examples of the neo-cons. The globalist culture promoted by the Congress for Cultural Freedom for several decades through the Cold War was primarily the formlessness of 'abstract expressionism' (the daubings of Jackson Pollock being particularly promoted), which was heralded by these cultural Bolsheviks in the service of globalisation as the United States' 'official art,' and which was aptly condemned by the Stalinists as 'rootless cosmopolitanism.'[303] It was a great paradox of history that the United States was promoting revolutionary decadence, while the USSR maintained a conservative position and saw the arts as reflecting the soul of the folk.[304]

---

302 Ibid., 114–18.

303 F. Chernov, 'Bourgeoisie Cosmopolitanism and Its Reactionary Role,' *Bolshevik: Theoretical and Political Magazine of the All-Union Communist Party*, no. 5, 15 March 1949, 30–41.

304 These subjects are detailed in Bolton, *Stalin: The Enduring Legacy*, 'Stalinism and the Art of Rootless Cosmopolitanism,' 28–54.

Wars in the Name of 'Multiculturalism'

As indicated by Peters and Ledeen, a one-size-fits-all world is being imposed by the United States. One must have 'democracy' whether one wants it or not. That is to say, one must have the 'freedom' to buy the consumer junk vomited over most of the world by the global corporations. If one resists (the so-called 'rejectionist regimes') there is the ultimate option of US, NATO, and UN bombs to explode the 'rejectionists' into oblivion, in the name of 'democracy' and 'human rights,' 're-educate' the 'liberated' people, and try the surviving leaders as 'war criminals.'

Hence, the two world wars were fought to inaugurate a new era of free-trade economics over the entire world,[305] and to put any regime that is reticent on notice that they too can expect 'total war.' One of the recent wars that epitomises the imposition of globalism by sheer force is that waged against Serbia. The proponents of Serb annihilation clearly stated that the Serbs were an anachronism that had to be defeated because they insisted on their own ethno-state. The Afrikaner Republic had to go for the same reason.

The Kosovar Albanians served as the present-day equivalent of the 19th-century *Uitlanders* in the Afrikaner Transvaal Republic. The *Uitlanders* justified British military invasion for the control of South Africa's mineral wealth by cosmopolitan mining interests. Kosovar Albanians justified NATO/UN invasion of Serbia to grab the mineral wealth of the region, again for cosmopolitan economic interests.

The war against Serbia is of interest for several major reasons. The war was undertaken against a people-culture-nation that sought to maintain their identity. While the war against the Serbs was launched with rhetoric about

---

305 The 'free trade' war aims were enunciated in both Wilson's 'Fourteen Points' and Roosevelt's 'Atlantic Charter.'

opposing the 'ethnic cleansings' of Kosovar Albanians faced with 'genocide,' Serb actions had been defensive rather than aggressive, and involved maintaining an integral part of Serbia. Even during the war there were occasional reports of Kosovar Albanian terrorism against Serbs, until increasingly the Serbs were depicted as the sole villains. However, the Albanian Muslim 'ethnic cleansing' of Serbs from Kosovo during the US/NATO war was the continuation of a process that had started long before to integrate the region into a 'Greater Albania.' During the war a British report stated of this anti-Serb 'ethnic cleansing' that 'The violence against Kosovo's dwindling Serb population increased on Monday night when nine mortar rounds were fired at a village in the U.S. sector, killing two young Serbs and injuring five.'[306]

'The people behind this are Albanians, they harass the population to get them to leave,' said Lieutenant Ryan Leigh of the U.S. 1st infantry division, which has a command post in Klokot. 'As to who's actually doing it, I couldn't really say. The United Nations refugee agency, UNHCR, estimates that only a tenth of Kosovo's Serb and Gypsy population now remain in the province, two months after K-For's arrived. . . . K-For's press centre said an elderly Serb woman was found murdered in her home in Pristina on Sunday. It is thought that the killing was a warning to the few remaining Serbs that they should leave. . . . Remembering the 14 Serb farmers massacred in their fields near Gracko last month, the men do what harvesting they can in armed posses. They do not trust K-For to protect them. . . . 'We've been satanised in the west so nobody is paying attention to what is happening here,' said another mourner, Rade Marinkovic, 45. . . . For the Serbs of Klokot, determined to stay, life is now a siege. They have no drinking water, their telephones have been

---

306 Chris Bird, 'Kosovan Serbs Under Siege,' *The Guardian*, 18 August 1999, http://www.guardian.co.uk/world/1999/aug/18/balkans1.

cut off and they dare not send their children to school in the next village when term starts on September 1. 'All my children are at home,' said one Serb woman. 'They are terrified they will be burned alive in the house. Where can I take my children? When will we be able to sleep?'[307]

While media reports depicted Kosovar Albanian terrorism against Serbs as reprisals for Serb atrocities against Albanian ethnics, the Serbs of Kosovo had long endured terrorism from Muslim and gangster organisations. Slobodan Milosevic invaded Kosovo to protect the Serb community from Muslim terrorists who had undertaken a long campaign to 'ethnically cleanse' Kosovo of Serbs.

The Kosovo problems originated with the artificial character of the Yugoslav state, whose multiethnic, multicultural federation was held together by the strongman Marshal Tito. Tito maintained the state by repressing nationalist tendencies among the different ethnic groups, so that no single ethnicity would achieve dominance. In particular Serbia, the largest region of Yugoslavia, was divided into two provinces, Kosovo and Vojvodina, while Albanian nationalism in Kosovo was repressed. By the late 1960s however, Albanian separatism focused on attacks on Serbian Orthodox churches. In 1981, 4,000 Serbs fled from Kosovo as anti-Serb riots escalated and Serbian Orthodox churches and graves were vandalised.[308]

In 1987, *The New York Times* reported that Kosovo was on the edge of civil war due to the ethnic cleansing by Kosovar Albanians against Serbs. The Yugoslav army had uncovered hundreds of Albanian terrorist cells within its ranks. In one instance an Albanian army conscript shot up his barracks killing and wounding his sleeping Serb bunkmates. 'Ethnic

---

307 Ibid.

308 'Minorities Leaving Yugoslav Province Dominated by Albanian,' Associated Press, 17 October 1981.

Albanians in Government have manipulated public funds and regulations to take over land belonging to Serbs,' the report stated. Serb churches had been attacked, wells poisoned, and crops burned. Serb boys had been knifed and young Albanians were being told by their elders to rape Serb girls. The *New York Times* article cited an Albanian nationalist as stating the goal is to incorporate parts of Macedonia, Montenegro, Serbia, and all of Kosovo into a Greater Albania. From 1980 to 1987, 20,000 Serbs and Montenegrins fled Kosovo because of Albanian violence.[309]

This was the situation when Milosevic brought the army into the province to rout the U.S.-funded 25,000-man Kosovo Liberation Army, a gangster empire of drug traffickers who were at the time regarded by the UN as a 'terrorist organisation.' How then did a bunch of gangsters become the darlings of the globalist Establishment and the so-called 'international community'? Milosevic in defending his people showed himself to be noncompliant to the dictates of the New World Order.

Just as U.S. President George W. Bush had called for all nations to enter a war against Iraq to build a 'New World Order,' Britain's sanctimonious Prime Minister Tony Blair called upon the world to 'enter a new millennium.' In an essay in *Newsweek* magazine Blair wrote: 'This is a conflict we are fighting not for territory but for values, for a new internationalism where the brutal repression of whole ethnic groups will no longer be tolerated, for a world where those responsible for such crimes have nowhere to hide.'[310]

Blair was laying down the ground rules for new wars in the name of 'a new internationalism' that will not tolerate any sense of national identity, and where ethnic groups will only be recognised and defended if by so doing the

---

309 *New York Times*, 1 November 1987.
310 Tony Blair, *Newsweek*, 19 April 1999.

broader agenda of globalisation is achieved. Here Orwellian doublethink is a convenient technique for selling the wars of the 'new internationalism,' or the other Orwellian principle enunciated in *Animal Farm*, which in this instance might be rendered as 'all ethnicities/nations/cultures are equal but some are more equal than others.' Albanian Kosovar ethnicity good; Serb Kosovar ethnicity bad.' Transposed further: 'The rights of indigenous peoples,' unless they are *White* indigenes such as Britons, Flemish, Afrikaners, French, et al., then the theme is changed to the 'rights of immigrants' *against* indigenes.' 'Majority rights' apply to South African Blacks, because the Afrikaners are the minority; whereas 'minority rights apply to Maoris because Whites in New Zealand are the majority. The criterion is how a majority or a minority might be of use to agitate in the service of globalisation and 'one world, one race.' Hence, Kosovar Albanians, at one time widely regarded as backed by terrorists, became the victims of villainous Serbs, because that is what served globalisation.

Other denizens of the globalist Establishment in the United States heralded the war against the Serbs as a crusade against any notion of ethno-nationalism or the ethno-state. In 1999 Susan Estrich, a law professor, a big name in the Democratic Party and a close friend of the Clintons, who was considered for a Cabinet post, described the war as 'the first war of the 21st century: a conflict not about communism, but about race and ethnicity.' She added that the prospect of America committing ground forces 'speaks well for the future.'[311] That year General Wesley Clark, commander of the NATO forces, stated: 'There is no place in modern Europe for ethnically pure states. That's the 19th-century idea, and we are trying to transition into the 21st century, and we are going to do it with multi-ethnic states.'[312]

---

311 Susan Estrich, April 1999, cited by Dr. William Pierce, 'The New World Order,' *Free Speech*, vol. 5, no. 4, April 1999, http://cdn.preterhuman.net/texts/unsorted/fs994d.html.

312 Wesley Clark, CNN interview, 25 April 1999.

Serb refugees leaving Kosovo, summer 1999.

Serbs were bombed to secure an Albanian ethnic state in Kosovo in the name of the 'new internationalism' that opposes ethnic states. Again, Orwellian doublethink was required.

President Clinton endorsed these views that there would be an ongoing crusade against any ethnicity wanting to preserve its identity when this became an obstacle to the New World Order. At the time anti-war activist and writer Justin Raimondo cogently wrote:

> The War Party never rests. No sooner is the war in Kosovo 'ended,' and the sky cleared of NATO's bombs, than war clouds immediately begin to gather on the horizon. 'In Africa or central Europe' intoned Clinton on the occasion of his visit to a Macedonian refugee camp, 'we will not allow—only because of differences in ethnic background or religion or racism—people to be attacked. We will stop that.' This underscores the quintessentially *leftist* nature of the new imperialism: the United States is now embarked on an international holy war against 'racism,' and woe unto those nations

who fail to live up to Clintonian standards of political correctness. 'We can do it now,' said Clinton, strutting and boasting before his Kosovar vassals, who greeted him like a conquering hero. 'We can do it tomorrow, if it is necessary, somewhere else.' Forewarned is forearmed.

To the Clintonians, and their British and German counterparts, the very idea of national sovereignty is a racist concept, since, by definition, it necessarily excludes other nationalities and often coincides with ethnicity. This is the true meaning of the 'Clinton Doctrine' now being enunciated, in fits and starts, by the administration: *the whole world is fair game!*

A crusade for multiculturalism in the post-Soviet world is a prescription for perpetual war. In Eastern Europe and Central Asia it means the reconstruction of the failed Soviet 'multinational' model, and a relentless military struggle against all form of separatism. That this conforms nicely to the plans of powerful business interests in the West—as I pointed out in my last column, where I discussed the brewing crisis of Azerbaijan—is sheer coincidence of course. The big oil companies and the big investment banking concerns have already signed contracts with the government of Azerbaijan: if the country now begins to break up into separate statelets, then the deal is off.[313]

Was there however another agenda of the globalists besides assisting Muslim terrorists and heroin traders to ethnically cleanse Serbs from Kosovo, while these same globalists claim to be waging a 'war on terrorism' against 'Jihadists' in other parts of the world? Kosovo includes one of the most mineral-rich areas of the world, which have been mined since Roman times. The iron and nickel mining and smelting plant of

---

313 Justin Raimondo, 'No Rest for the Wicked,' Behind the Headlines: Antiwar.com, 23 June 1999, http://www.antiwar.com/justin/j062399.html.

Ferronikeli, in Dreans, was one of the largest enterprises in Kosovo, which had previously been run by the Yugoslav state. Now, 'The entire complex is owned by foreign entities: by Cunico, a company owned by the Benny Steinmetz Group (BSG) Resources Ltd., and International Mineral Resources (IMR).' After a colossal explosion in 2011 and widespread pollution, including air toxicity, there have been protests, reinforced by 'the perception that a national natural resource had been sold to foreign tycoons at a ridiculously low price,' with accompanying payments to local politicians. *Haaretz* reported at the time, under the subheading, 'Riches of the Earth':

> May 3, 2006, was a significant date for the tottering Kosovo economy. On that day senior members of the local government joined with United Nations officials and international and local business at the headquarters of the UN Interim administration Mission in Kosovo (UNMIK) to celebrate the successful conclusion of the biggest privatisation deal signed since the end of the war with Serbia.[314]

The pretext for war was the refusal of the Serbs to sign the Rambouillet 'peace agreement' recognising the claims of the Kosovar Albanians, and presented as an ultimatum with the threat of war. The Serbs were willing to allow broad Albanian autonomy, but not the stipulated occupation of the region by NATO troops, and the imposition of NATO overlordship. The justification for the imposition of NATO martial law was the maintenance of Kosovo as a multicultural entity that would have nonetheless assured Albanian ethnic domination over the Serbs. The Rambouillet *diktat* pontificated in terms typical of globalist rhetoric since the days of Woodrow Wilson that a Constitution must be based on the recognition 'that the

---

314 'Israel Black Hole in Kosovo,' *Haaretz*, 12 August 2011, http://www.haaretz.com/weekend/magazine/israeli-black-hole-in-kosovo-1.378338.

preservation and promotion of the national, cultural, and linguistic identity of each national community in Kosovo are necessary for the harmonious development of a peaceful society.'[315] Such a multicultural edifice[316] in such a situation was designed to dispossess the Serbs. The proposals were designed to provoke, not to conciliate.[317]

Chapter Four of the agreement shows precisely what the globalists were after in seeking to deconstruct Serbia. This deals specifically with globalist demands regarding the Serb economy. Article I (1) states: '1. The economy of Kosovo shall function in accordance with free market principles.' Article II (1) of Chapter Four states that state-owned assets are to be privatised:

> 1. The Parties agree to reallocate ownership and resources in accordance insofar as possible with the distribution of powers and responsibilities set forth in this Agreement, in the following areas:

> (a) government-owned assets (including educational institutions, hospitals, natural resources, and production facilities).[318]

Rambouillet was the 'Fourteen Points' and the 'Atlantic Charter' all over again.

According to an article in *The Guardian* by Balkan affairs specialist Neil Clark, 'At the time, the rump Yugoslavia—then not a member of the International Monetary Fund, the World Bank, the World Trade Organization, or European Bank for Reconstruction and Development—was the last

---

315 Rambouillet Agreement: Interim Agreement for Peace and Self-Government in Kosovo, Chapter 1: Constitution, http://www.state.gov/www/regions/eur/ksvo_rambouillet_text.html.

316 Ibid., see Article VII: 'National Communities,' 1–7.

317 Richard Becker, 'Rambouillet a declaration of war disguised as a peace agreement,' *June 10, 2000 International Tribunal for U.S./NATO war crimes in Yugoslavia*, http://www.iacenter.org/warcrime/rbecker.htm.

318 Rambouillet Agreement, op. cit., Chapter Four, 'Economic Issues,' Article II (1).

economy in central-southern Europe to be uncolonised by western capital. "Socially-owned enterprises," the form of worker self-management pioneered under Tito, still predominated.' Clark wrote of Yugoslavia's industry being 75 per cent state or socially owned. 'In 1997, a privatisation law had stipulated that in sell-offs, at least 60% of shares had to be allocated to a company's workers.' Hence, profit-sharing was to continue as the basis of the Yugoslav economy.

> The high priests of neo-liberalism were not happy. At the Davos summit early in 1999, Tony Blair berated Belgrade, not for its handling of Kosovo, but for its failure to embark on a programme of 'economic reform'—new-world-order speak for selling state assets and running the economy in the interests of multinationals.[319]

Clark states that when the NATO bombing campaign started in 1999, state-owned companies, rather than military sites, were targeted. NATO destroyed only 14 tanks, but bombed 372 industrial facilities, although 'not one foreign or privately owned factory was bombed.'[320]

One of the first steps of the new administration was to repeal the previously mentioned 1997 privatisation law. Now 70 per cent of a company could be sold to foreign investors. The regime also enmeshed Serbia into the World Bank. The Trepca mining complex was seized by NATO troops.[321]

In 2004 the Kosovo Trust Agency (KTA), operating under the jurisdiction of the UN Mission in Kosovo (Unmik), was 'pleased to announce' the programme to privatise the first 500 socially owned enterprises (SOEs) under its control.[322] In 2008 the name of KTA was changed to the

319 Neil Clark, 'The Spoils of Another War,' *The Guardian*, 21 September 2004, http://www.guardian.co.uk/world/2004/sep/21/kosovo.comment.

320 Ibid.

321 Ibid.

322 Ibid.

more blatant Privatisation Agency of Kosovo (PAK).[323] Everything from shops and parcels of land to industries is up for grabs, as former SOEs are sold off in what are called 'waves' of privatisations.[324] PAK assures foreign investors of a freer hand in Kosovo, pointing out that all banks in Kosovo are privately owned; that there are 'abundant natural resources: lignite, lead, zinc, ferronickel and fertile agricultural land'; with

> Lignite reserves about 14 billion tonnes. New power plant will add 1,000MW capacity, GDP increase of 17%. Demand for investments in new coalmines. Huge deposits of lead and zinc (Trepça mines). Gold and silver, ferronickel and magnesium.[325]

PAK states in its 2011 report that, 'There are 600 SOEs listed in the PAK register.'

> Approximately 400 of them were considered viable businesses or have assets that are suitable for privatisation and the remaining 200 will be dealt through the liquidation process. To date close to 300 SOE's have been privatized in full or partially through creation of 619 NewCo's and an additional 175 liquidation sales of different assets have been successfully completed. It is therefore fair to say that with some notable exceptions, the majority of large SOE's have already been privatized and overall privatisation is well on its way to completion.[326]

Trepca, the jewel in the crown, is one of the most mineral rich regions in the world, and has been mined since Roman times. Although the shambles caused by the NATO/UN

---

323 Privatisation Agency of Kosovo, http://www.pak-ks.org/?page=2,4.

324 FAQ: What is PAK Selling?, http://www.pak-ks.org/?page=2,5.

325 'Why Kosovo?,' http://www.pak-ks.org/?page=2,35.

326 'The challenges facing the Privatisation Agency of Kosovo are considerable,' Information to Stakeholders, August 2011, p. 5.

invasion has suspended the operations of Trepca mining, it remains a priority for privatising. PAK states:

> Trepca is a conglomerate with assets and branches located in virtually all regions of the country including in the northern part of the Republic of Kosovo. Its extractable mineral wealth has been the subject of heated debate with expert opinions on valuation ranging from €8 to €12 billion. In the former Yugoslavia it was one of the largest employers with more than 20,000 workers. Trepça is made up of 40 subsidiary enterprises that include its main mineral and metallurgical components, processing capacities and other industrial products as well as supporting service activities for production, processing and technical support services. The majority of these are in the territory of the Republic of Kosovo but also abroad. Hence without any doubt Trepça has an extraordinary importance for the Republic of Kosovo and its citizens and is pivotal to the economy, society and politics of the country and indeed to some of its neighbours.

The Trepca conglomerate was not immune from political interference and interim measures during the Milosevic regime and parties with 'claims' against the assets started to emerge that resulted in suspension of executions as a result of a 'moratorium' imposed by the SCSC[327] following a request from the UNMIK SRSG. In November 2005, UNMIK issued a Regulation (2005/48) on Reorganisation and restructuring of certain enterprises. With the benefit of hindsight, it is clear that 2005/48 is less than ideal and, if used, would result in the control of Trepca's destiny being ceded to a private sector administrator. As a consequence, 2005/48 has been replaced with a new reorganization law that will ensure that reorganisation of Trepca is managed and controlled by the Agency for the benefit of the citizens of the Republic of Kosovo. The Agency will have the

---

327 Special Chamber of the Supreme Court.

power to engage the services of international mining and insolvency experts to design a reorganization plan that will be best suited to this complex enterprise together with specialised legal experts to address claims. The Agency remains convinced that any plan for revitalization of Trepça must happen as soon as possible but must comply with the internationally recognized standards in regards to the re-organization and restructuring of strategic enterprises. This will require significant engagement of all relevant stake-holders because successful revitalization of Trepça in essence implies that the enterprise should be freed from inherited problems and given the opportunity to flourish again.[328]

It can be noted that while PAK refers to the strategic importance of Trepca and its wide economic ramifications, the determination remains to privatise. The report goes on to say that Trepca has been operating at a loss, averaging 10 per cent of what it has produced. The aim is to liquidate Trepca and to 'Invite foreign direct investment from international mining groups with global reach . . . as the country's largest investment opportunity.'[329] Such is the reality of the war on Serbia, where 'Islamist' terrorists suddenly became 'freedom fighters,' backed by U.S. and NATO arms. The same situation transpired in Libya against Gadaffi, and in Syria against Assad as this is written.

Manipulation of Islam

The globalists and U.S. policy-makers are playing a duplicitous game in regard to Islam: The so-called 'Jihadists' or 'Islamists,' are paraded as the universal bogeymen that justify the 'global war on terrorism'; the 'Arab Spring' (another batch of well-planned and funded 'spontaneous' 'colour revolutions')[330]

328 'The challenges . . . ,' op. cit., p. 11.
329 Ibid., 'New Law on Reorganisation of Certain Enterprise,' p. 21.
330 K. R. Bolton, *Revolution from Above*, 'The Global Democratic Revolution,' op.

and the invasion and occupation of 'rejectionist' states. On the other hand, funding from globalist organisations and agencies of the U.S. government have supported 'Islamists' such as the Mujahideen when 'Islamists' were used to dislodge the Russians from Afghanistan, and similar organisations in Libya, Albanian Muslim terrorists in Serbia and the same types presently in Syria. These 'Islamists' can be called 'terrorists' or 'freedom fighters' as requirements dictate. The Kosovo Liberation Army had been designated originally by the U.S. State Department as terrorists and gangsters, but were armed to topple the Yugoslav state. The globalists have been playing the same game in supporting Muslim terrorism against Russia in Chechnya.

Today's 'Islamists' are a product of U.S. Cold War policy against Russia. Graham Fuller, when Deputy Director of the CIA's National Council on Intelligence, spawned the Mujahideen during the 1980s, recruiting fundamentalist Muslims for training in guerrilla insurgency against Soviet forces in Afghanistan. One of these trainees was Osama bin Laden. Al Qaeda was the product. Fuller, worked at the Pentagon, and at the RAND Corporation globalist think tank. Swiss journalist and author Richard Labévière cited a 1999 memo of Fuller as a basis for U.S. policy:

> The policy of guiding the evolution of Islam and of helping them against our adversaries worked marvelously well in Afghanistan against [the Russians]. The same doctrines can still be used to destabilize what remains of Russian power, and especially to counter the Chinese[331] influence in Central Asia.[332]

---

loc.

331 In this writer's opinion, the United States will not act against China. The two have symbiotic economies and the globalists headed up by Rockefeller, Soros and Goldman Sachs interests are profiting well from the Chinese status quo. Russia under Putin remains the primary globalist irritant. See Bolton, *Geopolitics of the Indo-Pacific, op. cit.*

332 Richard Labévière, *Dollars for Terror: The United States and Islam* (New York:

Babel, Inc.

Russia's main pipeline route out of the Caspian Sea basin transits through Chechnya and Dagestan. The 1994–1996 Chechen war, instigated by the main rebel movements against Moscow, served to undermine secular state institutions. The adoption of Islamic law in the largely secular Muslim societies of the former Soviet Union serves U.S. strategic interests in the region, as a means of destabilisation. Elsewhere, conversely, U.S./globalist policy pursues secularisation against Islam and all other traditional religions, as explained by Ralph Peters. The Soros networks are particularly assiduous in funding movements and individuals against traditional cultural, ethnic and national principles. 'Feminism' including so-called 'reproductive' rights' (abortion), is especially promoted by such globalist NGOs. 'Feminism' next to multiculturalism, is one of the most useful tools for globalist subversion in subverting traditional national and cultural structures.[333]

One of the numerous subversive organisations established to encourage 'regime change' in 'rejectionist' regimes is the American Committee for Peace in the Caucasus (ACPC), originally founded as the American Committee for Peace in Chechnya. This is a project of Freedom House, one of the primary globalist NGOs promoting 'regime change' around the world, in tandem with the Soros 'Open Society' network, USAID, the National Endowment for Democracy, *ad infinitum*.[334] ACPC, which is based at Freedom House, states of itself:

> Founded in 1999 to advocate for a political solution to the conflict in Chechnya that erupted into a war for independence with Russia in 1994, ACPC was at the helm of international NGO efforts to galvanize the U.S. and international policymaking community

Algora Publishing, 2000), 5–6.

333 K. R. Bolton, 'Feminism,' in *Revolution from Above*.

334 Ibid., 218–33.

on the implications of the conflict for human rights in Chechnya. As violence spread into other republics in the North Caucasus—Ingushetia, Dagestan, Kabardino-Balkaria, Karachay-Cherkessia and North Ossetia—ACPC concentrated its efforts on supporting human rights and rule of law, monitoring the trajectory of violence in the region, and advocating for peace and stability in the North Caucasus.[335]

The rhetoric about 'human rights' follows exactly the same agenda as the myriad of other NGOs, think tanks, and funds etc., in targeting any 'rejectionist' regime, from apartheid South Africa, to Milosevic's Serbia, to Assad's Syria to Putin's Russia. Whenever a state or statesman hinders some globalist objective, a sudden hue and cry goes up about 'human rights.' The formula does not change. The purpose is to undermine Russian policy in a patchwork of multiethnic republics by appeals to 'human rights,' 'civil society,' and 'democracy.' Hence in Dagestan, plagued by Muslim militancy, ACPC concluded in 2011:

Magomedov's appointment signalled the Kremlin's renewed reliance on clan politics as an instrument of control. His inability to launch a meaningful dialogue with adherents of Salafi Islam underscore the pitfalls of his limited mandate, made accountable to the federal centre as opposed to the Dagestani population. In the Russian political landscape, any attempts at changes by North Caucasus leaders will go awry without the Kremlin support, which suggests that the central government continues to favor ironfisted policies as opposed to reconciliation and aborts local efforts at practicing alternative approaches.[336]

---

335 'About ACPC,' http://www.peaceinthecaucasus.org/about.
336 Dagestan at Tipping Point, American Committee for Peace in the Caucasus, 2011, http://www.peaceinthecaucasus.org/sites/default/files/pdf/ACPC_paper_Dagestan.pdf.

After the bombing at the Boston marathon in 2013 allegedly by two Chechnyan 'Islamists,' the anti-Russia campaign of the ACPC received some criticism for portraying Russia as a villain in the region, and for spurning Russian warnings about Chechnyan terrorism. William Kristol, a seminal spokesman in favour of U.S. global hegemony, and a member of ACPC,[337] stated that although the Russian authorities had offered the United States 'a pretty detailed dossier of [bombing suspect Tamerlan Tsarnaev's] contacts,' he stated that the Russians were 'trying to get us to be suspicious of every Chechen who came to the U.S., especially of everyone who came as a political refugee.'[338] That is a dilemma of multiculturalism even for its chief backer, the United States: the chickens come home to roost. Many of those on the Chechnya-aiding ACPC, such as William Kristol, were also founders of the Project for a New American Century,[339] which drew up the blueprints for 'regime change' throughout the Middle East, a plan which is still unfolding. They were also enthusiasts for war against Serbia.[340]

However, there is another major factor in regard to globalisation and Islam. The globalists are manipulating Islam by different and in several respects, contradictory, means; which is to say, they are pursuing a *dialectical* strategy:

• As we have seen, a certain type of Muslim, the 'Islamists' or 'Jihadists' have been created by the globalists via their American proxies, to produce a

337 ACPC, members, http://www.peaceinchechnya.org/about_members.htm.

338 David Weigel, 'We Are All Russians Now,' *Skate*, 22 April 2013, http://www.slate.com/articles/news_and_politics/politics/2013/04/russia_warned_the_fbi_about_tamerlan_tsarnaev_how_american_neocons_originally.html.

339 Project for a New American Century, 'Statement of Principles,' 3 June 1997, http://web.archive.org/web/20070810113753/www.newamericancentury.org/statementofprinciples.htm.

340 Project for a New American Century, 'Balkans/Caucasus,' http://www.newamericancentury.org/balkans.htm.

controlled crises—the 'war on terrorism'—to justify globalist intervention in states that are regarded as 'rejectionist,' such as Iran, Iraq, Libya, and Syria.

• Conversely, those states that were or are fighting 'Islamists,' namely Serbia, Libya, Iraq, and Syria, and Russia vis-à-vis Chechnya, are targeted by the globalists as tyrannical for trying to suppress or contain their own Muslim militants, who receive globalist support.

• Muslim migrants,[341] especially to Europe, are used to establish ethnic enclaves and break down any remnants of European pride, while justifying increasingly oppressive measures against the European populations through 'human rights' laws and mass re-education of the young to discard the 'xenophobia' of their elders and embrace 'multiculturalism' as the exciting new wave of the future.

Having considered the first two points, we shall now turn our attention to a specific example of the globalist plan to destroy a European cultural and national identity by pushing multiculturalism in France via the use of Muslim migrants and their offspring.

---

341 Asians in New Zealand and Australia, Hispanics in the United States, etc., serve the same purposes.

Target: France

During 19–22 October 2010, Charles Rivkin, U.S. Ambassador to France, invited a 29-member delegation from the Pacific Council on International Policy (PCIP) to a conference in France, the stated purpose of which was to discuss Arab and Islamic relations in the country.[342] The meeting was part of a far-reaching subversive agenda to transform that entire character of France and in particular the consciousness of French youth. This programme focuses on the use of France's Muslim youth in a typically manipulative strategy behind the façade of 'human rights' and 'equality.'

The PCIP report stated of the conference:

> . . . The delegation further focused on three key themes. First, the group examined Franco-Muslim issues in France through exchanges with Dr Bassma Kodmani, Director of the Arab Reform Institute, and Ms Rachida Dati, the first female French cabinet member of North African origin and current Mayor of the 7th Arrondissement in Paris. A trip to the Grand Mosque of Paris and a meeting with the Director of Theology and the Rector there provided additional insight. Second, meetings with Mr Jean-Noel Poirier, the Vice President of External Affairs at AREVA (a highly innovative French energy company), and with Mr Brice Lalonde, climate negotiator and former Minister of the Environment, highlighted energy and nuclear policy issues and the differences between U.S. and French policies in these arenas. And finally, the delegation explored the connections between media and culture in California (Hollywood) and France in meetings at the Louvre, the Musée D'Orsay, and at

---

342 '2010 France Country Dialogue,' PCIP, http://www.pacificcouncil.org/page. aspx?pid=583.

179

FRANCE 24—the Paris-based international news and current affairs channel.[343]

The primary purpose was obviously on matters of a multicultural nature, including not only Arab and Islamic relations in France, but also importantly, a discussion on the impact of Hollywood 'culture' on the French; i.e. a major part of the 'culturally lethal' virus that Ralph Peters described as the most pervasive and subversive element of globalisation. Obama appointed Rivkin due to his role as a major fund-raiser for the President. His career has been in business, becoming head of two entertainment companies and gaining 'powerful friends' in Hollywood.[344]

The PCIP, of which Rivkin is a member, was founded in 1995 as a regional appendage of the omnipresent globalist think tank, the Council on Foreign Relations (CFR).[345] It is headquartered in Los Angeles, 'with members and activities throughout the West Coast of the United States and internationally.' Corporate funding comes from, among others: Carnegie Corporation of New York, Chicago Council on Foreign Relations, City National Bank, The Ford Foundation, Bill and Melinda Gates Foundation, The William & Flora Hewlett Foundation, Rockefeller Brothers Fund, The Rockefeller Foundation, United States Institute of Peace.[346] The PCIP is therefore yet another big player in the globalist network comprising hundreds of interconnected organisations, lobbies, 'civil society' groups, NGOs, and think tanks, associated with the U.S. Government, and with banks and other corporations.

---

343 '2010 France Country Dialogue,' ibid.

344 Nicholas Kralev, 'Being good at raising money doesn't make you a good diplomat,' *The Atlantic*, 19 March 2013, http://www.theatlantic.com/international/archive/2013/03/being-good-at-raising-money-doesnt-make-you-a-good-diplomat/274148/.

345 'Founded in 1995 in partnership with the Council on Foreign Relations,' PCIP, Governance, http://www.pacificcouncil.org/page.aspx?pid=373.

346 Corporate and Foundation funding: http://www.pacificcouncil.org/page.aspx?pid=513.

Early into his appointment as Ambassador, *The Los Angeles Times* described Rivkin as a '48-year-old Yale alum and Harvard Business School graduate with Russian Jewish parents,' who aims to promote American-style multiculturalism among France's bellicose *banlieues*[347] as the way of the future.[348] Prior to his appointment as Ambassador, Rivkin was California finance co-chair of the Obama Presidential campaign, raising $500,000—in a campaign that was heavily funded by the United States' oligarchy.[349] He had run an entertainment company, Wildbrain, and prior to that the Jim Henson Company,[350] and has stated that 'I do feel I understand the power of media.'[351]

Why France?

France has long been a thorn in the side of U.S. globalism because of its frequent (although not invariable) adherence to French interests around the world, rather than those of the manufactured 'world community.' France has followed the dictum of President Charles de Gaulle that they 'don't have friends, but only interests.' France is one of the few states left in Western Europe with the remnant of a national consciousness. She is therefore regarded as 'xenophobic' and in need of change. The best way of destroying any such sentiment is to weaken ethno-national consciousness and identity by means of 'multiculturalism.' Was it only a coincidence that the 1968 student revolt, sparked by the most puerile of reasons, occurred at a time both when the CIA was very active in funding student groups around the world, and when President de Gaulle was giving the United States a lot of trouble? De Gaulle did little to play along

---

347 France's ghettoised Third World ethnics.

348 Devorah Lauter, 'U.S. envoy in France is making the most of his opportunity,' *Los Angeles Times*, 24 April 2010, http://articles.latimes.com/2010/apr/24/world/la-fg-france-ambassador-20100425.

349 K. R. Bolton, 'Obama—cat's-paw of international capitalism,' [missing details]

350 Producers of the Sesame Street series that inculcated multiculturalism into preschoolers, with funding from the Ford Foundation.

351 Lauter, op. cit.

with American's post-war plans. He withdrew France from NATO military command. Even during World War II as leader of the Free French, he was distrusted by the United States.[352] Of particular concern would have been De Gaulle's advocacy of a united Europe to counteract U.S. hegemony,[353] especially as de Gaulle's vision of a united Europe included the Soviet Union. In 1959 he stated at Strasbourg: 'Yes, it is Europe, from the Atlantic to the Urals, it is the whole of Europe, that will decide the destiny of the world.' The expression implied détente between a future neutralist Europe and the USSR. In 1967 he declared an arms embargo on Israel and cultivated the Arab world. This is the type of statesmanship that globalists fear. With constant tension among disaffected Muslim youth, a backlash could see an intransigently anti-globalist, 'xenophobic' regime come to power, such as that of the Front National.

Of note in regard to the 2010 PCIP delegation is their interest in the influence of Hollywood on French culture. This might seem at first glance to be an odd concern. However Hollywood, as the symbol of international cultural excrescence, is an important factor in globalisation, in what amounts to a world culture-war, as discussed previously in regard to the Ralph Peters analysis. It is notable that the instigators of the 'Arab Spring' that swept through North Africa, reaching into Iran, were secularised youths without strong traditional roots, and enamoured by the products of global consumerism. These modernised youths are precisely the type that Ralph Peters described as being infected by the 'lethal culture' of Hollywood, MTV, etc., who could be mobilised and manipulated into overthrowing not only 'rejectionist' regimes such as that of Libya, but even regimes such as the Egyptian, that had traditionally been pro-U.S. but which did not accord with longer term aims

352 Simon Berthon, *Allies at War* (London: Collins, 2001), 21.
353 Aidan Crawley, *De Gaulle: A Biography* (London: The Literary Guild, 1969), 439.

for Africa and the Middle East. I have described elsewhere precisely how this was done during the 'Arab Spring' with a generation of North Africans as obsessed with 'social media' as their rootless counterparts in the West, at the instigation of U.S.-based globalists.[354]

So what are Rivkin and the U.S. State Department up to in France, that they should be so interested in the place of Hollywood and of Muslims in that nation?

The Rivkin Project for Subverting French Youth

When Rivkin invited a delegation of fellow PCIP members to France in 2010 he had outlined a program for the globalisation of France that involves the use of the Muslim minorities and the indoctrination of French youth with multiculturalism. The slogan invoked was the common commitment France and America historically had to 'equality.' Wikileaks released the 'confidential' Rivkin programme. It is entitled 'Minority Engagement Strategy.'[355] Here, Rivkin outlines a program that is a far-reaching interference in the domestic affairs of a sovereign nation and, more profoundly, seeks to change the attitudes of generations of Muslim and French youth so that they might be merged into a new globalist synthesis; or what might be called a new humanity: *Homo economicus*, or *Homo globicus*; what the financial journalist G. Pascal Zachary calls 'The Global Me.'[356] Rivkin begins by stating that his Embassy has created a 'Minority Engagement Strategy,' that is directed at Muslims in France. Rivkin states as part

---

354 K. R. Bolton, 'Twitters of the World Revolution: The Digital New-New Left,' *Foreign Policy Journal*, 28 February 2011, http://www.foreignpolicyjournal.com/2011/02/28/twitterers-of-the-world-revolution-the-digital-new-new-left/.
Tony Cartalucci, 'Google's Revolution Factory—Alliance of Youth Movements: Color Revolution 2.0,' *Global Research*, February 23, 2011, http://www.globalresearch.ca/index.php?context=va&aid=23283.
355 C. Rivkin, 'Minority Engagement Report,' U.S. Embassy, Paris, http://www.wikileaks.fi/cable/2010/01/10PARIS58.html.
356 G. Pascal Zachary, op. cit.

Muslim women demanding Shariah law for France

of the programme: '. . . We will also integrate the efforts of various Embassy sections, target influential leaders among our primary audiences, and evaluate both tangible and intangible indicators of the success of our strategy.'[357]

Rivkin is confident that France's history of ideological liberalism 'will serve us well as we implement the strategy outlined here . . . in which we press France. . . .' Note the phrase: 'press France.' America's global agenda is linked by Rivkin to his blueprint for transferring France into 'a thriving, inclusive French polity [that] will help advance our interests in expanding democracy and increasing stability worldwide.' The program will focus on the 'elites' of the French and the Muslim communities, but will also involve a massive propaganda campaign directed at the 'general population,' with a focus on the young.

The programme includes redefining French history in the school curricula to give attention to the role of non-French minorities in French history. It means that the Pepsi/MTV generation of Americans and their mentors in academe

---

357 Rivkin, op. cit.

184

will be formulating new definitions of French culture and rewriting French history to accord with globalist agendas. Towards this end: '. . . we will continue and intensify our work with French museums and educators to reform the history curriculum taught in French schools.' The U.S. 'elite' arrogates to itself the prerogative to refashion of culture and the very collective consciousness of another people, in order to reshape France for globalisation. This revision of French history and culture to accord with a multicultural, anti-national agenda has already been imposed within the United States itself for decades, to ensure that Euro-American consciousness is obliterated, in favour of the American 'melting pot,' while conversely 'Black Pride' and 'Hispanic Pride' (*La Raza*) have been promoted as a dialectical battering ram against American Whites. Ultimately the aim remains to create a nebulous mass called 'Americans' out of a melting pot.

'Tactic Number Three' is entitled: 'Launch Aggressive Youth Outreach.' As in other states targeted by the U.S. State Department and their allies in the Soros network, Freedom House, Movement.org, the National Endowment for Democracy, Solidarity Center,[358] and so forth, disaffected youth are the focus for change. Leading the charge on this effort, the Ambassador's inter-agency Youth Outreach Initiative aims to 'engender a positive dynamic among French youth that leads to greater support for U.S. objectives and values.' Can the intentions be stated any plainer? It is cultural and political Americanisation. It is here that we can most easily get past the cant and see what is behind the strategy: to form a generation 'that leads to greater support for U.S. objectives and values' (*sic*). These 'U.S. objectives and values' will be sold to the French as 'French values' on the basis of the liberal-humanist ideals

---

358 K. R. Bolton, 'The Globalist Web of Subversion,' *Foreign Policy Journal*, 7 February 2011, http://www.foreignpolicyjournal.com/2011/02/07/the-globalist-web-of-subversion.

that instigated both the 1776 American Revolution and the 1789 French Revolution. The young French will be taught to think that they are upholding French traditions, rather than acting as the useful idiots of Americanisation, and the concomitant *idiocracy*[359] of the global shopping mall. A far-reaching program incorporating a variety of indoctrination methods is outlined by Rivkin:

> To achieve these aims, we will build on the expansive Public Diplomacy programs already in place at post, and develop creative, additional means to influence the youth of France, employing new media, corporate partnerships, nationwide competitions, targeted outreach events, especially invited U.S. guests.[360]

The program directed at youth in France is similar to that directed at the youth that formed the vanguard of the 'velvet revolutions' from Eastern Europe to North Africa. Potential leaders are going to be recruited by the U.S. State Department in France and cultivated to play a part in the future Americanised France:

> We will also develop new tools to identify, learn from, and influence future French leaders. As we expand training and exchange opportunities for the youth of France, we will continue to make absolutely certain that the exchanges we support are inclusive. We will build on existing youth networks in France, and create new ones in cyberspace, connecting France's future leaders to each other in a forum whose values we help

---

359 Coined from the 2006 movie, *Idiocracy*, where the United States' population has been dumbed-down dysgenically; the most intelligent pursuing careers rather than having families, while the idiots proliferate and are addicted to the banality of mass entertainment. The United States is led by a ghetto Black and his Cabinet includes a youngster who won the post in a game-show. 'Advertising, commercialism, and cultural anti-intellectualism have run rampant and dysgenic pressure has resulted in a uniformly stupid society . . .' 'Idiocracy,' http://en.wikipedia.org/wiki/Idiocracy.

360 Rivkin, op. cit.

to shape—values of inclusion, mutual respect, and open dialogue.[361]

Here Rivkin is advocating something beyond influencing Muslims in France. He is stating that a significant part of the programme will be directed towards cultivating French youth in 'American' ideals, behind the façade of French ideals. The State Department and corporate allies and allied NGOs intend to 'shape their values.' The globalist programme for France is stated clearly to be the re-education of French youth. One would think that this is the most important role of the French state, the Catholic Church and the family; the latter two in particular.

As in the states that are chosen for 'velvet revolutions' part of the strategy includes demarcating acceptable political boundaries. In the context of France it is clear that the demarcation of French politics cannot include any elements of so-called 'xenophobia' which in today's context would include a return to the grand politics of the De Gaulle era. Hence, 'Tactic 5' states:

> Fifth, we will continue our project of sharing best practices with young leaders in all fields, including young political leaders of all moderate parties so that they have the toolkits and mentoring to move ahead. We will create or support training and exchange programs that teach the enduring value of broad inclusion to schools, civil society groups, bloggers, political advisors, and local politicians.[362]

Rivkin is outlining a programme to train France's future political and civic leaders. While the programmes of U.S. Government-backed NGOs such as the National Endowment for Democracy are designed to develop entire

361 Ibid.
362 Ibid.

programs and strategies for political parties in 'emerging democracies' (*sic*), this can be rationalised by stating that there is a lack of experience in liberal-democratic party politics in certain states. The same can hardly be used to justify America's interference in France's party politics. Towards this end Rivkin states that the 1,000 American English language teachers employed at French schools will be provided with the propaganda materials necessary to inculcate the desired ideals into their French pupils: 'We will also provide tools for teaching tolerance to the network of over 1,000 American university students who teach English in French schools every year.' The wide-ranging programme will be coordinated by the 'Minority Working Group' in 'tandem' with the 'Youth Outreach Initiative.' One of the issues monitored by the Group will be the 'decrease in popular support for xenophobic political parties and platforms.'[363] This is to ensure that the programme is working as it should, to block the success of any 'extreme' or 'xenophobic' party that might challenge globalisation. Hence, one might conclude that the Front National, is or will be the target of agencies of the U.S. Government.

Rivkin clarifies the subversive nature of the programme when he states: 'While we could never claim credit for these positive developments, we will focus our efforts in carrying out activities, described above, that prod, urge and stimulate movement in the right direction.'[364] What Rivkin is describing is a covert operation to fundamentally change the character of French youth and society and to interfere with the French political process.

What would the reaction be if the French Government through its Embassy in Washington undertook a program to radically change the United States in accordance with 'French national interests,' inculcating through an

363 Ibid.
364 Ibid.

'aggressive outreach program' focusing on youth, 'French ideals' under the guise of 'American ideals on human rights'? What would be the response of the U.S. Administration if it were found that the French Government was trying to influence the attitudes of Afro-Americans, American-Indians, and Latinos? What if French officials were ordered to take every opportunity to 'press' U.S. officials to ask why there are not more American Indians in Government positions? What would be the official U.S. reaction if it were found that French-language educators in American schools and colleges were trying to inculcate American pupils with ideas in the service of French interests, and to reshape attitudes towards a pro-French direction in foreign policy?

Multicultural Programmes Sponsored by U.S. Government

What the globalist agenda is for French youth can be seen in what the United States has for decades imposed upon American youth with programmes such as 'Black History Month' (February) in which a history of Africans and Afro-Americans is invented, where Cleopatra and Hannibal are portrayed as Black Africans. Black History Month was formally recognised by the U.S. Government in 1976.[365] Black History Month has been extended to Canada,[366] Britain,[367] and France, and is being extended throughout the world via UNESCO. Black History Month in France in February 2013 featured events held by 'the mainstay American cultural institutions such as The American

---

365 'President Gerald R. Ford's Message on the Observance of Black History Month,' 10 February 1976, *Gerald R. Ford Presidential Library and Museum*, University of Texas, http://www.ford.utexas.edu/library/speeches/760074.htm.

366 Citizenship and Immigration Canada, http://www.cic.gc.ca/english/multiculturalism/black/background.asp.

367 Black History Month UK, http://www.black-history-month.co.uk/sitea/BHM_FAQ.html.

Church, The American Library, The American Embassy, or Dorothy's Gallery' (American Center for the Arts).[368] A feature of Black History Month in France is the denigration of its colonial heritage, which, as with apartheid in South Africa, slavery and segregation in the United States, and colonialism in other European states, serves as a convenient method of social engineering; namely the inculcation of a guilt complex especially among the young. Hence in 2013 the public activities of the 'Beyond Colonialism' Association were organised to coincide with Black History Month.[369]

In 2010, the year that the Rivkin memo was issued, the U.S. Embassy in Paris sponsored a symposium featuring Afro-American expatriate Dr. Monique Wells, who runs a travel agency called 'Black Paris.' She spoke on the theme 'Black Paris and the Myth of a Colorblind France.' The lecture and discussion were evidently of the type structured to promote a guilt complex among the Europeans present, while promoting a sense that French culture owes much to American Negro input.

> The lecture was given in three parts: part one—physical traces of African Americans in Paris (i.e. names on buildings, street signs, etc.); part two—the African-American presence in Paris which continues to permeate the city sometimes impalpably so. During this segment Dr. Wells also confronted the question 'Is France color blind?,' examining it from both a cultural and historical perspective; part three—was a slide show of images of the contemporary Diaspora in Paris.[370]

Wells stated that Paris and France culturally owe much to

---

368 'Spirit of Black Paris,' http://spiritofblackparis.blogspot.co.nz/2013/02/whats-focus-of-black-history-month-in.html.

369 Ibid.

370 Monique Wells, 'Black Paris and the Myth of a Colorblind France,' Embassy of the Untied State, Paris, 9 February 2010, http://france.usembassy.gov/events100209.html.

US Ambassador Rivkin speaking at event for Black History Month in Paris

Africans: 'Paris has changed and is the way it is because we continue to be here. We're not the only force that drives the French way of life but the African-American contribution is definitely not insignificant to the culture of this city and by extension of this nation.'[371]

Music, particularly jazz, made major inroads into French culture, and now a new generation of French youth are being Africanised via hip hop:

> Gospel music is very much appreciated in France; however the biggest contribution from African-Americans was jazz music. The famous jazz club Caveau de la Huchette has attracted many top jazz musicians such as Lionel Hampton, Art Blakey, and Sidney Bechet. Hip-Hop is another genre that has permeated French youth culture, not only in music but in fashion, slam poetry/spoken word, graffiti, and dance.[372]

---

371 Ibid.
372 Ibid.

Note that Wells states this corporate-generated Afro-American ghetto subculture has 'permeated' French youth not only in music, but in fashion and in speech, which the French have so assiduously attempted to preserve in its purity.

Wells' presentation concluded with a discussion, seemingly as a type of 'group therapy' session long popular in the United States among corporate and government organisations, and political and religious cults, as a method of imposing conformity of opinions through induced guilt.[373] Hence, 'The positive feed-back allowed audience members from different racial backgrounds to interact and discuss racial inequalities experienced in Paris; not just among Blacks but among others outside the traditional construct of mainstream French.'[374] The *a priori* assumption is that 'the traditional construct of mainstream French' is still not sufficiently open to cultural subversion from alien sources.

One project of particular concern that was exposed in France was the U.S. backing of an immigrant lobby. Such U.S. sponsorship of NGOs via the National Endowment for Democracy, Freedom House, USAID, and many others, is generally directed at states marked for 'regime change,' such as Libya, Syria, Iraq, Serbia, former Soviet bloc states, etc. However, in 2011 Abdelaziz Dahhassi, described like many U.S. dupes as a 'human rights activist,' set up a 'think tank to find new ways of fighting ethnic and religious discrimination in France,' with 'backing from the U.S. State Department.'[375]

---

373 K. R. Bolton, *The Psychotic Left* (London: Black House Publishing, 2013), 190–92.

374 M. Wells, op. cit.

375 Anita Elash, 'U.S. accused of meddling in France's immigration policies,' *Globe & Mail*, 17 February 2011, http://m.theglobeandmail.com/news/world/europe/us-accused-of-meddling-in-frances-immigrant-policies/article1910663/?service=mobile.

The *Globe & Mail* specifically points to the support given by the United States to groups as part of the Rivkin programme, and pointed to the cultivation of Muslim youth by the United States. Such 'leadership programs' are a long-used method of influencing potential leaders of states marked for 'regime change,' and have been used since the days of the Cold War, when the U.S. was trying to take over from Europe's colonial rule in Africa and elsewhere, as we have previously seen. The *Globe and Mail* report states of the programme:

> A U.S. embassy official in Paris said the program focused on building relationships with potential leaders in Muslim groups and other minorities, mainly by inviting young up-and-comers to participate in the U.S.-sponsored International Visitor Leadership Program. The program has traditionally sent members of the white French elite on educational visits to the United States. Last year, about a third of French participants belonged to minority groups, mostly Muslims.[376]

It also seems that U.S. diplomats actually encourage discontent and legitimise insurgency from within Muslim enclaves in France by visiting 'troubled immigrant suburbs' and inviting youths to U.S. Embassy functions. It might well be asked whether the U.S. Embassy is recruiting radical Muslim youth leaders for direction as cadres against France, just as youths in Serbia, Ukraine, Georgia, Egypt, Morocco, Tunisia, Libya, and so forth, have been selected, funded, and trained to agitate in states marked for 'regime change'? In 2009, the U.S. Embassy helped fund a mural project in the Paris suburb of Villiers-le-Bel, where there had been violent riots in 2007.[377] Three wall daubings included two other suburbs, undertaken under the direction of three muralists from the Mural Arts

---

376 Ibid.
377 Ibid.

Target: France

American filmmaker Zachary Taylor and co-founder
of Discover Paris! Monique Y. Wells

Program (MAP) of Philadelphia, which the U.S. Embassy
described as having worked for 25 years on murals that
bring urban populations together;[378] a euphemism for what
in liberal-speak is called 'empowering' ethnic enclaves.
Rivkin inaugurated the first of the murals in September
2009 before 200 guests at Martin Luther King Middle
School, the first mural honouring King.[379] Hence, the
message of U.S. officialdom to volatile ethnic minorities in
France is to look to the example of Martin Luther King,
whose sit-downs and other so-called 'passive resistance'
strategies were designed to provoke violent confrontations
with the authorities of local communities.[380] Note the fact
that there is even a 'Martin Luther King Middle School' in

---

378 'A dialogue between local citizens, artists and urban spaces: Three murals are
 born in Bagnolet, Bondy and Villiers-le-Bel,' U.S. Embassy in Paris, http://
 france.usembassy.gov/event090726.html.

379 'Ambassador inaugurates in Paris suburbs Franco-American exchange program
 on mural art,' U.S. Embassy in Paris, 19 September 2009, http://france.
 usembassy.gov/event090919.html.

380 Martin Luther King, 'Letter from a Birmingham Jail,' 1963, http://mlk-kpp01.
 stanford.edu/index.php/resources/article/annotated_letter_from_birmingham/.

France. King was just the type of Black 'Uncle Tom' that the globalists love; an integrationist, in contrast to 'Black separatists' and the 'Nation of Islam' that also emerged among Blacks, repudiating assimilation in favour of Black racial consciousness,[381] with a widespread belief that the 'Whites' who were responsible for Black woes, including slavery, were often Jews.[382] When King (and now also President Obama) are upheld by the United States as a beacon towards which the non-White ethnic minorities of the world can turn, they are providing a black face—as with Nelson Mandela also—for an oligarchical slavery of all races.

American news media have referred to the U.S. State Department as a primary influence in pushing multicultural agendas in France. In a report for *The Christian Science Monitor*, Anita Elash wrote that 'The U.S. embassy in France has become a key promoter of Muslim and minority rights as part of a long-term strategy to ease the threat of terrorism.'[383] As we have seen from the Rivkin memo, the U.S. strategy goes well beyond the globalist catchphrase of heading off Muslim radicalism, which, as we have also seen, has been backed by the U.S. in Serbia, Afghanistan, Chechnya, Libya, Syria, and elsewhere. Islamic migration and the support of Muslim enclaves in Europe are used to fundamentally change the character of Europe.

Returning to the activities of Abdelaziz Dahhassi, Elash states that 'it was the U.S. State Department that helped Mr. Dahhassi's Lyon-based Association for the Convergence of

---

381 'A Summing Up: Louis Lomax Interviews Malcolm X,' 1963, http://teachingamericanhistory.org/library/document/a-summing-up-louis-lomax-interviews-malcolm-x/. Here Malcolm X refers to Martin Luther King as an 'Uncle Tom' subsidised by 'whites.'

382 *The Secret Relationship Between Blacks and Jews*, vol. 1 (Boston: Historical Research Department, Nation of Islam, 1994).

383 Anita Elash, 'In France, U.S. advocacy for Muslim rights raises more than a few hackles,' *Christian Science Monitor*, 17 February 2011, http://www.csmonitor.com/World/Europe/2011/0217/In-France-US-advocacy-for-Muslim-rights-raises-more-than-a-few-hackles?nav=topic-tag_topic_page-storyList.

Respect and Diversity finally get off the ground. . . . "I'm not saying we couldn't have done it without them, but their support is very important," he says. "The Americans have a very interesting vision which can be very enriching for France."[384] Here we have an example of how the globalists are channelling Muslim migrant discontent in multicultural Europe into an 'American vision'; that is, a cosmopolitan vision designed to make the 'American Dream' of accumulating consumer goods the Universal Dream in a Global Shopping Mall, as alluded to with pride by the Afro-American expatriate in Paris, Dr. Wells at her U.S. Embassy-sponsored seminars. Elash reported in 2011:

> Over the next several months, U.S. embassy staff will work with Dahhassi to secure funds and expertise from public and private U.S. sources to help establish the think tank's program. Dahhassi says the focus will be to 'find another approach' to addressing racism directed at all minority groups in France, and that it will likely include a debate over the divisive issue of whether France could benefit from an affirmative-action program.[385]

Such a programme of Affirmative Action, based on the U.S. model, would see ethnic minorities given favouritism in employment and university placements, with lesser qualified applicants being promoted over better qualified French Whites. Such a programme would also likely see applicants to medical schools, for example, be selected on the basis of their minority ethnicity rather than their academic accomplishments. That is a price of 'ending racism.'

The Rivkin offensive is part of a long-time programme of undermining French identity. France, like much of the rest of the world, is however fighting a losing battle against

384 Ibid.
385 Ibid.

globalisation. Jeff Steiner's column 'Americans in France' refers to the manner by which the French at one time resisted the opening of the fast food franchise McDonald's as 'part of an American cultural invasion.' Steiner wrote:

> . . . That seems to be past as McDonalds has so become a part of French culture that it's not seen as an American import any longer, but wholly French. In short, McDonalds has grown on the French just like in so many other countries.
>
> I've been to a few McDonalds in France and, except for one in Strasbourg that looks from the outside to be built in the traditional Alsacien style, all McDonalds in France that I have seen look no different than their American counterparts.
>
> Yes, there are those that still curse McDo (They are now a very small group and mostly ignored.) as the symbol of the Americanization of France and who also see it as France losing its uniqueness in terms of cuisine. The menu in a French McDonalds is almost an exact copy of what you would find in any McDonalds in the United States. It struck me as a bit odd that I could order as I would in the United States, that is in English, with the odd French preposition thrown in.
>
> If truth were told, the French who eat at McDonalds are just as much at home there as any American could be.[386]

This seemingly minor example is actually of much importance in showing just how a culture as strong as that of, until recently, an immensely proud nation, can succumb, especially under the impress of marketing

---

386 Jeff Steiner, "Americans in France: Culture: McDonalds in France," http://www. americansinfrance.net/culture/mcdonalds_in_france.cfm.

towards youngsters. It is an example *par excellence* of the standardisation that American-imposed corporate culture entails. It is what the globalist oligarchy desires on a world scale, standardisation right down to what one eats. It is notable that the vanguard of the initial resistance to the opening of McDonald's came from farmers, a traditionalist segment of Europe's population that are becoming increasingly anomalous, and will under the globalist regime become an extinct species in the process of agricultural corporatisation, where the family farm becomes extinct.

Nonetheless, given France's historical role of maintaining sovereignty in the face of U.S. interests, she remains one of the few potentially annoying states in Europe; hence her being first on the line of the globalist offensive using multiculturalism. However, the concern remains, as alluded to in the Rivkin memo, that the French, despite their acceptance of McDonald's, and their liking for American trash TV, will translate the remnants of their 'xenophobia' into the election to office of a stridently anti-globalist party, as reflected in the electoral ups and downs of the Front National, whose policy would not be in accord with either U.S. foreign policy, or with privatisation and cultural Americanisation. Hence the Front National, like other anti-globalist parties, can be attacked with red-herring slogans about 'racism' and 'hate' to deflect from the real concern, which is opposition to globalisation. The militants of the Left with slogans such as 'Open Borders' hardly credit being regarded as opponents of globalisation, when they accept the fundamentals of globalist ideology. This is a major reason for Rivkin's far-reaching subversive and interventionist program to assimilate Muslims into French society, which in so doing would also have the result of casting French consciousness into a more thoroughly cosmopolitan mould. The intention is clear enough in the Rivkin Embassy documents where it is stated that the Embassy will monitor the effects of the 'outreach' program on the 'decrease in popular support for xenophobic political parties and platforms.'

Some conservative observers immediately recognised the U.S. agenda, criticising the United States for trying to undermine French values by imposing failed U.S. policies on how to deal with ethnic minorities:

> 'They are criticizing us because we are not the United States, or more precisely, because we do not resemble them,' blogger Christine Tasin wrote on a website for The Republican Resistance, a non-partisan group established last year to defend what it sees as French values. '[It] is a strategic plan to get France to do whatever the U.S. wants'?[387]

Ivan Rioufol, of the conservative newspaper *Le Figaro*, stated that 'The American analysis, which seems to say that the France of the future will be the France of the immigrant suburbs, is very disparaging to native French people.'[388]

Multicultural Europe Pushed by the United States

While France is among the greatest challenges to deconstruct through multiculturalism, because of its persistent suspicion of the United States, she paradoxically has a fatal flaw: the French Republic must at least pay lip-service to the ideals of the 1789 French Revolution; the same ideals which had also inspired the American Revolution of 1776. Hence, as the Rivkin memo mentions, multiculturalism can subvert France through an appeal to the Republic's extreme liberal foundations. The founding slogan of the French Republic was 'Liberty, Equality, Fraternity,' which

---

387 Elash, *Globe & Mail*, op. cit.
388 Ibid.

leaves France open to globalist subversion by manipulating its own foundation myths, and Rivkin et al. have been quick to recognise this.

However, the globalist offensive is intended to bring ruin to the traditional foundations of the whole of Europe. The European Institute (EI), Washington-based, despite what its name suggests, was founded to promote the subservience of Europe to the United States, as part of a common globalist drive. The Institute states that it has the backing of 'top level representatives from the U.S. Administration and Congress, the European Commission, Council and Parliament, European Embassies, major foundations and global corporations from both Europe and the United States.'[389] It is therefore yet another of the seemingly endless NGOs, think tanks, fronts and lobbies pushing the globalist agenda.

The co-chair of the EI Board is Yves-André Istel, formerly a director of Lehman Brothers and other banks, and 'currently Senior Advisor to Rothschild Inc. and a member of its Investment Banking Committee,' among much else.[390] As with other such organisations, EI combines a wide range of luminaries from finance, industry, policy-making and academia.[391] Therefore when EI gives an opinion, it does so as a significant think tank among the globalist network. EI states of Rivkin and of the United States' multicultural agenda not just in France but across Europe:

The U.S. State Department has some new pro-active policies toward Muslims and other minorities in Europe that seem to mark a salient change. For example, Charles Rivkin isn't your traditional American ambassador in

---

389 European Institute, 'Mission,' http://www.europeaninstitute.org/200905301/Welcome-and-Mission/welcome-and-mission.html.

390 http://www.europeaninstitute.org/Board-Biographies/yves-andre-istel.html.

391 'Board of Directors,' http://www.europeaninstitute.org/200905302/Boards/boards.html.

Paris: a political appointee with a career background in entertainment, he is regularly spotted doing things like this: hosting hip-hop artists and ethnic-minority politicians at embassy receptions; inaugurating a large art mural in Villiers-le-Bel, the site of major urban riots in 2007; visiting a youth cultural center and engaging in debates with the audience; dropping in on embassy-sponsored seminars on social issues and engines of change; or surprising French high school students by bringing along Hollywood star Samuel L. Jackson for a discussion about his growing up in the segregated American South. . . . Since taking up his post in summer 2009, Rivkin has pursued a vigorous public effort to connect with the poorer, multiracial suburbs of major French cities . . .[392]

Rivkin goes where the French Government does not, with the purpose of harnessing ethnic resentment into a globalist device that can be wielded to subdue France. That is clear enough from the actions of Rivkin, and comments in the Rivkin memo and descriptions such as those of the EI, which must of course be read between the lines of rhetoric about 'human rights.' It should be noted also from the above passage that State Department interference is also being directed at 'other minorities in Europe.' The report continues:

In what amounts to a significant but largely unreported shift in U.S. diplomacy, embassies are broadening their traditional focus on national elites and established leaders in politics, trade-unions and the like, and expanding the mix to include under-represented minorities. In France, this new focus has been dubbed by Rivkin as a 'Minority Engagement Strategy' aimed

---

392 Garrett Martin, 'In Smart-Power Shift, U.S. Now Actively Cultivating Muslim Minorities in the EU,' *European Affairs*, April 2011, http://www.europeaninstitute. org/EA-April-2011/in-smart-power-shift-us-now-actively-cultivating-muslim-minorities-in-the-eu.html.

at helping potential leaders in the Muslim *banlieues* learn the tools of U.S.-style democratic change. Part of this outreach (and its political acceptability) is that it includes mainstream French leaders, hoping to raise consciousness in their ranks about the advantages of overcoming social exclusion and promoting real diversity and not just pay lip service to the notion of it. This new U.S. approach is now being applied in many democratic countries (and in some, notably in the Middle East, that aspire to be democratic)—an effort to walk the walk that goes with the pro-democracy talk of public diplomacy emanating from Washington.[393]

What should be noted here is that:

1. Ethnic minority leaders are being tapped along with so-called 'national elites' (leaders in politics business and labour) as delegations for indoctrination into globalism.

2. The inclusion of 'mainstream leaders' ensures acceptability of a strategy to radicalise ethnic agitators, without causing alarm among the targeted states' government.

3. The inclusion of the 'national elites' allows them to be indoctrinated into multiculturalism, especially when they are part of the same programmes that include the ethnic minorities, allowing for a heavy does of inculcated self-guilt and showing that the 'American Dream' is superior to centuries of European values and traditions.

4. Muslims in *banlieues* learn the tools of U.S.-style 'democratic change,' which sounds suspiciously like they are being trained and indoctrinated with the same techniques that have long been used to foment the 'colour revolutions' in states marked for 'regime change.'

393 Ibid.

Babel, Inc.

The State Department's International Visitor Leadership Program (IVLP), which selects potential leaders for training, is now focusing on ethnic minority leaders; 'now targeting promising young people from Muslim and other minority communities.'[394] Those chosen are brought to the United States on tours to see the wonders of the American Dream. They include 'an influx of youthful or young professional "outsiders" that the U.S. embassy considers "promising" in their own communities and perhaps eventually on a larger, even national stage.'[395] What seems flagrant is that the then-U.S. Secretary of State, Hillary Clinton, 'recently noted, many of the leaders of the Egyptian movement that overthrew the old regime in Egypt had "benefited from the visitation program"—by which she meant the State Department's IVLP outreach and training.'[396] These youths, who sparked the supposedly 'spontaneous' rioting in Egypt, which brought down a hitherto friendly regime that had become awkward to deal with,[397] had been trained in the United States. Garrett states for *European Affairs* that:

> The French case is particularly interesting because France has traditionally been wary of any 'U.S. influence' liable to infiltrate the nation. But the current innovation in U.S. outreach seems to enjoy a benign reception and even encouragement in Paris both in government and in the Muslim community.[398]

Garrett relates the United States' recent inroads into France to both 'deft political management,' and the processes of globalisation: 'In fact, this American policy seems to be benefiting from an astute analysis in Paris of domestic

---

394 Ibid.
395 Ibid.
396 Ibid.
397 K. R. Bolton, 'What's Behind the Tumult in Egypt?,' *Foreign Policy Journal*, 1 February 2011, http://www.foreignpolicyjournal.com/2011/02/01/whats-behind-the-tumult-in-egypt/2/.
398 Garrett, op. cit.

political imperatives in a globalizing world, and also from deft U.S. diplomatic management.'[399]

> The program goes beyond 'talent-scouting and wooing' to include a more ambitious, grass-roots effort aimed at actively encouraging leaders of minorities in France and in other countries across Europe and seeking to help them learn more about how to take full advantage of the potential for democratic change in their societies.[400]

The United States regards the presently disaffected and unassimilated ethnic minorities, not only in France, but 'across Europe,' as the up-and-coming leaders of a melting-pot Europe that is no longer identifiably European. This is also indicated by Garrett's comparison of the U.S.-directed programmes with the experiences of Obama as a community leader in Chicago, which was the start of his long march to the White House (keeping in mind the patronage Obama received from the United States' oligarchs). Garrett states however that the programme was initiated by President George W. Bush, 'to export some of the American experience of minority integration to other countries in Europe and the Middle East: now it is touted in Washington as part of the tool kit of "smart power" as advocated by Mrs. Clinton to creatively promote transatlantic cooperation and American diplomatic interests.'[401] Note that Garrett cites then Secretary of State Clinton as openly stating that these programmes in the name of 'human rights' and democracy' are in reality nothing but masks for the expansion of globalist interests, described as 'transatlantic cooperation and American diplomatic interests.' In referring again to the Rivkin memo, Garrett describes what the United States is trying to impose on France:

---

399 Ibid.
400 Ibid.
401 Ibid.

France, with its five to six million Muslims (an estimated one-tenth of the population) is obviously an important test case for this newer form of outreach. 'Diversity' in France has been official dogma that in practice is often largely ignored. Perhaps because the current French government is aware of this contradiction, the U.S. embassy has made no secret of its work: officials have relied on 'an annual public affairs budget of $3 million' to sponsor or fund a large number of small-scale programs, including 'urban renewal projects, music festivals and conferences.' They have 'formed a network of partnerships with local governments, advocacy groups, entrepreneurs, students and cultural leaders in the troubled immigrant enclaves outside France's major cities'—to coach them, support them and encourage them—with a view to turning cultural outsiders and social rebels into part of broadening French national elite. Just how direly restricted the current French elite can appear, not only to Americans but also to French leaders themselves, emerges from another passage in the Wikileaks cable from U.S. embassy-Paris . . .[402]

Here we see:

1. France is a test case for a multimillion dollar programme that is aimed at being replicated throughout Europe, among ethnic minorities, and as previously indicated, not only Muslims.

2. The U.S. plays on the French Republic's founding doctrine of revolutionary liberalism to undermine the 'xenophobia' that has maintained French culture. The United States can claim that its programmes are merely expressing the true French Republican heritage, rather than foreign or subversive.

---

402 Ibid.

3. The State Department is recruiting, training and indoctrinating bellicose ethnic agitators to become the new 'French governing elite.'

In a move that has been repeated many times in many states that have experienced 'spontaneous' (*sic*) 'colour revolutions,' across North Africa and the former Soviet bloc, the U.S. Embassy in Paris has 'built up one of the best networks and contacts with minorities in civil society'. . . .[403]

> Thus, in June 2010, the embassy co-sponsored a seminar for French participants on how to help minorities build a political base. For two days, Karen Finney, a communication strategist for the Democratic Party, and Cornell Belcher, who had worked as a pollster for the Democratic Party, coached seventy local elected representatives and members of associations on how to communicate, fund and manage a political campaign.[404]

This would seem to be a flagrant interference in the political process of a sovereign nation. The U.S. State Department is targeting certain ethnic political blocs, which— with Muslims forming 10 per cent of the population in France— can have a marked influence on electoral outcomes at all levels of society. Is the globalist strategy in France any different from that of the U.S. State Department, the National Endowment for Democracy, Freedom House, Soros' networks, etc., in training and funding agitators to foment the 'colour revolutions' across North Africa, Central Asia, Russia and Eastern Europe, to bring about 'regime change'?

In addition to the IVLP that grooms potential leaders, the U.S. Embassy has also arranged trips to the United

---

403 Ibid.
404 Ibid.

States by eight hip hoppers as part of a musical exchange programme with Harlem, and has assisted Reda Didi, founder and head of the think tank *Graines de France*, which aids 'minority politicians,' with a delegation to go to Chicago as guests of Senator William Burns, to learn about 'community organising.'[405]

Garrett states that U.S. Embassies across Europe are under instruction to be 'open to Muslims' and 'to court second- and third-generation immigrants.'[406] These are the bellicose, ghettoised youths that cause riots throughout Europe, which the U.S. seeks to 'court.' It would be naïve to think that the globalists intend this 'courtship' as a means of 'taming' these second and third generation 'immigrants' by assisting with their acculturation into the host society. Rather, they are being trained in techniques of ethnic agitation, sent to the United States to learn from Black street organisers, and returned to Europe as agitators against their hosts. They are being formed into a power bloc that is expected by the United States to become the new leadership of Europe. These second and third generation 'immigrants' have become rootless and deracinated. Hence they are ripe for inculcation with the bastardised subcultures that serve globalist interests, such as hip hop, which are far removed from the traditions of Islam, but are part of the 'lethal culture' described by Ralph Peters.

Le Figaro reported of the hip hop delegation that one of the delegation came back to France full of enthusiasm for the 'American Dream,' stating: 'We're back with another vision of the country. It is one thing to see the United States on television and another to come breathe the country, its energy, its movement. Everything is hip-hop here.' In Harlem the youth felt that they were meeting their 'ancestors.' They were inspired by meeting the Black poet

Abiodun Oyewole,[407] a veteran of the Black Panthers, an urban guerrilla group of the 1970s. Hence, the second and third 'immigration' generation in France see their hopes in the United States, and they feel kinship with Afro-Americans. Their traditional culture and authority of their elders is replaced by U.S. ghetto subcultures, lacking depth of tradition. It is a phenomenon that is gripping non-White ethnic minorities the world over, from the Maoris and Polynesians in New Zealand to the descendants of West Indians in Britain, who are becoming detached form tribal and ethnic roots and forming new youth subcultures formed in tandem between the American ghettoes and the global music and fashion corporations with the zealous aid of the U.S. State Department. They are on their way to becoming the next breed of humanity: *Homo globicus.*

The U.S. push in France and elsewhere in Europe comes at a time when other European leaders, such as then French President Sarkozy, German Chancellor Merkel and British Prime Minister David Cameron, have backtracked on the workability of multiculturalism, and have suggested reverting instead to the melting-pot of assimilation.[408] The U.S. strategy in Europe remains however to promote multiculturalism rather than assimilation into the host cultures. The aim of globalisation is to target unassimilated ethnic communities for inculcating not with their own heritage or with the heritage of the host community but with what Ralph Peters calls America's 'lethal culture' of consumerism, MTV, Big Macs, and Coca-Cola, to create a new generation that belongs to nothing in particular and everything in general.

---

407 Laure Mandeville, 'De jeunes rappeurs français "ambassadeurs" des USA,' *Le Figaro*, 4 March 2010, http://www.lefigaro.fr/international/2010/03/04/01003-20100304ARTFIG00534-de-jeunes-rappeurs-francais-ambassadeurs-des-usa-.php.

408 'EU Leaders Rejection of "Multiculturalism" Aimed at Far-Right Demagogues,' European Affairs,' March 2011, http://72.249.31.51/March-2011/rejection-of-multiculturalism-by-eu-leaders-aimed-at-far-right-demagogues-41.html.

This vision of a multicultural 'Europe' is 'Europe' in name only, and perhaps one day the name will be changed altogether. U.S. Embassies throughout Europe have been given the lead from the Rivkin programme. The murals project in France was broadened with Deborah MacLean, public diplomacy officer at the U.S. Embassy in Copenhagen, using the programme 'to reach out to ethnic minorities in Denmark,' stating: 'We wanted to encourage these youths to realize that it is okay to be different.'[409]

When expressions such as 'okay to be different' are used by the multiculturalists, it is important to realise that this is doublethink. What is being formed through multiculturalism is a uniform global culture based on production and consumption that is unhindered by ethnic, religious, moral and cultural traditions. What these ethnic minority youths are being encouraged to adopt is not the perpetuation of the ethnic traditions of their parents or grandparents, but primarily American-derived pseudo-culture, where young migrants of Third World descent adopt Martin Luther King and Barack Obama as role models and hip hop as their preferred art form, with all the manufactured accoutrements that go with it.

While the Rivkin programme and others of similar type across Europe are being promoted often with references to a strategy of pacifying the disaffected Muslim ghettoes, especially in France, as part of a cunning plan to thwart anti-Americanism, this is not the primary purpose. We have already seen the character of the multicultural 'outreach' programmes undertaken by the U.S. State Department, with Rivkin stating that the aim is to change the character of France itself and especially of French youth.

Gilles Kepel, a French academic and expert on Islam in the Paris suburbs, or *banlieues*, said of the U.S. programme,

409 Sherry C. Keneson-Hall, 'Bridging Culture's,' *State Magazine*, U.S. State Department, Washington, February 2010, p. 13; http://www.state.gov/documents/organization/136475.pdf.

'that it was more than anti-Americanism among Muslims that concerned State Department officials.'[410] Kepel stated:

> They [State Department] sort of thought that the French were characterized by a sort of political elite that was non-mixed, that was too white, too male, too old, and that if the country was not more pluralistic, then it would become weaker, and a weaker France was not good as an ally, so they started to reach out to the banlieues.[411]

Kepel is accurately perceiving that the U.S. strategy is to change the very character of the French nation and the French people and culture. Nicolas Dupont-Aignan, a centre-right Member of Parliament, perceptively asked:

> How will answer the U.S. government if the French government decided to go in some suburbs of the United States to say to the people, 'You are not very well treated by your government, and we are going to help you. You are going to travel in France, be agent for us.' It is not acceptable.[412]

Benjamin Pelletier, a French commentator on international cultural influence, also pertinently asked: 'What happens when you have a certain segment of the young population that has been influenced by another country acting in its own national interest? Isn't there a risk of fracturing national cohesion?'[413]

Among the 'activist' groups assisted by the U.S. State

---

410 Amy Bracken, 'Ambassador Charles Rivkin and American Diplomacy in Paris Suburbs,' *The World*, 10 January 2013, http://www.theworld.org/2013/01/american-diplomacy-paris/.

411 Amy Bracken, quoting Kepel, ibid.

412 Nicolas Dupont-Aignan, ibid.

413 Benjamin Pelletier, ibid.

Department is the Brigade Against Anti-Black Racism.[414] This is a Black militant organisation that portrays France as a 'Negrophobe state.' Brigade 'activists' were recently arrested for violence against police, when the 'activists' started a fracas outside a presidential event celebrating the abolition of Black slavery.[415] The Brigade is supported by the extreme Left in France,[416] being aligned with the African Socialist International, a revolutionary communist organisation.[417] The stated aim of the Brigade is to 'focus on Hidden Racism Performed by the French state.'[418] The United States seems to be trying to encourage a strategy of tension in order to pressure France to self-destruct as a European nation. The United States is treating France like a state that is marked for 'regime change.'

Elsewhere in Europe, in Bulgaria a Blues musician, Steve James, held 'workshops on the benefits of embracing a multicultural society.'

'America is a melting pot and nowhere is that more evident than in our artistic culture and in our music,' said James. 'Every form of pop music and folk music in America is a direct result of our being a multi-ethnic culture.' James conducted master's classes with students from the Music Academy in Plovdiv, Bulgaria, and workshops at three other Bulgarian schools, reaching out to students from ages 8 to 18. 'Some of these people were really experienced and talented musicians, but they had never seen anyone play this kind of music.'[419]

414 Bracken, ibid.

415 M. Molard, 'Member of Brigade anti-Negrophobia summoned to Court,' Street Press, 16 May 2013, www.streetpress.com/tag/brigade-anti-negrophobie.

416 'Solidarity Brigade Anti Negrophobia,' 14 May 2013, www.convergencedesluttes.fr/index.php?.

417 Vannessa Thompson, 'African Liberation Day Paris Unites Africans across Europe in Struggle for African Liberation,' Burning Spear, 12 June 2012, http://uhurunews.com/story?resource_name=ald-paris-unites-africans-to-complete-the-struggle-to-liberate-africa-africans-at-home-and-abroad.

418 'Opposition grows against racial violence,' Fria Tidnigen (Sweden), 15 June 2013, www.fria.nu/.

419 Sherry C. Keneson-Hall, op. cit.

The American hip-hop group Cypress Hill at the
Bulgaria New International Music Festival

Young Bulgarians learn how 'hip' it is to embrace American-style multiculturalism, with little or no understanding of the way the United States has for decades being falling apart at the seams with racial strife, ghettoisation, crime, infrastructural breakdown, and educational dysfunction where there is a large Black population; let alone the snare of having their own cultural identity replaced by the inherently rootless character of 'pop music.' It is also notable that Bulgaria is one of the ex-Soviet states where the globalist fear an upsurge in militant nationalism, and where institutions such as George Soros Open Society networks invest much largesse in ensuring that there is no resurgence of the 'Right.'[420]

---

420 Rightist parties resisting both globalisation and multiculturalism are significant in Eastern Europe, including the Ataka Party in Bulgaria.

De-Europeanising Europe

> The European Union should do its best to undermine the homogeneity of its member states.
> —Peter Sutherland, House of Lords, 2012.

The European Union project was from its inception ironically named. This union of Europe was never intended to be anything but a phase towards a Universal Republic (in Masonic terminology) or a 'new world order,' as it is now generally called by pundits, politicians, businessmen and diplomats. Grand Orient Freemasonry wanted a secularised Europe, with all the traditions that make Europe what she is, obliterated, in the name of science and 'enlightenment.' That is now largely what we have. When these ideas came to bloody fruition in the French Revolution, France was regarded as the herald of a new era, much like some people regarded the USSR, and how many globalists regard the United States. Hence, in 1792 the French Convention called for the creation of 'La République Universelle.'[421] During the latter part of the 19th century the idea of a 'United States of Europe' was revived with renewed impetus, led by a well-funded Freemason named Count Richard Coudenhove-Kalergi, who became known as the 'father of European union.' The Austrian Masonic magazine, *The Beacon*, stated of Coudenhove-Kalergi's programme that 'it is a Masonic work,' an opinion reiterated in recent years by high Masonic initiates in Europe.[422] While the early Masonic role in what is now called globalisation and the 'new world order' cannot be elaborated here,[423] what is of significance is that Coudenhove-Kalergi's idea of Europe

---

421 K. R. Bolton, introduction to Hilaire Belloc, *Europe and the Faith* (London: Black House Publishing, 2013), 25.

422 Marian Mihaila, 'European Union and Freemasonry,' *Masonic Forum*, http://www.masonicforum.ro/en/nr27european.html#b_22.

423 See this author's introduction to Belloc, *Europe and the Faith*, and a book on the role of secret societies in politics, forthcoming from Arktos Media, London, 2013.

was multicultural in character. Coudenhove-Kalergi was of Austro-Hungarian and Japanese parentage.[424] Coudenhove-Kalergi in 1925 clearly stated the globalist ideal that is being pursued today,

> The man of the future will be of mixed race. Today's races and classes will gradually disappear owing to the vanishing of space, time, and prejudice. The Eurasian-Negroid race of the future, similar in its appearance to the Ancient Egyptians,[425] will replace the diversity of peoples with a diversity of individuals.[426]

Coudenhove-Kalergi added that the Jews would form a 'new spiritual nobility' to take over leadership from the old European nobility whose influence had been largely obliterated,[427] and it should be added in significant part through Masonic revolutions such as those in France, Russia and throughout much of the rest of Europe.[428]

This precisely explains the globalist alchemy of multiculturalism: to break down all differences—in the name of promoting 'differences'—to re-create a formless mass of 'individuals without bonds to 'space,' 'time' or 'prejudice,' or what we can call one's rootedness to land, heritage, and destiny, and consciousness of identity. The goal is the elimination of the idea of a collective identity and consciousness, or indeed of community and society. This is what had been unfolding in the United States for decades: a collection of individuals tenuously held together in the

424 Mihaila, 'European Union and Freemasonry.'
425 Coudenhove-Kalergi's ethnological knowledge is flawed: the dark-skinned Egyptians were predominantly of the Mediterranean sub-branch of the Europoid. John R. Baker, *Race* (Oxford: Oxford University Press), 518. The 'black' presence was primarily through Nubian slaves.
426 Richard Nikolaus von Coudenhove-Kalergi, *Praktischer Idealismus* (Vienna: Paneuropa Verlag, 1925), 20, 23, 50.
427 Ibid.
428 See this author's forthcoming book on secret societies from Arktos Media, London, 2013.

name of the Constitution and the Bill of Rights, and the pursuit of the 'American Dream' of endless consumption. The glue of money that is supposed to hold the lot together gradually becomes unstuck as ethnic minorities, Blacks, Hispanics, and increasingly others, see the 'American Dream' as becoming ever more distant, and resort again to their own ethnic heritages by segregating themselves into their own communities, whether in towns or in jails. This is the 'Dream' that U.S. State Department programmes lecture young Europeans that they should adopt as a superior lifestyle choice to their own ancestral traditions.

Also of relevance was that Coudenhove-Kalergi relates that he was funded by Max Warburg of the international banking dynasty, initially with 60,000 gold marks, arranged by their mutual friend Baron Louis Rothschild in 1924. Coudenhove-Kalergi stated that Warburg's funding of the Pan-European movement 'contributed decisively to its subsequent success.'[429] A leading Masonic initiate, Dr. Mihaila, has stated that Coudenhove-Kalergi was also funded by 'American Masons who wanted to create thus according to the American model (the first Masonic state in history) the United States of Europe.'[430] What Mihaila is stating is that united Europe was from the start founded on the Masonic ideals that were at the birth of the United States, and later manifested in the French Revolution. The globalists want to remake the entire world in the image of the United States, although the project is not now solely in the hands of Freemasons, and has picked up its own momentum through the refocusing of international finance, especially since World War II, to New York.

429 Richard Coudenhove-Kalergi, *Pan Europe* (Vienna: Paneuropa Verlag, 1923), quoted in Kalergi, *An Idea Conquers the World* (London: Hutchinson, 1953).
430 Mihaila, 'European Union and Freemasonry.'

'Undermining Homogeneity'

Is the push for a multicultural Europe being promoted by influences other than the U.S. State Department? We have seen that it is also an intrinsic part of corporate globalist doctrine, Masonic doctrine, and in general the agenda of sundry organisations and ideologies aiming for a world state. There cannot be 'one world' without 'one race,' as each distinct entity would inevitably resegregate if left to its own devices.

In 2012 Peter Sutherland stated in an address to the House of Lords EU Home Affairs, Health and Education Sub-Committee inquiry into the EU's Global Approach to Migration and Mobility, that 'the European Union should do its best to undermine the homogeneity of its member states.' A 'key argument . . . for the development of multicultural states' was the aging of the indigenous European populations, which need replacing by non-European migrants in the interests of economic growth. Sutherland stated that ethnic and cultural homogeneity cannot survive 'because states have to become more open states, in terms of the people who inhabit them, just as the United Kingdom has demonstrated.'[431]

BBC News reported that Sutherland told the committee:

> The United States, or Australia and New Zealand, are migrant societies and therefore they accommodate more readily those from other backgrounds than we do ourselves, who still nurse a sense of our homogeneity and difference from others. And that's precisely what the European Union, in my view, should be doing its best to undermine.[432]

---

431 Brian Wheeler, 'EU should "undermine national homogeneity" says UN migration chief,' BBC News, 21 June 2012, http://www.bbc.co.uk/news/uk-politics-18519395.
432 Ibid.

Here Sutherland is stating that societies such as the United States, Australia, and New Zealand, having been established by colonists from Europe, are considered 'migrant societies.' Indeed, a key argument of multiculturalists in defending non-European immigration to these states is that 'we are all immigrants.' Therefore Australians and New Zealanders do not have a legitimate right to object to mass Asian immigration for example, or White Americans to mass Hispanic immigration. Further, Australia and New Zealand, having had their roots to Britain in particular and Europe in general, weakened since World War II, with the demise especially of the British connection, have not developed a vigorous European nativist culture with which to resist globalisation. European nations however, with their centuries of tradition for all Europeans to readily see and appreciate if they still have the spirit to do so, have the cultural heritage for a multiplicity of vibrant ethnic nationalisms that are being reasserting in the rise of Rightist parties such as the Front National in France, Jobbik in Hungary, Golden Dawn in Greece, and Ataka in Bulgaria.

Sutherland states that the EU bureaucracy should wage a culture war against the vestiges of European consciousness in order that Europeans will more readily accept their own demographic displacement by non-European migrants, whose proliferation will mean the demise of future generations whose forebears were born, lived, and died in Europe. Instead, Europe's future population will increasingly consist of those whose forebears were born, lived and died north and south of the Sahara, Pakistan, India . . . Without roots in the soil of the EU states to which they migrate and breed new generations, ever more rootless, a new 'Eurasian-Negroid' non-race of individuals of the type Coudenhove-Kalergi envisioned, will fill the void of the European.

Sutherland speaks with the authority of a globalist that

few others possess. A former Attorney General of Ireland, Sutherland has been described by Mickey Kantor, U.S. Trade Representative, as 'the father of globalisation.'[433] Sutherland is the UN's special representative for migration, head of the Global Forum on Migration, chairman of Goldman Sachs International, and a former chairman of British Petroleum. He has been Director General of GATT (General Agreement on Tariffs and Trades), now known as the World Trade Organization. He is an attendee of the ultra-secret meetings of the Bilderberg Group,[434] an annual gathering of the world power elite; and according Professor Costa, Sutherland has been a director of the World Economic Forum, is currently Honorary Chairman of the Trilateral Commission,[435] the European Institute, the European Roundtable of Industrialists and the advisory Council of Business for New Europe, Chair of the London School of Economics Council, and what Costa described as the 'financial adviser' to the Vatican.[436] In 1998 he was recipient of the David Rockefeller International Leadership Award.[437]

Sutherland has often spoken of a 'European identity,' a 'soul of Europe,' and the need for a European unity transcending old national rivalries. All are laudable, indeed essential ideas. Yet above them all Sutherland and other globalists who founded and sustain the EU, like Coudenhove-Kalergi, stand for a diversity of 'individuals' that define a 'European identity' on a wholly bogus globalist conception that is doublespeak for the repudiation of 'European identity.'

---

433 Cited by Professor Kenneth J. Costa, introducing Peter Sutherland at the Gretham College Lectures, 8 March 2011, http://www.gresham.ac.uk/lectures-and-events/leadership-at-a-time-of-transition-and-turbulence-a-conversation-with-peter.

434 Wheeler, BBC News, op. cit.

435 The Trilateral Commission is a globalist think tank founded by David Rockefeller, head of the famous globalist dynasty, which aims to bring together political and business interests across Europe, North America and Asia.
See also: 'Peter Sutherland,' Vox, http://www.voxeu.org/person/peter-sutherland.

436 Costa, op. cit.

437 'Peter Sutherland,' Vox, op. cit.

While Sutherland talks of 'Christianity' as being the basis of this European 'individualism,' along with the French Revolution and the Enlightenment, which overthrew the traditional religions and cultures of Europe, Sutherland states: 'My conclusion is that a European identity exists because of the shared belief in a universal equality that is not defined by race, gender or religion. In particular it is one that provides equal freedom under a shared moral code. It is grounded in the Christian teaching on the brotherhood of man.'[438] Again, it is a universalistic creed, with an appeal to the *spiritual* universalism of Christianity to break down all distinctions as to 'race, gender and religion,' a mass levelling that might better be defined as communism than Christianity, or at least than the Gothic Christianity upon which Europe's High Culture was founded and for which it fought against Turk and Mongol.[439] Hence the globalist 'Europe' as expressed by Sutherland, is one that is open to all and sundry, until she is nothing but a land-mass holding a population-mass of rootless 'individuals' who respond to the needs of production and consumption.

In finding a doctrine that can re-create this 'Europe' of 'human rights' Sutherland has recourse to 'a conception of solidarity reflected in a commitment to what Ludwig Erhard described as the "social market economy."' Again, Sutherland attempts to sell this as a Christian ideal. He quotes Shirley Williams as defining this as 'a free market curbed and regulated to conform to social goals.' These social goals are better termed social engineering. Economics is used to impose this restructuring of identity. As we have seen, the character of the global free market is to undermine ethnic and cultural barriers that impede the free flow of labour, money, and technology. The currency speculator George Soros promotes the 'social

---

438 Peter Sutherland, 'Values and Leadership in Europe,' 2008, http://petersutherland.co.uk/tag/nationalism/.
439 Hilaire Belloc, *Europe and the Faith* (London: Black House Publishing, 2012).

market economy' with his vast fortune through a myriad of NGOs across the world in what he calls the 'open society.' It is the means by which the mass of individuals might be integrated into a consumer society peaceably, and indeed become pacified into accepting a state of 'soft enslavement' with the enticement of consumer goods, of which Ralph Peters wrote.

It is Sutherland's views on migration into Europe and its relationship to 'universalism' or globalisation that is the primary concern here. Of this Sutherland states:

> Migration policies too can only be properly developed through European policies and again these should be influenced by the concept of the equality of man. Without arguing that it is possible to have unrestricted migration we should surely recognise that there is a contradiction between our former condemnation (on grounds of human rights) of the Soviet Union in its refusal to permit people to leave and the case made by some that we have no obligation at all to permit migrants to enter Europe. Globalisation is not just about trade, it is above all about people and our policies should start from a multilateral dialogue that links development with migration and an understanding that migrants have rights including to the maximum extent possible the right to legally enter host countries. On the other hand we must unequivocally also uphold the rights we believe in within our own societies and not permit a mistaken concept of multiculturalism to require us to derogate from them.[440]

This latter matter of multiculturalism actually challenging rather than supporting the concept of the globalist 'open society' is a major dilemma for globalists and the politicians on the ground floor, who must face a volatile electorate that

---

440 Sutherland, 'Values and Leadership in Europe.'

might turn sharply to the Right. Multiculturalism is from the globalist viewpoint a method for the disintegration of traditional concepts. However, what is required is not a multiculturalism where the elders and the religious leaders retain influence over the new generations born in Europe to migrant parents. Rather the aim is for the creation of a deracinated new generation that can be melded into a melting pot culture that serves global marketing needs.

The type of 'multiculture' that is sought by the globalists is what we have seen being promoted by the U.S. State Department, forging a generation of hip hoppers, watching MTV, and buying Coca-Cola and Big Macs, instead of reading the Koran, praying to Mecca, and living in stable families in which parents are respected. That is not the 'Europe' of 'universalism and 'equality' that Sutherland, Rivkin, Soros, et al. have in mind. They want feminism, where the woman becomes part of the production process; factory fodder. They want youngsters who spend money on the latest fashions and are not constrained by religious modesty. Hence, Sutherland states that Europe must 'unequivocally also uphold the rights we believe in within our own societies,' and not allow migrants coming in with traditional moral and religious and social beliefs to undermine the 'social market economy.' Therefore the appeal of Sutherland to Catholic traditions is disingenuous. A traditional Catholic of the type whose forebears formed the real Europe prior to the Masonic French Revolution and the Age of Enlightenment, to which Sutherland et al. appeal, will have more in common with a traditional Muslim than a Rivkin, Sutherland, or a Soros, while there will be a commonality of behaviour between new generations of both migrant and European youth who have become rootless consumers, wearing the same fashions, speaking the same street talk, listening to the same music, eating the same fast food. What is really wanted by the globalists is not multiculturalism in the true sense of self-contained and self-sustaining cultures, but a consumer monoculture. It is a dilemma and paradox.

While Sutherland is critical of the nation-state and of the petty nationalism that has caused rivalry and wars among Europeans, a critique with which the advocates of a real Europe, such as Sir Oswald Mosley,[441] Otto Strasser,[442] Jean Thiriart,[443] and Francis Parker Yockey[444] would concur, his condemnation of petty nationalism is also a condemnation of its extension as a pan-European nationalism. The globalists who founded the European Union and its predecessor, the European Economic Community, did so not to create a European Nation, but an economic edifice as part of a global economic structure, that includes other regional economic blocs, or 'free trade areas,' as they are called, such as the 'Pacific Rim' and NAFTA. Indeed, the founding of the Trilateral Commission by David Rockefeller in 1973, of which Sutherland was its 'Honorary European Chairman' (2001–10),[445] was to promote these economic regions as part of the globalisation process.[446] These blocs are designed to reflect the convenience of trade, not the unity of a heritage. That is why New Zealand and Australia, both still predominantly of European descent, have over the past few decades, been referred to as parts of Asia, and why advocates of a united Europe from Coudenhove-Kalergi to Sutherland, can refer to a new 'Europe' that

---

441 Oswald Mosley, *Europe: Faith and Plan* (Euphorion Books, 1958). See also: 'Oswald Mosley' at Black House Publishing, http://blackhousepublishing.co.uk/index.php?route=product/category&path=62.

442 K. R. Bolton, 'Otto Strasser's New Europe,' Counter-Currents Publishing, http://www.counter-currents.com/2011/05/otto-strassers-new-europe-part-one/.

443 Jean Thiriart, 'Europe as Far as Vladivostok,' http://www.amerika.org/texts/europe-as-far-as-vladivostok-jean-thiriart/.

444 Francis Parker Yockey, *Imperium* (Wermod and Wermod, 2013 [1948]), http://shop.wermodandwermod.com/books/philosophy/imperium-the-philosophy-of-history-and-politics.html.

445 'Leadership,' The Trilateral Commission, http://www.trilateral.org/go.cfm?do=Page.View&pid=32.

446 'The Trilateral Commission,' http://www.trilateral.org/.

is based on hyper-individualism rather than any form of collective cultural and ethnic identity, where migrants can be accepted on the basis that they will meld in to a common cosmopolitan Europe-wide milieu. Hence, Sutherland attacks any sense of difference among peoples and cultures:

> A passionate belief in breaking down barriers and borders does not sit comfortably with a sense of identity which, in the last analysis, often stresses a belief in particular national virtues. By implication this stress on the relative strengths of one's own people often suggests that others do not share them. There is essentially something triumphalist about patriotism.[447]

By the same measure, the 'European patriotism' or nationalism advocated by Napoleon, Mosley, Strasser, Thiriart and Yockey, must be as equally objectionable to the globalist proponents of this 'European Union,' as the petty nationalisms of the nation-state. A real United Europe or a European Nation is a higher form of patriotism as Mosley for example, explained in his post-World War II thinking, and is nothing if not having her own sense of identity, difference and barriers. Such a European Nation as proposed by Mosley et al. would mean Europe as a self-contained economic bloc (autarky), in contrast the globalist aim of Europe one of several free trade regions in a global economy.

Challenge from the Right

A concern, stated in the introductory remarks of the House of Lords report referred to above, was the rise of radical Rightist parties in Europe in response to immigration from the Third World:

---

447 Peter Sutherland, 'Being Irish—A Personal Reflection,' 3 August 2000, http://petersutherland.co.uk/article/ireland-articles/global-agenda-world-economic-forum-magazine-5/.

Whatever the benefits—economic and cultural—of migration, it has frequently proved controversial. Europe in the early twenty-first century is no exception. The rise of far right political parties in many Member States, which reflect and sometimes stoke fears among the electorate about immigration to Europe from the Islamic world among other things, has provoked policy responses from the more mainstream parties in government. Member State concerns and controversies are invariably reproduced at the EU level.[448]

Immigration is one of the most apparent aspects of globalisation, and the Right would inherently put a break on a major aspect of globalisation, although its economic and financial policies are often woefully inadequate to meet the challenges. The response of the Left, including the extreme Left, to globalisation, regardless of the riots against globalisation summits, etc. means little or nothing in stopping the process. 'Open Borders' and 'One Race: the human Race' are the facile slogans that are shared by corporate CEOs and Leftists alike.

Multiculturalism as a social control mechanism was publicly exposed in 2009 by Andrew Neather, a former adviser and speech-writer to British Prime Minister Tony Blair, and Labour Home Secretaries Jack Straw and David Blunkett. Neather stated that: 'The huge increases in migrants over the last decade were partly due to a politically motivated attempt by ministers to radically change the country and "rub the Right's nose in diversity."' There was a fear however of a backlash, particular among Labour's working class supporters. Hence, the supposed economic benefits of immigration were focused upon; a key element in globalist propaganda for multicultural immigration.

---

448 'Summary,' House of Lords, European Union Committee, 'The EU's Global Approach to Migration and Mobility,' 18 December 2012, http://www. publications.parliament.uk/pa/ld201213/ldselect/ldeucom/91/91.pdf.

Neather wrote in *The Evening Standard* that the 'major shift' in immigration policy was based on a 2001 policy paper by the Performance and Innovation Unit, a think tank based in the Cabinet Office. Neather wrote that 'the final published version of the report promoted the labour market case for immigration but unpublished versions contained additional reasons,' according to a report in *The Telegraph*.[449] Neather wrote:

> Earlier drafts I saw also included a driving political purpose: that mass immigration was the way that the Government was going to make the UK truly multicultural. I remember coming away from some discussions with the clear sense that the policy was intended—even if this wasn't its main purpose—to rub the Right's nose in diversity and render their arguments out of date.[450]

Neather stated that 'as well as bringing in hundreds of thousands more migrants to plug labour market gaps, there was also a "driving political purpose" behind immigration policy. He defended the policy, saying mass immigration has "enriched" Britain, and made London a more attractive and cosmopolitan place.'[451] Neather stated exactly what the intent of multicultural immigration is: to change the foundations of a society.

---

449 Tom Whitehead, 'Labour threw open Britain's borders to mass immigration to help socially engineer a "truly multicultural" country, a former Government adviser has revealed,' *The Telegraph* (London), 23 October 2009, http://www.telegraph.co.uk/news/uknews/law-and-order/6418456/Labour-wanted-mass-immigration-to-make-UK-more-multicultural-says-former-adviser.html.

450 Ibid.

451 Ibid.

'Hip Hop Diplomacy'

Hip hop is America
—U.S. Secretary of State
Hillary Clinton

There's a youth culture in the country that is large, very different and transcends ethnic cultures.
—Gregory Fortuin,
New Zealand Race Relations Commissioner, 2006.

The use of Afro-American ghetto subcultures in the promotion of globalisation has already been referred to in the promotion of hip hop by the U.S. State Department among youth of the migrant communities in France and elsewhere in Europe. While hip hop, rap, and other subcultures are promoted as expressions of 'revolt' by disaffected and alienated youth, 'revolts,' including feminism, the New Left, and psychedelia, and the current 'colour revolutions,' they are bogus and fermented, directed and funded by the corporate globalists.[452]

A well documented account on the corporate takeover and use of hip hop and rap has been written by Lewis Weaver, who states that hip hop, created by coloured youth in the Bronx, New York in the 1970s, was taken over by the large corporations from the early 1990s and 'infused with messages of materialism.'[453] He writes:

> Hip Hop is currently being used by large corporations to be exploited for profits, reinforce capitalistic ideals as well as a tool to adversely effect Black and Latino Youth. Once corporations began to see the earning potential of rap music, the exploitation began.[454]

---

452 Bolton, *Revolution from Above*.
453 Lewis Weaver, 'Corporate Exploitation of Hip Hop,' 15 May 2013, http://itzarap.wordpress.com/2013/05/15/corporate-exploitation-of-hip-hop/.
454 Ibid.

Since the time *Rapper's Delight* by the Sugarhill Gang sold million of records, corporations began to see the potential of hip hop not only in terms of profits, but as a means of promoting and selling their products. Referring to Budweiser's sponsorship of Jay-Z as an example of hip hop artists as marketing tools, Weaver states:

> Corporations realize this influence artists have, and use them as 'guinea pigs' to promote their products and make millions in revenue. Jay-Z being endorsed by Budweiser was a tactic to promote and build a new consumer base for profits. These corporations do not care about the underlying effects of their messages. Alcoholism is a problem in the African American community. Someone who is influential in the black community like Jay-Z, is not helping this problem by endorsing a beer company.
>
> You can see how and why companies use these artists as exploitation tools to promote their products, they will not only attract a new consumer base but they will also increase sales of their products. Adding an artist as the face of a corporation's product adds instant credibility to the mind of consumers. Companies like Adidas backed by Run-DMC and Nike backed by Spike Lee and Michael Jordan, turned into hip hop branding.
>
> Hip Hop culture and corporate America have basically become business partners. This partnership is in the form of paid product placement. This paid product placement is used to influence music listeners by the forced entry or obtrusion of the product in a song or video.[455]

---

455 Ibid.

Hip Hopping Over the World

While hip hop is used as a corporate advertising gimmick, is there a broader agenda in which it is used to subvert nations, peoples, and cultures in what Ralph Peters called the United States' 'lethal culture'? The question can be answered with a definitive 'yes.' As indicated by the sponsorship of hip hop by the U.S. Embassy in Paris, this product of deracination and alienation within the United States is particularly well suited as a social control mechanism to recruit deracinated and alienated youth to the 'American Dream' from around the world. Something similar had already been undertaken during the Cold War with the use of jazz and abstract expressionism, sponsored primarily through the CIA front, the Congress for Cultural Freedom.[456]

The campaign is called 'Hip Hop Diplomacy' and is officially sponsored by the U.S. State Department.

Hishaam Aidi, a Fellow of the Open Society Institute in New York, and therefore close to the centre of the globalisation offensive, writes of the use of hip hop:

> The State Department began using hiphop as a tool in the mid-2000s, when, in the wake of Abu Ghraib and the resurgence of the Taliban, Karen Hughes, then undersecretary of state for public diplomacy, launched an initiative called Rhythm Road. The programme was modelled on the jazz diplomacy initiative of the Cold War era, except that in the 'War on Terror,' hip hop would play the central role of countering 'poor perceptions' of the US.
>
> In 2005, the State Department began sending 'hip hop envoys'—rappers, dancers, DJs—to perform and

---

456 Bolton, *Revolution from Above*, 138–43.

US backed Hip-Hop rapper Sphinx (right) performed in
Egypt calling for Hosni Mubarak to stand down.

speak in different parts of Africa, Asia and the Middle
East. The tours have since covered the broad arc of
the Muslim world, with performances taking place
in Senegal and Ivory Coast, across North Africa, the
Levant and Middle East, and extending to Mongolia,
Pakistan and Indonesia.[457]

The hip hoppers not only stage performances but hold
workshops. The aim is stated to be not just to be as a
propaganda outreach to Muslims, but as a means of selling
the 'American Dream' around the world and therefore
has the potential to create dissent; again in line with what
Ralph Peters explained about the lethality of 'American
culture.' 'The tours aim not only to exhibit the integration
of American Muslims, but also, according to planners, to
promote democracy and foster dissent.'[458] How 'democratic'

---

457 Hishaam Aidi, 'Levering hip hop in U.S. foreign policy,' AlJazeera, 7 November 2011,
     http://www.aljazeera.com/indepth/opinion/2011/10/2011103091018299924.
     html.
458 Ibid.

a state is, is literally rated by globalist organisations such as Freedom House and the National Endowment for Democracy. A low rating is liable to get one bombed.

This 'hip hop diplomacy' acts in tandem with another global programme fostered by the U.S. State Department in association with social media giants such as Google, Facebook, and Twitter. This is the use of social media among youth, which has played an important role in the 'colour revolutions' in ex-Soviet bloc states and elsewhere, including the recent 'Arab Spring.'[459]

Secretary of State Hillary Clinton stated during a CBS News interview that, 'Hip hop is America. You know it may be a little bit hopeful, because I can't point to a change in Syrian policy because Chen Lo and the Liberation Family showed up. But I think we have to use every tool at our disposal.' She was referring to a rap group sent by the State Department in April 2010 to perform in Damascus, Syria.[460]

Noting that rap and hip hop provided the lyrics and music of the revolts throughout North Africa in 2011, Aidi states that 'as security forces rampaged in the streets, artists in Tunis, Cairo and Benghazi were writing lyrics and cobbling together protest footage, beats and rhymes, which they then uploaded to proxy servers. These impromptu songs—such as El General's *Rais Lebled*—were then picked up and broadcast by Al Jazeera, and played at gatherings and solidarity marches in London, New York and Washington.'[461]

459 For the use of social media in fomenting revolt, see Bolton, 'Twitterings of the Revolution,' in *Revolution from Above*, 235–40. This strategy is conducted under the auspices of the Alliance of Youth Movements, also known as Movements.org, sponsored by Google, MTV, Pepsi, YouTube, Facebook, et al., and in 'public partnership' with the U.S. State Department, and was founded by the CEOs of Howcast and Google. They hold seminars with such agencies of U.S. foreign policy as the RAND Corporation and Freedom House.
460 Hishaam Aidi, op. cit.
461 Ibid.

'Hip Hop Diplomacy'

Referring to the use of jazz during the Cold War, Aidi draws parallels with the present use of hip hop and rap:

> The jazz tours of the Cold War saw the U.S. government send integrated bands led by Dizzy Gillespie, Louis Armstrong, Duke Ellington and Benny Goodman to various parts of Africa, Asia and the Middle East to counter Soviet propaganda about American racial practices, and to get people in other countries to identify with 'the American way of life.'

> The choice of jazz was not simply due to its international appeal. As historian Penny Von Eschen writes in her pioneering book *Satchmo Blows Up the World*, in the 1950s, the State Department believed that African-American culture could convey 'a sense of shared suffering, as well as the conviction that equality could be gained under the American political system' to people who had suffered European colonialism. Similar thinking underpins the current 'hip hop diplomacy' initiatives. The State Department planners who are calling for 'the leveraging of hip hop' in U.S. foreign policy emphasise 'the importance of Islam to the roots of hip hop in America,' and the 'pain' and 'struggle' that the music expresses.[462]

In so doing the United States projects itself with a revolutionary, even messianic, mission to refashion the world in its own image. Hip hop is another means of subverting the traditional cultures of the world and recreating a global monoculture behind the façade of 'diversity.' The real 'diversity' of the world, the real 'cultural enrichment' is with the traditional cultures, religions and ethics that globalisation is destroying in the name of 'freedom.' The subversive intentions of hip hop for the globalists is described by a Brookings Institution report which

462 Ibid.

232

states that 'hip hop reflects struggle against authority,' and expresses a 'pain' transcending language barriers, according to Aidi.[463] Hence, when the State Department promotes hip hop among alienated youth it does so as a means of undermining 'authority,' not just in Muslim states, but in European states such as France, with the aim of fundamentally changing the traditions of Europe, as Rivkin and others have plainly stated. The globalists go so far as to co-opt the most extreme of Black revolutionist doctrines, Aidi stating of the Brookings Institution report:

> Moreover, note the authors, hip hop's pioneers were inner-city Muslims who 'carry on an African-American Muslim tradition of protest against authority, most powerfully represented by Malcolm X.' The report concludes by calling for a 'greater exploitation of this natural connector to the Muslim world.'[464]

While there is really nothing that connects the Muslim world with the Black separatism of Malcolm X, it is apparently a contrived, Americanised version misnamed 'Islam' that the United States plans to use to subvert traditional Islam and bring Muslim youth over to a bastardised version that has U.S. roots. The black separatism promoted by Malcolm X was not the type of 'Afro-American civil rights' that the globalists wanted within the United States at the time, but it is now apparently suitable for export under State Department auspices. It is a means, in the name of 'Islam,' of detaching youth from their elders and their traditional ethics, to be converted to a religion contrived in the United States. Shall we see generations of new 'Muslims' bow toward New York rather than Mecca?

The authors of the Brookings report point out that 'arts and culture' have the capacity to 'move and persuade audiences

---

463 Ibid.
464 Ibid.

and to shape and reveal identities.'[465] That is precisely the aim of the globalists: to 'shape identities' that conform to the requirements of globalisation. The image-changing methods can take the 'form of a play, a TV reality show, a novel, or hip-hop music.' None of this seems to relate to traditional Islam of any type.

Joshua Asen and Jennifer Needleman, who have been credited as the founders of 'hip hop diplomacy' state that the programme grew out of the 'use of Hip Hop music as a cultural diplomacy tool for government, corporate, and non-profit partners to reach young audiences in target regions, such as the Middle East and North Africa.' It is notable how Asen and Needleman state the aims of the U.S. government, corporations and 'non-profit partners,' converge. They trace the origins to 'The pilot program, called "I Love Hip Hop in Morocco," [which] launched the first Hip Hop festival in Morocco in 2005, with a 3-city concert series featuring the leading Moroccan rap and breakdance groups, and became a feature-length documentary film, which has screened at festivals and universities worldwide.'[466] The hip hop festival in Morocco was sponsored by the Coca-Cola Company (a big player in globalisation) and the U.S. Embassy.[467]

A recent tour as part of the State Department's U.S. Music Aboard stopped off at New Zealand, where it was hosted by the U.S. Embassy. The band, 'Audiopharmacy,' is described by the U.S. Embassy as 'an up-and-coming hip hop/reggae/dub band from San Francisco.' The Embassy explains that the band combines styles from across the

---

465 Kristina Nelson and Cynthia P. Schneider, 'Mightier than the Sword: Arts and Culture in the U.S.-Muslim World Relationship,' Brookings Institution, June 2008, http://www.brookings.edu/research/papers/2008/06/islamic-world-schneider.

466 Joshua Asen and Jennifer Needleman, 'Hip Hop Diplomacy: About Hip Hop culture and geopolitics,' http://hiphopdiplomacy.org/about/.

467 Ibid., 'Case studies,' 'I Love Hip Hop in Morocco, June 2005,' http://hiphopdiplomacy.org/case-studies/.

Babel, Inc.

world and 'tours the world using music to build a global sense of community.'[468] It is hybrid music for a hybrid, globalised world. It is explained further that

> Audiopharmacy is part of a San Francisco-based artist collective (known as Audiopharmacy Prescriptions) that includes avant-garde musicians, dancers, DJs, photographers, filmmakers, writers, activists, philosophers, and body healers who express their shared consciousness and world view through different means.[469]

> Funded by the State Department, AMA sends American musicians overseas to engage with global audiences and share America's rich musical heritage, including Blues, Bluegrass, Cajun, Country, Folk, Latin, Native American, Gospel, Hip hop/Urban, Indie Rock, Jazz, Punk, R&B, Zydeco, and more.[470]

The message from the United States to the world is that anyone can be anything they like and adopt the lifestyle they like if they accept the nihilistic 'freedom' offered by the United States and make the 'American Dream' their dream too. It is the 'global me' lauded by Zachary et al. One's birth, which is also to say one's birthright and heritage, are of no consequence as anyone can reinvent themselves. This state of perpetual individual flux is another form of 'planned obsolescence' also known as following fashions and trends, and creates an ever-expanding market. A stable and slowly evolving culture, what we call the *Classical*, rooted in land and people, is as useless for ever-expanding markets as an automobile that runs excellently forever. There must be high sales-turnovers whether for cars or for music. It is turning

468 U.S. Embassy, New Zealand, Audiopharmacy dispenses hip hop and more,' http://blogs.newzealand.usembassy.gov/ambassador/2013/04/audiopharmacy-dispenses-hip-hop-and-more/.
469 Ibid.
470 Ibid.

the arts into a commodity, and is why many artists in the epochal aftermath of World War I—such as Ezra Pound, D. H. Lawrence, T. S. Eliot, et al.—were concerned about the impact of mass merchandising literature, theatre, and music, etc., on the quality and durability of the arts.

The U.S. Embassy in New Zealand alludes, without specifically saying so, to the origins of this international music programme in the context of the Cold War when, as we have previously seen, music and other forms of culture, were used as a psychological weapon. The present-day programme is a continuation of that Cold War weapon,

> The AMA program traces its roots back to the great American *Jazz Ambassadors* of the 1950s and 1960s, when the U.S. Government sent the likes of Louis Armstrong, Benny Goodman, and Duke Ellington abroad to spread human truth and foster goodwill. Today's AMA artists are a different generation but just as fine ambassadors of American culture and people-to-people connections without borders.[471]

'Without borders' is the crux of the matter. Sold as something idealistic, 'people-to-people,' the road to peace and brotherhood, something sponsored by the U.S. State Department should rather obviously be considered as nothing more than a tactical manoeuvre to bring the world under the iron heel of globalism as a softer method than the bombs that have been dropped on Iraq or Serbia. If a regime needs bringing down by means other than bombs and US/NATO/United Nations troops, or by economic sanctions, then waves of alienated youth, fed on MTV, Twitter, Facebook, and Coca-Cola, can be brought onto the streets, 'spontaneously,' to create a 'colour revolution.'

This description by Dr. Curtis Sandberg, Senior Vice

---

471 Ibid.

President for the Arts Meridian International Center, on Jazz Ambassadors is instructive:

> More than 50 years ago, at the height of the Cold War, there was little room for intercultural dialogue—and U.S. government officials looked at how to bridge the gap. European powers were giving up long-held possessions in Asia, Africa and the Pacific, and a competition developed between the Soviet Union and the United States to court these newly independent nations.
>
> One of the ways the USSR accomplished this was through culture—folk and classical music, and an established school of dance. In this battle for the "hearts and minds" of the world's peoples, the United States developed an unlikely but remarkably effective response to Soviet initiatives: building international friendships through jazz. Music that was unique to America and represented a fusion of African and African-American cultures with other traditions was a democratic art form that helped others to understand the open-minded and creative sensibility of our country.[472]

Here we see a number of important points that support the contentions of this book:

1. As we have seen, the post-World War II era became a scramble between the United States and the USSR to fill the places vacated by the war-ravished and bankrupted European colonial powers. The United States was at least as active in backing anti-colonial and anti-European movements as the USSR.

2. The USSR since the time of Stalin had rejected much of the Bolshevik doctrine[473] in favour of a new Slavic

---

472 Curtis Sandberg, 'Does jazz have a healing role in a world divided by conflicting ideologies?,' Jazz Ambassadors, http://www.meridian.org/jazzambassadors/.

473 Bolton, *Stalin: The Enduring Legacy*, 28–54.

empire that was based on a return to traditional culture; and condemned 'rootless cosmopolitanism' in the arts as a strategy for imposing a 'one world state.'[474] Ironically, the USSR fought against what most of the 'Right' accused the Soviet Union of promoting, when in fact the real subversive power was the United States.

3. Countering Soviet 'folk culture' the United States promoted African beats through jazz, as it now does through hip hop and rap.

Ghetto Whores and Pimps for Toddlers: Bratz and Flavas

Moreover, the creation of younger generations of consumers has even descended to the level of forming pre-teens into mass consumer markets, with their own fashion and make-up trends and music, and dolls such as 'Bratz'[475] promoting 'street wise' ghetto fashions for children. Some who object to it are describing this as a type of corporate paedophilia. Bratz is a series of dolls, multi-ethnic, and dressed and made-up in modes suggestive of ghetto whores and pimps, that are marketed to pre-school girls. Accoutrements include colouring books, school bags, make-up, clothes, a movie, a television series, music, video games, board games, etc. MGA Entertainment markets the dolls. They were first released in 2001. MGA has received criticism for the dolls being made by cheap labour in China. The American Psychological Association has considered the products as part of the corporate 'sexualisation of children.' The creation of a whole new global mass market based on children, down to toddlers, is concomitant with the same processes used to create new mass markets through multiculturalism. Of this the American Psychological Association stated:

---

474 'Welcome to Bratz: The only girls with a passion for fashion,' MGA, http://www.bratz.com/.

475 *Bratz*, MGM Entertainment. See www.bratz.com.

Although extensive analyses documenting the sexualization of girls, in particular, have yet to be conducted, individual examples can easily be found. These include advertisements (e.g., the Skechers 'naughty and nice' ad that featured Christina Aguilera dressed as a schoolgirl in pigtails, with her shirt unbuttoned, licking a lollipop), dolls (e.g., Bratz dolls dressed in sexualized clothing such as miniskirts, fishnet stockings and feather boas), clothing (thongs sized for 7- to 10-year-olds, some printed with slogans such as 'wink wink'), and television programs (e.g., a televised fashion show in which adult models in lingerie were presented as young girls). Research documenting the pervasiveness and influence of such products and portrayals is sorely needed.[476]

A rival line of multi-ethnic ghetto pimps and whores, Flavas, was launched by Mattel in 2003. The name derives from a hip hop term and the whole hip hop style is promoted, including speech, style, and 'attitude.' The Mattel promotion of the line, aimed at girls aged 8 to 10, stated,

Mattel asks girls: What's your Flava? In an all-new line of fashion dolls. Flava, according to *Hip Hoptionary: the Dictionary of Hip Hop Terminology*, means personal flavor or style. . . . With the introduction of Flavas (pronounced Flay-vuhz) the first reality based fashion doll brand that celebrates today's teen culture through authentic style, attitude and values Mattel created a hot hip-hop themed line that allows girls to express their own personal flavas. . . . Reflecting how today's teens change their looks based on their personality and mood of the moment, Flavas will also feature multiple looks of the same character in every product wave.[477]

---

476 'Sexualization of Girls,' American Psychological Association, http://www.apa.org/pi/women/programs/girls/report.aspx.

477 'Mattel asks girls: What's your Flava? In an all-new line of fashion dolls,' Mattel, 29 July 2003, http://investor.shareholder.com/mattel/releasedetail.

Hip-Hop multi-ethnic fashion dolls created by Mattel

Here the supposed idealism of corporate multiculturalism works in tandem with the 'sexualization of children,' as a method of creating a new market. Moreover, the corporations are creating youth identities right down to pre-teens. A feature of this Mattel-created identity is the fluidity of character for girls that is promoted: the *planned obsolescence of personality* to maintain the constancy of markets. This pitch to children is the same marketing technique that is a feature of globalisation in general, and what makes this culture 'lethal.'

Gregory Fortuin, a South African Coloured and supporter of the ANC who became Race Relations Commissioner in New Zealand, observed that 'There's a youth culture in the country that is large, very different and transcends ethnic cultures.'[478] This is a cogent description of what the

cfm?releaseid=115032.
478 Fortuin speaking at River of Life Church, Kapiti, New Zealand, 26 February 2006 (*Kapiti Observer*).

globalists aim for on a worldwide scale. While Fortuin saw it as a progressive development that would obliterate ethnic divisions, what he was lauding was the globalist 'crucible' that works throughout the world to forge youth into a standardised consumer market that is not rooted in a specific tradition, but comes out of a ragbag of everything. These progressive liberals do not seem to realise that this 'youth culture' is a form of what the liberal-Left would otherwise condemn as 'American cultural imperialism.' However, because it is derived from the ghettos it is acceptable, like jazz before it, and is even regarded as laudable.

Purse Strings

As a strategy for the breaking down of separate cultural and ethnic identities across the world, the multicultural agenda that to a considerable extent emanates from the United States, is not only for export but also for the home market. While military strategist Ralph Peters refers to America's 'lethal' culture undermining traditional states, the cultural virus that it exports dominates the United States itself. The U.S. oligarchy is as zealous to impose cultural nihilism on the United States as on any other nation. Because these oligarchs are not loyal to anything other than their money or their own dynasty, the United States is to them just the current host of their parasitic activities.

The oligarchy has no more interest in seeing the development of an *American* people,' an *American* nation,' and an *American* culture,' than it does in seeing the maintenance or revival of peoples, nations, and cultures anywhere else in the world. What is the American people, nation, and culture other than a diversity of individuals held together by a way of life called the 'American Dream' which is nothing more than the pursuit of money, and a superficial 'patriotism' based on loyalty to legalistic documents: a Constitution and a Bill of Rights, heralded as 'patriotism' when a war needs fighting in the interests of faraway investments? The oligarchy that rules the United States is no more 'American,' than its counterparts elsewhere, past and present, have been 'British,' 'French,' 'Dutch,' or 'German.' If the United States self-destructs due to the parasitism of the oligarchy on its host, that oligarchy would be looking to pack its bags and ensconce itself elsewhere. When America has shown signs of developing a strong nativist nationalism, such as the movement that was emerging around Senator Joseph McCarthy, it has been crushed by the oligarchs and their dupes in the news media, Congress, and Senate.[479]

---

479 K. R. Bolton, 'McCarthy's Threat to the Globalist Establishment,' in *Revolution*

Hence, the oligarchs residing in the United States have promoted the destructive multicultural agendas in their own land of residence as enthusiastically as they have promoted the same agendas around the world. Elsewhere I have extensively documented the funding of a broad range of subversive cultural and political movements and ideologies around the world and within the United States.[480] Here we shall examine the funding of specifically multicultural agendas, movements and doctrines by these sources.

NAACP and Corporate Funding

We have previously seen the concern the first president of the National Association for the Advancement of Colored People, Walter White, had in regard to the organisation's funding by non-Negro, and primarily Jewish banking sources. He was worried that such funding would allow the plutocrats to direct the course of the organisation. In 2004 the issue became public, when questions were raised as to whether corporate funding had changed the character of the NAACP.

Despite assurances by the NAACP leadership, sources worried that corporate funding from the likes of Microsoft, Exxon, PepsiCo and others 'compromised its effectiveness of the nation's oldest civil rights watchdog might hesitate to bite the hand that feeds it, they reason.'

'Under the leadership of Kweisi Mfume, former president of the National Association for the Advancement of Colored People, the organization increasingly forged relations with Wall Street and solicited millions of dollars from corporations' . . . Lots of companies do. The NAACP's $27 million annual budget is marbled with

---

from Above, 40–41.

480 Bolton, *Revolution from Above*, passim.

contributions from the nation's leading corporations. But how much Wall Street gives is anybody's guess.[481]

The NAACP was founded on the initiative of Jacob H. Schiff, one of the most significant figures of Wall Street. Others included such oligarchs as Felix Warburg and Herbert Lehman. They were world power wire-pullers as are Soros and Rockefeller today. If they not only funded, but even founded an organisation such as the NAACP, they did so with a long-range purpose in mind, as do today's oligarchs. It would be very naïve to think that these corporations invest so much money on an Afro-American organisation promoting assimilation because they are kindly, or merely as a pay-off to be left alone.

While NAACP records of corporate donors are not revealed by the organisation, the donors can be tracked down from the sources. Additionally despite the impression given by the 2004 *Baltimore Sun* article, the NAACP has always been the recipient of corporate largesse, from its foundation in 1909 to the present. Although the NAACP runs at a deficit, the wealthy oligarchy has always poured its millions into the organisation, as they have with sundry other Leftist/liberal causes.[482] The Ford Foundation gave the NAACP $1,000,000.[483] The NAACP Legal Defense and Education Fund (NAACP-LDF), founded as a separate entity in 1940, specialising in litigating in the Courts, and achieving the landmark decisions that ended school segregation, has been the focus of Ford Foundation largesse. The grants from 2009 to 2012 that Ford gave the NAACP-LDF total $7,050,000.[484]

---

481 Greg Barrett and Kelly Brewington, *The Baltimore Sun*, 13 December 2004,' cited by History News Network, http://hnn.us/articles/corporate-funding-raises-ethical-questions-naacp.

482 Bolton, *Revolution from Above*, passim.

483 James Bock, 'Gifts, Foundation grant ease NAACP's deficit,' *Baltimore Sun*, 19 November 1994, http://articles.baltimoresun.com/1994-11-19/news/1994323100_1_ford-foundation-naacp-grant.

484 Ford Foundation Grants, 'NAACP,' http://www.fordfoundation.org/Grants/

Mexican-American Legal Defense and Education Fund (MALDEF)

The Hispanic equivalent of the NAACP Defense and Education Fund is MALDEF, which not only received Ford Foundation largesse, but also is 'the creation of the Ford Foundation.' The grants from Ford during 2009–2012 total $4,300,000.[485]

The example of how the oligarchs virtually created a new ethnic group within the United States, the 'Hispanic,' is instructive. Until the 1960s the problems of Mexican immersion was primarily economic, with the demand for cheap labour, as it had been the prior century with the importation of Asian coolies. However during the 1960s 'identity politics,' and the 'civil rights' movement arose, especially to integrate the South, where Segregation would have been as burdensome to the expansion of a modern economy as had by the Old South of the slave-owning era, and for the same reasons that the Afrikaner had to be overthrown in South Africa. The Ford Foundation expanded its ethnic outreach to Spanish speakers in the United States to mould previously diverse nationalities into a new entity, the 'Hispanic,' and indeed a new race, *La Raza*. Until the creation of MALDEF by the Ford Foundation, those Mexicans who migrated to the United States regarded themselves as 'Whites' and desired to assimilated with White America.

Prior to MALDEF, Mexican-Americans were represented by the League of United Latin American Citizens (LULAC), founded in 1929. Joseph Fallon, demographics and immigration researcher, writes of LULAC that it 'was a middle-class, patriotic organization of U.S. citizens of Mexican descent whose activities centred primarily on

---

Search.
485 Ibid., MALDEF.

education,' committed to traditional 'Americanism.' They promoted the assimilation of Mexican-Americans into the majority 'Anglo' culture, stressed that they were 'Americans,' and insisted on proficiency in the English language, opposing any notion of Mexican enclaves within the United States. 'LULAC endorsed immigration control and supported President Eisenhower's "Operation Wetback" which deported a million illegal aliens back to Mexico.' However, from the mid-1950s LULAC changed direction to espouse the reversal of its original aims, including the classification of Mexican-Americans as a separate, non-White entity. As a radicalised Hispanic organisation it received funding from the major corporations, such as AT&T.[486]

MALDEF emerged in 1967 as a rival of LULAC and in imitation of the NAACP-LDF. 'Seed money' for MALDEF was given by Ford after Jack Greenberg, president of the NAACP-LDF, arranged for Peter Tijerina, State Civil Rights Chairman for the LULAC chapter in San Antonio, to meet Bill Pincus, head of the Ford Foundation. Fallon writes:

> Pincus agreed to advance Tijerina 'seed money' to create a five-state 'Mexican-American' organization modelled after the NAACP-LDF. This new organization would pursue civil rights litigation on behalf of 'Mexicans' as the NAACP-LDF was doing on behalf of blacks. Tijerina became MALDEF's first executive director, and, in 1970, Mario Obledo, former Texas Attorney General, became General Counsel. After MALDEF was established by 'seed money,' the Ford Foundation then awarded the organization a five-year grant in excess of $2 million. . . . MALDEF was a creation of the Ford Foundation in more ways than just funding.

---

486 Joseph Fallon, 'Funding Hate—Foundations and the Radical Hispanic Lobby—Part III,' *The Social Contract* 11, no. 1 (Fall 2000) http://www.thesocialcontract.com/artman2/publish/tsc1101/article_912.shtml.

The Ford Foundation soon took control of virtually all important matters from where the headquarters should be located, to the appointment of its executive director, and the type of legal cases it should pursue.[487]

MALDEF's funding derives mainly from corporations and foundations; in particular the Carnegie Corporation, the Ford Foundation, and the Rockefeller Foundation. It has received generous funding from the Ahmanson Foundation, the AT&T Foundation, the David and Lucile Packard Foundation, the John D. & Catherine T. MacArthur Foundation, the Joyce Foundation, the Open Society Institute, and the Verizon Foundation.[488]

La Raza—The Race

The National Council of La Raza was established in 1968 originally as the Southwest Council of La Raza. Henry Santiestevan, former head of the Southwest Council of La Raza, wrote that 'it can be said that without the Ford Foundation's commitment to a strategy of national and local institution-building, the Chicano movement would have withered away in many areas.'[489] Ford grants for 2009–2013 total $6,650,600.[490]

LaRaza's 'corporate champions' include: Bank of America, Wal-Mart, J. P. Morgan Chase & Co., Shell Oil, FedEx Corporation, Google, and others.[491] Its 'Corporate Board of Advisors' includes representatives from AT&T, Bank of

---

487 Ibid.

488 'Discover the Network,' http://www.discoverthenetworks.org/printgroupProfile. asp?grpid=6156.
    The reader is referred to 'Discover the Network' as a convenient references for cross-referencing the interconnections and activities of the Foundations.

489 William F. Jasper, 'Silk Hats and Brown Berets,' *The New American* 12, no. 4, 1996.

490 Ford Foundation Grants, National Council of La Raza, op. cit.

491 La Raza, 'Corporate Champions,' http://www.nclr.org/index.php/support_us/ corporate_champions/corporate_board_of_advisors/.

Babel, Inc.

America, Chevron, Citibank, the Coca-Cola Company, Comcast NBCUniversal Telemundo, ConAgra Foods, Inc., Ford Motor Company, General Mills, Inc., General Motors, Johnson & Johnson, Kraft Foods, McDonald's Corporation, MillerCoors LLC, PepsiCo Inc., Prudential Financial, Shell, State Farm Insurance Companies, Time Warner Inc., Toyota, UPS, Verizon, Wal-Mart, and Wells Fargo.[492]

The mission of La Raza, according to the biography of its current president, is to make 'Hispanics an integral part of the 'American Dream':

> As someone who has experienced the promise of the American Dream firsthand, Janet Murguía has devoted her career in public service to opening the door to that dream to millions of American families. Now, as a key figure among the next generation of leaders in the Latino community, she continues this mission as President and CEO of the National Council of La Raza (NCLR), the largest national Hispanic civil rights and advocacy organization in the United States.[493]

Here we get to the crux of why these ethnic minority lobbies are supported by corporate America; it is for the same reason why globalists fund ethnic minority agendas around the world: as part of the 'One World' concept, and the creation of *Homo globicus*, presently unfolding in its most advanced form in the United States. The 'American' is *Homo globicus* in the process of actualisation, and the 'American Dream' is the globalist monoculture in the process of actualisation, championed in the name of 'diversity.'

The Rockefeller Foundation is a major contributor to La

492 La Raza, 'Corporate Board of Advisors,' http://www.nclr.org/index.php/support_us/corporate_champions/corporate_board_of_advisors/.
493 NCLR President and CEO, http://www.nclr.org/index.php/about_us/leadership/.

Raza, the NAACP, and many other immigrant and ethnic groups. The Foundation's purpose 'through grantmaking' is 'to spread the benefits of globalization to more people in more places around the world.'[494]

League of United Latin American Citizens (LULAC)

LULAC claims to be the oldest and largest Hispanic organisation in the United States. It is worth noting the long list of 'corporate partners' that are represented on LULAC's advisory board, while keeping in mind that such organisations as LULAC are helping to open the U.S. borders to Latino immigrants which, while undertaken in the name of 'human rights,' serves corporate interests in terms of an expanded market and labour force. Such lobbies are kept in line by corporate money. LULAC's 'corporate advisory board' comprises: Altria Group, Inc., American Airlines, Amgen, Anheuser-Busch Inc., AT&T, Bank of America, BlueCross BlueShield Association, Burger King Corporation, The Coca-Cola Company, Comcast Corporation, Cox Enterprises, Inc., Denny's, Inc., Diageo, Exxon Mobil Corporation, Ford Motor Company, General Motors Company, The Home Depot, JPMorgan Chase & Co., McDonald's Corporation, Mead Johnson Nutrition, MillerCoors LLC, National Cable & Telecommunications Association, The Procter & Gamble Company, Pfizer Inc, Shell Oil Company, Southwest Airlines Co., Sprint Nextel Corporation, Time Warner Cable, Tyson Foods, Inc., Univision Communications, Inc., Verizon Communications Inc., Wal-Mart Stores, Inc., The Walt Disney Company, Western Union, and Yum! Brands Inc.[495]

---

494 Rockefeller Foundation, 'What we fund,' http://www.rockefellerfoundation.org/grants.
495 LULAC, 'Corporate Alliance,' http://lulac.org/about/corpall/.

Note that many of these corporations are also involved in a multitude of ethnic, Hispanic, Black and other lobbies, and include key globalist corporations, bankers, junk food merchants, and oil interests.

Emma Lazarus Fund

We have previously considered the poetical enunciation of the melting-pot for the United States by the early Zionist Emma Lazarus, whose sonnet on the United States' mission to accept the outcasts of the world adorns the Statue of Liberty. Hence, the fund that globalist speculator George Soros established in 1996 specially for the sponsoring of immigration lobbying was named after Lazarus: the Emma Lazarus Fund. When Soros sponsors an organisation or cause you can be certain that it is for an important political objective in advancing the 'new world order.' The umbrella organisation for Soros is the Open Society Institute formed in 1993 as an international network of foundations in more than 50 countries supporting a range of programs, according to its website. Soros money funds feminism, and pro-abortion and marijuana liberalisation, including the Drug Policy Alliance. The Soros agenda is to break down the traditional, structures of states in order to make them suited to a globalised economy.[496]

The Emma Lazarus Fund was set up by the Open Society Institute to operate for the year 1996–97 for the purpose of dispensing grants totalling $50,000,000 to pro-immigration lobbies and projects. Among the dozens of recipients of Soros largesse were the National Council of La Raza and MALDEF. A major focus was to support projects to assist in the naturalisation of Latinos. While not much remains in evidence for the existence of the Emma Lazarus Fund, having dispensed its $50,000,000, immigration lawyers Siskind and Susser have lauded the work of Soros

---

496 Bolton, *Revolution from Above*, 222–27.

as a great humanitarian gesture, while ensuring that readers appreciate that this is another generous gesture for humanity by a 'Jewish philanthropist':

> It might strike a person as odd that one of America's richest men would decide to take a leading role in calling for a more tolerant, open attitude toward immigration. But when one learns the man is George Soros, perhaps this is not surprising. Soros, profiled earlier this month on the popular television newsmagazine 60 Minutes, has a reputation for being a tough businessman, but also one of the world's leading philanthropists. Until recently, he was best known for giving money to help promote open societies in Eastern Europe.
>
> But recently Soros chose to tackle the issue of immigration. Soros knows first hand the importance of an open immigration policy. He is, after all, a Hungarian Jew who survived the Holocaust and knows that for many, the right to immigrate can be a matter of life and death.
>
> Recently Soros created the Emma Lazarus Fund, an initiative of Soros' Open Society Institute. Emma Lazarus was the 19th Century Jewish-American poet whose famous words from her poem 'The New Colossus' welcoming impoverished immigrants to American shores are on a plaque on the Statue of Liberty. The poem, beginning with the famous words 'Give me your tired, your poor . . .' is one of the most famous in American literature and is now synonymous with America's welcoming historical attitude to immigrants.[497]

Note how these immigration lawyers play on the theme

---

[497] Siskin and Susser Immigration Lawyers, 'Non-Profit corner—The Emma Lazarus Fund,' http://www.visalaw.com/98dec/31dec98.html.

of 'The Holocaust' in relation to promoting 'open immigration' to the United States. Any objections to the globalist agendas on immigration and multiculturalism are howled down with the spectre of 'The Holocaust.'

While it would be superfluous to further detail the organisations and the millions that have been dispensed by globalist corporations, funds, and foundations, the reader is invited to search the grant-making databases of the likes of the Rockefeller Foundation, Ford Foundation, Open Society Institute, and major globalist corporations such as AT&T, Coca-Cola, Pepsi, interconnected and associated with U.S. government agencies such as the State Department, in a seemingly endless network.'[498]

Case Study: Wal-Mart

Something of the Big Business strategy in backing both open immigration and in seeking to control immigration lobbies through financial patronage, can be seen in the example of the two-pronged relationship Wal-Mart has towards Mexican migrant workers. Wal-Mart lauds itself as both a major employer of Mexicans and a major contributor to Hispanic lobbies, including MALDEF and National Council of La Raza. Yet at the same time Wal-Mart has been prosecuted for the exploitation of Mexican illegal aliens. Its commitment to the lowest prices is extracted at the pressure it puts on suppliers to provide the cheapest products to the extent that Wal-Mart suppliers are relocating to cheap labour countries such as China. That is the reality of globalisation.

In Mexico itself, Wal-Mart is that state's largest private sector employer, with 209,000 workers. Another salient

498 K. R. Bolton, 'The Globalist Web of Subversion,' *Foreign Policy Journal*, 7 February 2011, http://www.foreignpolicyjournal.com/2011/02/07/the-globalist-web-of-subversion/.

example of the reality of globalisation, with an aesthetic and cultural implication, was the building in 2004 of a stark, utilitarian Wal-Mart building near the Mayan pyramid of the small market town of San Juan de Teotihuacán. A news report stated:

> As they have for centuries, the merchants here ply their trade midway between the ruins of giant pyramids built by the Maya and the stone steeple of the town's main Catholic church, which Spanish monks founded in 1548.
>
> Now another colossus from a different empire is being built in the shadow of the pyramids, a structure some merchants and other townsfolk here say threatens not only their businesses but their heritage. In December, an ugly cinderblock building rising from the earth is to house a sprawling supermarket called Bodega Aurrera, a subsidiary of Wal-Mart of Mexico.
>
> How Wal-Mart got permission to build a superstore on farmland supposedly protected under Mexican law as an archaeological site has vexed the merchants here, who freely accuse the town, the state and the federal Institute of Anthropology and History of corruption.
>
> The opponents charge Wal-Mart with trampling on their Indian heritage and suggest that the backhoes clawing at the earth on the site are destroying irreplaceable relics.
>
> But an economic reality underlies this dispute—Wal-Mart has not only built stores throughout Mexico, but has taken over several other chains. It is the largest private employer in the country, and wherever this American retail titan erects a new outlet, the local merchants tend to disappear, or at least lose business.[499]

---

499 James C. McKinley Jr., 'No, the Conquistadors Are Not Back. It's Just Wal-Mart,'

This is the actual meaning of globalisation, the reality behind the façade of the corporate sponsorship of 'diversity.' Meanwhile, in the United States, Wal-Mart promotes itself as the champion of the Mexican migrant, which it also finds to be a convenient source of exploitable labour. Hence, in a press release to a Hispanic business news site, Wal-Mart informed Hispanic readers about its issuing of a bilingual 'fiesta guide' to help celebrate Cinco de Mayo. Wal-Mart boasted of being the largest private employer of Hispanics in the United States (as it is across the border), as well as sponsoring organisations such as the Hispanic Association of Colleges and Universities, National Council of La Raza, Lulac Women's Conference in Texas, La Prensa Foundation, National Association of Hispanic Publications, and the New Mexico Alliance for Hispanic Education.[500]

While indulging in self-promotion of its humanitarian support for Hispanics in the United States, the previous year (2003) the FBI raided 60 Wal-Mart stores across 21 states and arrested 250 illegal immigrants who had been employed by Wal-Mart as janitors from contractors. The FBI also raided Wal-Mart's headquarters in Arkansas and removed documents. An FBI official stated that wiretaps had been used to record meetings between Wal-Mart executives and contractors. In 2004 a court ordered Wal-Mart to pay 83 workers unpaid overtime, 'in the second phase of a trial that highlighted working conditions at the nation's largest private employer.' 'Wal-Mart, the world's largest retailer, made employees at 18 Oregon stores work unpaid overtime from 1994 to 1999. About three dozen similar suits against the retailer are pending nationwide.'[501]

The New York Times, 28 September 2004, http://www.nytimes.com/2004/09/28/international/americas/28mexico.html?_r=0.

500 'Wal-Mart Creates Fiesta Guide to Help Customers Celebrate the Flavor and Fun of Cinco de Mayo,' HispanicBusiness.com, 2 May 2004.

501 'Judge: Wal-Mart Must Pay 83 for Overtime,' *Houston Chronicle*, 18 February 2004.

Representative George Miller of the House Education and Workforce Committee, stated after an investigation in 2004 that 'Substandard pay and health care benefits for Wal-Mart workers allow the firm to charge very low prices that force nearby stores to slash their workers' pay and benefits in order to compete.'[502] Despite Wal-Mart's indignation at such accusations and investigations, the complaints persist to the present. At protests outside the annual conference of Wal-Mart shareholders in Arkansas, workers drew attention to grievances not only in the United States, but also the use by Wal-Mart of manufacturers in such states as Bangladesh. One Wal-Mart employee was quoted as stating that,

> irregular hours left her unable to pay for healthcare for her family. One week she could work eight hours, the next 40. 'Healthcare costs do not change, but my pay and hours do,' she said. She said the instability left her unable to keep up with her premiums. 'We need public assistance to survive. Living in low-income housing, relying on food stamps, not being able to afford healthcare, is not my definition of providing a good job,' she said.[503]

There are reports that employees who complained about conditions suffered 'retaliation,' including dismissal. Representative Miller raised the same matters in 2004. This is the real face of globalisation, behind the donations to ethnic minority lobbies and the eagerness of these corporations to promote 'open borders.' What is notable is the zeal by which many 'ethnic' leaders, spokesmen, and lobbies accept donations from such corporations, and even award prizes to their directors and CEOs in the cause

---

502 Charles Burress, 'Wal-Mart foes detail costs to community Public subsidizes workers, study says,' *San Francisco Chronicle*, 17 February 2004.

503 Dominic Rushe and Paul Harris, 'Walmart workers speak out: "I do not earn enough. I cannot survive like this,"' *The Guardian*, 6 June 2013, http://www.guardian.co.uk/business/2013/jun/06/walmart-workers-speak-pay-conditions.

of 'minority rights.' In 2013 the Association of Hispanic Advertising Agencies (AHAA) gave Wal-Mart its 'first Marketer of the Year' award at its annual conference in Miami.

'AHAA's criteria for the award included a top-down commitment to Hispanic and other multicultural marketing, significant spending, and incorporating Hispanic into the company's overall strategy with measurable accountability. 'Walmart spent about $60 million on Hispanic marketing alone in both 2011 and 2012. At the ANA conference last October, Mr. Rogers said that 100% of Walmart's growth in sales is going to come from multicultural customers, leading the company to decide to at least double its spending to reach those customers in 2013.'[504]

---

504 Laurel Wentz, 'Walmart Is First Marketer of the Year at AHAA Conference,' AdAge/Hispanic, 1 May 2013, http://adage.com/article/hispanic-marketing/walmart-hispanic-group-s-marketer-year/241243/.

Conclusion:

The Multicultural Dilemma

The Stranger within my gate,
He may be true or kind,
But does not talk my talk—
I cannot feel his mind.
I see the face and the eyes and the mouth,
But not the soul behind. . . .

—Rudyard Kipling, *The Stranger*

The agenda of the globalists is to use multiculturalism as a transition phase towards the melting-pot of an integrated global workforce and consumer market. Multiculturalism implies 'diversity,' but the melting-pot in what Emma Lazarus and Israel Zangwill termed a 'crucible' implies a nebulous mass. It is akin to alchemy where various substances are placed into a crucible to make something entirely new; in this instance a new human being: what I have here called *Homo globicus*. It is a dialectical tactic of using the pretence of 'diversity' and of supposed 'respect' for all the cultures of the world, to impose a standardised global system.

A multicultural world is the polar opposite of a 'multicultural nation' or 'society.' The latter is a misnomer.[505] A nation or society implies a community of shared heritage and a common outlook. A nation and a society are founded on a dominant culture. Where there is more than one culture within a territory, there exists in embryo the potential for another nation and another society. The apartheid

---

505 For descriptions of the various often contradictory versions of multiculturalism, see Cameron McKenzie, *The Menace of Multiculturalism*, 1997, http://archive.org/stream/TheMenaceOfMulticulturalism/MMC_djvu.txt.

system developed by Dr. Verwoerd was designed to work as a number of semi-independent culture-nations existing within a South African confederation; apartheid meaning 'separate development,' or 'apartness.' It was a noble experiment, but flawed insofar as it could not proceed to fruition as long as South Africa relied on Black labour. Segregation in the Southern states of the United States had the same flaw. While both systems were imperfect, they were better than what has resulted in either the United States or South Africa.

A 'multicultural world' is the Earth in its natural state of being: different cultures, peoples and ethnicities existing within their own territories, inter-relating but not amalgamating, under the popular saying: 'good fences make good neighbours.' They can trade peacefully, exchange ideas, and provide assistance, without the need for some hegemonic world state. Alternatives to the present concept of the nation-state, which is based on 18th-century notions of legal contacts between individuals in the form of constitutions and the like, on the ruins of the traditional social nexus of Church and Monarch, might include what the Russian geopolitical analyst Professor Alexander Dugin has called 'vectors,' or geopolitical blocs of nations with common interests. Such geopolitical blocs would be more suitable for world order and cooperation than the one-size-fits-all universalism of the United Nations Organization, or globalist regional groupings such as NAFTA or the European Union, again based on legalistic economic contracts. Such new blocs moreover would recognise the status of more rather than fewer nation-cultures. For example, in Europe there are many stateless peoples such as the Flemish, Bretons, and Basques, who have been incorporated into artificial state constructs devoid of historical basis. The Afrikaner remnant in South Africa could be accorded status within a European confederation in such a new European geopolitical bloc. The Bolivarian concept inaugurated among South American republics by the late Hugo Chávez is an example of an already functioning bloc that resists globalisation.[506]

However, the globalists see economics rather than blood ties and shared heritage and similarity of outlook as the basis for both regional groups and a 'new world order.' When they impose multiculturalism upon a state it is done with the intention of wrecking the foundations of that state for the purpose of fitting it into a global economic structure. It is designed to wreck, not to 'celebrate diversity' or any other such claptrap.

Liberal apologists of multiculturalism and conservative antagonists both begin from faulty and contradictory foundations. As politicians they are caught in a trap of trying to make systems promoted by globalists workable.

The liberals acclaim multiculturalism as a 'celebration of diversity' and use nonsensical terms such as 'unity in diversity.' The mental rationalisation requires 'doublethink.' When an organism attempts to 'celebrate unity in diversity' the result is cancerous. The result in a liberal society is that the host culture—most likely Christian and European at root—is forced to retreat into oblivion in the name of 'tolerance,' and enforced where necessary by draconian laws, which include imprisonment for sceptics. Therefore, for example, chapels in hospitals will become religiously neutral, Christian holidays will be renamed, and Christmas decorations, prayers in schools, and public nativity scenes will become passé. A report on the situation in the United States stated:

Frosty the Snowman is tolerable, but the ACLU[507] has

---

506 On new geopolitical blocs, see K. R. Bolton, *Geopolitics of the Indo-Pacific* (London: Black House Publishing, 2013).
507 American Civil Liberties Union, a long-running liberal law lobby.

Conclusion

threatened to sue a school in Colorado for permitting Jingle Bells, which makes Jewish students no longer feel welcome. In New York City public schools, menorahs and Islamic symbols are acceptable, but not nativity scenes. Teachers in Sacramento have been forbidden to use the word Christmas in the classroom, Illinois state government employees forbidden to say 'Merry Christmas' on the job.[508]

However, the particularly awkward factor of maintaining a multicultural society for liberal politicians is that many of the imported cultures are extremely illiberal, and in recent years, to preserve the liberal secular humanism of the West, the politicians are abandoning multiculturalism and returning to the old policy of assimilation or the 'melting-pot.' The problems with illiberal cultures particularly focus on the attitudes of some forms of Islam towards women, and hence this affronts feminist sensibilities. Therefore, when Muslims settle in a typically liberal state, multicultural tolerance and 'respect for differences' does not extend to their treatment or attitude toward women, including their own wives and daughters. If the liberal society was truly multicultural then it should 'celebrate' such differences. They are expected to conform to the laws of the land in this respect. It is here that the real intent of multiculturalism is shown to be a sham. The liberal expects the migrant to become liberalised and secularised, and this is a reason why the U.S. State Department focuses on transforming Muslim youths in France and other states, so that a generation emerges that has rejected the traditions of their elders, under the pretence of 'respecting different cultures.' As we have seen, globalist values are imparted through the contrivance of bastardised cultural forms such as 'Muslim hip hop' (*sic*). Professor Lauchlan Chipman pointed out the liberal quandary when he wrote:

---

508 Lionel Shriver, 'Nativity scenes are out, carols are banned, and don't dare wish anyone merry Christmas: the festive season, US-style,' *The Guardian*, 7 December 2005, http://www.guardian.co.uk/theguardian/2005/dec/07/features.g2.

. . . here's the rub. In many cases these values are neither liberal nor pluralist. Support for the values of some communities means support for a sheltered, separate, limited and thoroughly sexist upbringing for daughters, for example. It means, for some communities, inculcating racial and ethnic mythologies theoretically irrelevant to the future of Australia, but politically, and literally, explosive if developed here . . .[509]

Hence, in this central problem of feminism and illiberal migrants, a particularly large amount of money is spent, especially by the Rockefeller, Ford, and Soros funds, on promoting feminism, including liberalised abortion laws, within the Third World. Feminism, which was funded and fostered in the West by the global oligarchy and CIA as part of an agenda to use the anti-Soviet Left, has been just as useful in subverting traditional societies as multiculturalism.[510]

One can see the dilemma of multicultural for liberal societies when, for example, President Sarkozy pushed for the banning of the burqa in France in 2011, describing the traditional dress as an affront to the principles of the French Republic, which is to say liberal-humanist principles. Among the results of the burqa ban, a riot broke out in June 2013 in a Paris suburb after police tried to arrest a woman for wearing the burqa, with 60 people attacking the police. Forty riot police were required to restore order.[511] The dilemma is the conflict between Muslim tradition and Western liberalism. Liberal societies are increasingly

---

509 Lauchlan Chipman, 'The Menace of Multi-Culturalism,' *Quadrant*, September 1980, 3. Lauchlan is Emeritus Professor, Faculty of Humanities and Social Sciences, Bond University, Queensland.

510 K. R. Bolton, *Revolution from Above*, 160–200.

511 Nabila Ramdani, 'France's burkha ban sparks violence across Paris after police try to arrest woman for wearing a veil and pregnant woman is attacked for covering her face,' *Daily Mail*, 13 June 2013, http://www.dailymail.co.uk/news/article-2341113/Frances-burkha-ban-sparks-violence-Paris-police-try-arrest-woman-wearing-veil-pregnant-woman-attacked-covering-face.html.

Conclusion

deciding that this type of multiculturalism is unworkable and that there now has to be a reversal of policy, to return to the old method of assimilating migrants into the mainstream of liberal society rather than, as hitherto, avidly promoting the continuation of ethnic enclaves.

In 2011 Britain's David Cameron, Germany's Angela Merkel, and France's Nicolas Sarkozy made a public confession of the rather obvious, that multiculturalism has failed. Sarkozy stated: 'My answer is clearly yes, it is a failure. . . . Of course we must all respect differences, but we do not want a society where communities coexist side by side.' Referring specifically to the Melting-pot idea, Sarkozy added: 'If you come to France, you accept to melt into a single community, which is the national community, and if you do not want to accept that, you cannot be welcome in France. The French national community cannot accept a change in its lifestyle, equality between men and women and freedom for little girls to go to school.' Around the same time, David Cameron 'called for an end to the "passive tolerance" of divided communities and said members of all faiths must integrate into wider society and accept core values.' 'German Chancellor Angela Merkel, Australia's former Prime Minister John Howard and former Spanish Prime Minister José Maria Aznar have also said in recent months that multicultural policies had not successfully integrated immigrants.'[512]

The Russian president, Vladimir Putin, who is the only White politician coming close to the conception of a White statesman, has also expressed Russia's repudiation of multiculturalism, but Putin is likely to have a far more profound understanding of the dynamics involved than that his lesser counterparts in Western Europe. Russia has

---

512 'Nicolas Sarkozy joins David Cameron and Angela Merkel view that multiculturalism has failed,' *Daily Mail*, 11 February 2011, http://www.dailymail.co.uk/news/article-1355961/Nicolas-Sarkozy-joins-David-Cameron-Angela-Merkel-view-multiculturalism-failed.html.

Russian President Vladimir Putin

its own traditional national idea and even its own sense of mission that is of a religious character[513] and contra the United States' 'manifest destiny.' Putin has said of multiculturalism:

> In Russia live Russian. Any minority, from anywhere, if it wants to live in Russia, to work and eat in Russia, should speak Russian, and should respect the Russian laws. If they prefer Sharia Law, then we advise them to go to those places where that's the state law. Russia does not need minorities. Minorities need Russia, and we will not grant them special privileges, or try to change our laws to fit their desires, no matter how loud they yell 'discrimination.' We better learn from the

---

513 For a consideration of the Russian national idea and sense of mission in the world, see K. R. Bolton, 'Spengler and Russia,' in Troy Southgate, ed., *Spengler: Thoughts and Perspectives*, vol. 10 (London: Black Front Publishing, 2012), 89–138.
Also see Nikolai Berdyaev, *The Russian Idea* (New York: Macmillan, 1948), and N. V. Gogol, *Taras Bulba & Other Tales* (1842), Project Gutenberg, http://www.gutenberg.org/files/1197/1197-h/1197-h.htm. For Russia's place in geopolitics vis-à-vis Asia and Europe, see K. R. Bolton, *Geopolitics of the Indo-Pacific* (London: Black House Publishing, 2013).

suicides of America, England, Holland and France, if we are to survive as a nation. The Russian customs and traditions are not compatible with the lack of culture or the primitive ways of most minorities. When this honourable legislative body thinks of creating new laws, it should have in mind the national interest first, observing that the minorities are not Russians.[514]

Note the focus on the requirement of migrants to now 'integrate' into the mainstream, which is to say, the liberal, globalist consumer society culture that now dominates the West and is continually spreading. The globalists seek a common cultural, moral and social denominator. The hope of the globalists is in the youth who can all be melded into one nebulous mass around the nexus of MTV, Twitter, hip hop, and Coca-Cola. The potential for this has already been seen by the way Muslim youth were manipulated by globalists during the so-called 'Arab Spring,' and the way the poorest and most alienated of France's Muslim youth are embracing the 'American Dream' courtesy of the U.S. State Department.

The conservative response to the liberal and globalist agendas is muddled, conservatism having long lost its direction epically in the Anglophone world. They have insisted on maintaining the old patronising attitude of assimilating non-White migrants into White society, on a premise that is really the same as that of the liberal and the globalist: that culture can be changed like clothes. Hence, all migrants, no matter how diverse their origins, can be welded together into a common citizenship. The conservative seeks conformity with a nation, the globalist, conformity over the entire Earth. Unfortunately, the values of the 'West' maintained by 'conservatives' have for several centuries at least, undergone such subversion from a variety of political, economic, and

---

514 Vladimir Putin, Russian president, addressing the Duma (Russian Parliament) on the tensions with minorities in Russia, 4 February 2013.

religious sources, that little remains, and what remains is little more than a defence of 'free enterprise economics' and individualism which are not traditionally conservatism, but Whig liberalism. The 'conservatives' have for decades not often known what they are trying to conserve. What emerges from today's conservatives, for example, in opposing 'special rights and privileges' for ethnic minorities, is an attitude that every individual has the same chance to economically prosper in a free market society, if they work had enough. That is why, for example, conservatives will welcome Chinese and other Asian immigrants, because they 'work hard' and their children study hard at school. They want to 'make it' in the consumer society.

The conservative of this type no longer considers questions of culture and identity. Identity to this bogus 'conservatism' is shaped in the crucible of the consumer society; an attitude that is similar to the corporate globalists in trying to create one world, one race. The conservative instead tries to create 'one people, one nation,' but on the same faulty premises that individuals are infinitely malleable, according to dogma. A manifestation of this 'conservative' position is the One Nation Party that was founded in Australia, and the same attitudes in New Zealand, with a tentative new party forming in 2013, called the 'One Law4All' Party based on eliminating the increasingly intrusive demands of the Treaty of Waitangi and 'Maori separatism.' This is condemned as 'apartheid' in favour of the Maori, as distinct from the apartheid in favour of the Afrikaner. The National, New Zealand First, and Act parties, as well as a now defunct One New Zealand Party, have also expressed similar 'one law' ideas. In the year 2000 Winston Peters, leader of the New Zealand First Party, and of Maori descent, condemned the 'social apartheid' of certain state programmes exclusively for Maoris, while *The Dominion* newspaper alluded to such policies as 'having no place in a multi-racial society.'[515]

---

515 Mike Butler, 'Separate and Privileged,' in John Robinson et al., *Twisting the*

Conclusion

While European-New Zealanders are right to object to the manner by which they are being perpetually conned into granting billions in money and assets to Maori, with so-called 'final settlements' under the Treaty of Waitangi that have been ongoing for over a century, the 'One Law' advocates assume that separatism per se is wrong, whether of the 'White' or 'Brown' variety. Hence, they claim to be the genuine 'anti-racists,' because they do not believe in any race-based law, either for Maori or White, or that New Zealand needs any political party based on race, such as the Maori or Mana parties. This approach harks back from the mid-1800s to the mid-1970s when the old British colonial attitude of trying to make the Maori into 'brown-skinned whites' was the policy; that is, a policy of the 'Melting-pot.' Indeed, when Maori chiefs signed the Treaty of Waitangi in 1840 they were each greeted by Governor William Hobson with a handshake and the declaration 'we are now one people,' as all denizens of New Zealand now came under the protection of the British Monarch. Hence, the nation-building exercise of the British Empire was based on legalistic contractualism, and this remains so in New Zealand, although the interpretation of this 1840 contract has for decades been hotly disputed, invariably to the disadvantage of the Whites.

As the demographics changed with a large Polynesian population and now more specially, Asians and Africans, the policy became one of multiculturalism, within the context of giving the Maori privileged recognition as the 'indigenous people' through modern reinterpretations of the Treaty. The 'conservative' reaction is to reinforce the idea of New Zealand as a multicultural society rather than a bicultural one, and hence claim again that in opposing Maori privileges under the Treaty of Waitangi they are promoting New Zealand's diversity.[516] They thereby hope to avoid, albeit unsuccessfully, accusations of 'racism.'

Treaty: A Tribal Grab for Wealth and Power (Wellington, New Zealand: Tross Publishing, 2013), 283.

516 Ibid.

It is not really surprising then when the embryonic 'One Law4All' party quotes the communist dupe and rabble-rouser Martin Luther King, the Rastafarian musician Bob Marley, and the free market philosophers Ayn Rand and Thomas Sowell, all condemning 'racism.'[517] Such 'conservatives' also applaud the 'rainbow nation,' South Africa, because its post-apartheid economy has been put on the course to globalisation and privatisation, albeit one that is in a shambles and will remain so. The conservative answer is that 'we are all New Zealanders.' Like 'American,' the definition means little other than as citizens in a piece of real estate. There is no real identity with which to resist globalisation.

The answers to the problems of immigration and race relations are neither multiculturalism nor assimilation. The system politicians have been swinging between the two while none work. The answer will not be found among the run-of-the-mill 'conservative' assimilationists or the Far Left whose principles of 'open borders' and 'one race, the human race' are no different from that of the oligarchs they think they are opposing.

One does not solve any problem by trying to change or suppress 'human nature.' Ethnos is at the foundations of human consciousnesses and subconsciousness. It forms our identity, our sense of who we are, where we have come from, where we belong, and where we might be going. To muddle this in the cause of an ideology or to expand global markets is the type of *hubris* that will lead to a fall.

We are now beginning to understand very much more about human motives having a biological basis, although this is regarded as heresy by liberals and Leftists, and is in general antithetical to the very premises of sociology. Among the innate characteristics of humans is that of a preference for what is most like oneself that has a biological, including an ethnic, basis.

---

517 'One Law for All,' One Law4All Party, Auckland, New Zealand.

Conclusion

According to a study headed by Dr. Elizabeth Phelps of New York University, published in *Nature Neuroscience*, a review of previous brain scanning studies show that the same circuits in the brain that allow one to recognise which ethnic group a person belongs to overlap with others that drive emotional decisions. The result is that even the most self-consciously liberal and egalitarian of people will unconsciously possess an innate tendency to make decisions based on another's race, and therefore people will harbour so-called 'racist' views without being conscious of it. The research shows a network of brain regions, the amygdala, dorsolateral prefrontal cortex, and the anterior cingulate cortex, are important in the unintentional implicit expression of racial attitudes. These brain areas together the functional connectivity among them, are critical for this processing of ethnic recognition. Dr. Phelps states:

> Evidence from neuroscience has been vital in clarifying the nature of how intergroup cognition unfolds. Moreover, the neuroscience of race has been useful in pointing the way toward the type of new behavioural evidence needed to answer questions of not only what happens when intergroup cognition is at stake, but whether and how change is possible in real human interactions. How to use this knowledge from brain and behaviour to further extend basic knowledge and to drive applications is the obvious next generation of questions that we must pose. If good people who intend well act in a manner inconsistent with their own standards of egalitarianism because of the racial groups to which 'the other' belongs, then the question of change takes on new and urgent meaning. This urgency requires that we attend to the evidence about how our minds work when we confront racial and other group differences. Thus far, we have obtained modest evidence about these processes as they operate in our brains, unbeknownst to our conscious selves. The question of what we will do with these insights awaits an answer.[518]

---

518 Rob Waugh, 'Racism is "hardwired" into the human brain—and people can be

Babel, Inc.

It is notable that Dr. Phelps, even when confronted with hard science, maintains an ideological bias, not in regard to how such innate characteristics should be recognised as a positive when formulating social policy, but as to how they might be repressed or eliminated in order to follow the same 'egalitarian' policies and dogmas regardless of the new findings of science. It is assumed by Dr. Phelps that it is the 'egalitarians' who are the 'good people.' This liberal pantheon of the 'good' must include those who slaughtered millions in the name of 'equality,' from Jacobin France to Bolshevik Russia to Jonestown.

Rather than the guillotine, firing squad, concentration camp, and 're-education' labour battalion, it has been suggested that such reshaping of the human conscious and unconscious can be accomplished through medication. Recent research has suggested that a common blood pressure drug can reduce 'inbuilt racism.' An Oxford University study has found that Propranolol, which blocks the peripheral 'autonomic' nervous system, 'reduces racial bias because such subconscious thoughts are triggered by the autonomic nervous system.' Sylvia Terbeck, lead author of the study, published in the journal *Psychopharmacology*, states,

Our results offer new evidence about the processes in the brain that shape implicit racial bias. Implicit racial bias can occur even in people with a sincere belief in equality. Given the key role that such implicit attitudes appear to play in discrimination against other ethnic groups, and the widespread use of propranolol for medical purposes, our findings are also of considerable ethical interest.[519]

prejudiced without knowing it,' *Daily Mail*, 26 June 2012, http://www.dailymail.co.uk/sciencetech/article-2164844/Racism-hardwired-human-brain--people-racists-knowing-it.html.

519 Stephen Adams, 'Blood pressure drug "reduces in-built racism,"' *Daily Telegraph*, 7 March 2012, http://www.telegraph.co.uk/health/healthnews/9129029/Blood-

Conclusion

The obvious point has arisen as to the possibilities of being able to medicate 'racism' out of existence. It is not for a moment entertained even by those involved in the hard, physical sciences, who should know better, that perhaps such 'inbuilt racism' and the innate neurological basis of recognising differences, has evolved over millennia as an essential survival mechanism, like the ability to recognise snakes as dangerous without the need to learn each time from first-hand experience. This is what is meant by instinct, but intellectuals, communists, and CEOs think that instinct can and should be overridden for the sake of achieving an ideological aim.

Political scientist Dr. Robert D. Putnam of Harvard University has argued that ethnic diversity causes a decrease in community trust. His studies refute the assumption that inter-ethnic relations will engender better understanding among diverse ethnic groups. His study is based on 40 communities and 30,000 individuals in the United States. The results include less interest in local politics with an increased perception that one's vote and views do not matter, less likelihood of working on community projects, of giving to charity or of volunteering, fewer close friends, more time watching television as the prime source of entertainment, etc.[520] This indicates empirical evidence for the contention that multiculturalism destroys the cohesion of a society and undermines community, which is based on commonality of outlook, shared experiences, and customs.

Despite attempts at criticism and claims that the findings of Putnam only apply to the United States because of the legacy of Black slavery, the research on the 'hardwiring' of so-called 'racism' in the brain indicates that something more far-reaching is at work in the development and

---

pressure-drug-reduces-in-built-racism.html.

520 Robert D. Putnam, '*E Pluribus Unum*: Diversity and Community in the Twenty-first Century,' *Journal of Scandinavian Political Studies* 30, no. 2 (June 2007), 137–74.

maintenance of a community, a society and a nation, that are partly formed by recognising one's differences from outsiders. There seems to be a convergence of evidence that 'diversity' engenders distrust and lack of community spirit.

By now it will hopefully be apparent to the reader that multiculturalism and immigration are symptoms rather than causes of decline. These symptoms can only be halted and reversed by addressing the root cause: the rise of plutocracy (rule by money). Many of the parties that oppose immigration and multiculturalism have economic policies that do not get to the root of problems, and at most see import controls as a panacea.[521] Globalisation, and all of its symptoms, such as immigration, multiculturalism, and the debasement of youth and tradition, cannot be treated unless the foundation of this power is eliminated. That power emanates from the international economic, trade, and banking system.[522]

The bottom line is that the fight against ethno-cultural debasement is a fight against globalisation. The Left, regardless of its vehement anti-globalisation rhetoric, and even its violent anarchist protests, is not only useless, but often serves as the foot soldiers of international capital by confronting the Right, and giving the 'Establishment' the excuse to delegitimise Rightist debate.[523]

---

521 For a survey of Rightist parties and movements that include policies challenging the globalist financial system, and those who have a policy of free trade economics, see K. R. Bolton, 'Breaking the Bondage of Usury: Where is the Right?,' *Ab Aeterno*, no. 14 (January–March 2013), 22–32.

522 For an explanation of the international banking and economic systems, and theories, individuals, and movements that have opposed this system, see K. R. Bolton, *The Banking Swindle: Money Creation and the State* (London: Black House Publishing, 2013).

523 For example, the recent fracas in France, where an anarchist was accidentally killed after he and his comrades attacked several Rightist youths. The result was that despite the incident being an unprovoked attack from the anarchists, a Rightist group that did not have any association with those involved was outlawed, and the incident was played up as an excuse to smear the entire radical Right in France. See K. R. Bolton, 'Leftist Humbuggery in France: The Death of Clément Méric,' Counter-Currents Publishing, 10 June 2013, http://www.counter-currents.com/2013/06/leftist-humbuggery-in-france-the-death-of-

Conclusion

Opposition to multiculturalism, immigration, and other globalist agendas must be aspects of a holistic Rightist opposition to globalisation. This might require re-evaluating the present conception of the 'nation-state' and the types of 'nationalism' being promoted by the Right. The centralised 'nation-state' in large part derives from the anti-Rightist, that is to say anti-Traditionalist, ideas of the 18th-century Enlightenment, culminating in the American and French revolutions, and rests on legalistic concepts that define 'citizenship' and 'nationhood' as 'social contracts' designed to ensure harmonious relations between individuals.[524] States based on this 18th-century political legacy are adjudicators between individuals rather than guardians of a community, and are not conducive to building real national identities.

Nations might have to readjust their present boundaries to reflect ethnicity rather than economics, to decentralise rather than centralise power, as well as seek out new confederations based on geopolitics rather than trade. Within multicultural states there exist by definition a multiplicity of embryonic nations and peoples. These might maintain a confederation of ethno-cultural communities like the ethnic cantons of Switzerland. Other states are artificial constructs that do not reflect historical realities. In a genuinely organic European confederation based on a sense of destiny rather than a fixation on economics, new nations would emerge with the break-up of such artificial state constructs, granting autonomy to stateless peoples such as the Tyroleans, Basques, Burgundians, Lombards, Flemish, Bavarians, Saxons, et al.[525] Others, especially

---

clement-meric/.

524 See, for example, the U.S. Constitution and Bill of Rights, and the French Declaration on the Rights of Man and the Citizen. Today's legalistic documents designed to impose world order, such as the United Nations Charter, UN Declaration on Human Rights, etc., are based on the same 18th-century doctrines.

525 Leopold Kohr, *The Breakdown of Nations* (London: Routledge and Kegan Paul, 1986), 194–95.

those that are beleaguered, such as the Afrikaners, might retreat into more defensible enclaves, such as Orania, which has achieved remarkable degree of self-sufficiency, based on permaculture and has its own local currency, while having a population of only 1,000. Most importantly the Afrikaners at Orania do their own labour, and are not at all reliant on non-Afrikaner workers. It can only be hoped that Orania will serve as the basis for a new Afrikaner republic.[526] The United States adopted a more realistic approach to the Indian nations than to its African population, and subsequent immigrants. Despite its moral posturing against apartheid and its multicultural offensive around the world, the United States has maintained its Indian reservations as a more effective form of apartheid than the Afrikaner model.

In New Zealand, while we have the anomaly of 'conservatives' opposing Maori separatism as 'apartheid,' and the liberal-Left supporting Maori separatism due to its reliance on 'identity politics,' such separatism is more realistic than trying to make 'one people' out of 'two,' although the sharing of an island land-mass in the face of common—albeit as yet unperceived—challenges from Asia—provide the basis for a return to a bicultural state, the sound foundations of which were destroyed from the 1960s with a deliberate government policy to urbanise the rural-based Maori communities. The possibilities for a Maori renewal that need not encroach upon the European New Zealander exists by encouraging a resurgence of Maori tribal authority that is rural based. Again, much that is presently problematic between the two peoples could be cleared away by addressing the financial and economic system that burdens both peoples, rather than basing such relations on the red-herring of ideology-driven

---

526 K. R. Bolton, 'Orania: Lessons from the Afrikaner Ethnic Community,' Counter-Currents Publishing, 4 June 2013, http://www.counter-currents.com/2013/06/oranialessons-from-the-afrikaner-ethno-community/.

Conclusion

reinterpretations of history based on an anti-White guilt complex.[527]

Another factor is the need for all those who are called

'Identitarians' in Europe to unite against the common enemy: the global oligarchy, and to put an end to its power before the multitude of problems it has caused can be solved. One such form of cooperation is the Unrepresented Nations and Peoples Organization, which includes the Afrikaners represented by the Rightist 'Freedom Front Plus' party.[528] Again, the Orania Afrikaners are conscious of what is required:

> We simply believe in the right of all cultural groups to practice their own culture, language, religion and traditions in a fair way. We also strongly believe in self-determination and therefore support the efforts by the Flemish people in Belgium, the German speaking people in South Tyrol (Italy), the Catalans in Spain and the French speaking people in Quebec (Canada) as they strive for greater self-determination.[529]

Once the edifice of plutocracy is demolished, including the eclipse of hegemonic powers such as the United States and China, the way can be cleared for all peoples around the world to reorient their relations on the basis of mutual good will, rather than being used as both economic cogs and cannon fodder in globalist schemes for a new world order.

---

527 K. R. Bolton, *The Parihaka Cult* (London: Black House Publishing, 2012).

528 UNPO, 'Afrikaner,' http://www.unpo.org/members/8148.

529 Jaco Kleynhans, Orania Movement CEO, 'Insight into Orania,' *Südafrika—Land der Kontraste*, 21 March 2012, http://2010sdafrika.wordpress.com/2012/03/21/insight-into-orania/.

Index

Index

Index

Index

Index

Index

9 780992 736521